BOLLINGEN SERIES XI

HEINRICH ZIMMER

(1890–1943)

Works in English, completed and edited
by Joseph Campbell

1946

MYTHS AND SYMBOLS IN
INDIAN ART AND CIVILIZATION

(BOLLINGEN SERIES VI)

1948

THE KING AND THE CORPSE

Tales of the Soul's Conquest of Evil

(BOLLINGEN SERIES XI)

1951

PHILOSOPHIES OF INDIA

(BOLLINGEN SERIES XXVI)

1955

THE ART OF INDIAN ASIA

Its Mythology and Transformations

IN TWO VOLUMES

(BOLLINGEN SERIES XXXIX)

HEINRICH ZIMMER

THE KING
AND THE CORPSE

TALES OF THE SOUL'S CONQUEST OF EVIL

EDITED BY JOSEPH CAMPBELL

BOLLINGEN SERIES XI

PRINCETON UNIVERSITY PRESS

Published by Princeton University Press, 41 William Street,
Princeton, New Jersey 08540
In the United Kingdom: Princeton University Press,
Chichester, West Sussex

THIS IS THE ELEVENTH IN A SERIES OF WORKS
SPONSORED BY BOLLINGEN FOUNDATION

Library of Congress Card No. 48-6544
ISBN 0-691-01776-X (paperback)

Second edition, with index, 1956
First Princeton/Bollingen Paperback printing, 1971
Ninth paperback printing, 1989
Tenth printing, for the Mythos series, 1993

Princeton University Press books are printed on acid-free paper
and meet the guidelines for permanence and durability of the
Committee on Production Guidelines for Book Longevity of the
Council on Library Resources

16   15   14   13   12

Printed in the United States of America

EDITOR'S FOREWORD

At the time of his sudden death, in the spring of 1943, Dr. Zimmer was still working on the material for the present volume. All of the tales were represented in more than one version, some in English, some in German. The manuscript margins carried many jottings; three chapters had been published in earlier forms, in Europe and India; and there were outlines for projected augmentations. None were in a final state. Nevertheless, the moment the editor put his hand to them—co-ordinating the scattered jottings, amplifying the narratives from the original sources, and revising on the basis of numerous conversations with Dr. Zimmer himself during the months just preceding his death—the book came to life, arranged itself, and developed in what now seems the one inevitable way.

For advice and assistance in this task, my thanks are given to Mrs. Peter Geiger and Mrs. Margaret Wing. The late Dr. Ananda K. Coomaraswamy generously read the galleys, offered valuable suggestions, and supplied a few supplementary notes to complete the references. The latter appear in bracketed footnotes, with his initials.

For the earlier versions, the reader is referred to the following publications: *Die kulturelle Bedeutung der komplexen Psychologie*, edited by the Psychological Club of Zurich, Verlag Julius Springer, Berlin, 1935, "Die Geschichte vom indischen König mit dem Leichnam"; Heinrich Zimmer, *Weisheit Indiens*, L. C. Wittich Verlag, Darmstadt, 1938, "Abu Kasems Pantoffeln," "Die Geschichte vom indischen König mit dem Leichnam"; *Prabuddha Bharata*, Mayavati, Almora, Himalayas, Sept.-Dec., 1938, "The Story of the Indian King and the Corpse"; *Corona*, Zweimonatsschrift, edited by Martin H. Bodmer, Verlag der Corona, Zurich, 1936, "Abu Kasems Pantoffeln," 1939, "Merlin."

J. C.

New York City, September 9, 1947

CONTENTS

Editor's Foreword   v

List of Plates   ix

The Dilettante among Symbols   1

PART I

Abu Kasem's Slippers   9

A Pagan Hero and a Christian Saint   26

Four Romances from the Cycle of King Arthur

    I. Gawain and the Green Knight   67
    II. The Knight with the Lion   96
    III. Lancelot   131
    IV. Merlin   181

The King and the Corpse   202

PART II

Four Episodes from the Romance of the Goddess

    I. The Involuntary Creation   239
    II. The Involuntary Marriage   264
    III. The Voluntary Death   285
    IV. Shiva Mad   296

On the Siprā Shore   307

Index   317

LIST OF PLATES

following page 164

1. **Head of the Dancing Shiva**
   South Indian bronze, X century, Madras Museum
   (Photo: Van Oest, in *Ars Asiatica* III)

2. **The First Kiss**
   From a French manuscript of the XII century
   (Reproduced from Henry Yates Thompson, *Illustrations from One Hundred Manuscripts*, London, 1916, courtesy of Chiswick Press)

3. **The Knight of the Cart**
   See plate 1

4. **The Sword Bridge**
   See plate 1

5. **Four Cards of the Tarot: The Fool, The Hanged Man, Death, and The World (The Dancing Hermaphrodite)**
   From the Atouts of an Italian Tarot series of the early XIX century.
   (Courtesy of the United States Playing Card Company)

6. **Pārvatī**
   South Indian bronze processional image, late XI or early XII century. Possibly the portrait of a deified queen
   (Photo courtesy of the Freer Gallery of Art, Washington, D.C.)

THE KING
AND THE CORPSE

THE DILETTANTE AMONG
SYMBOLS

Story-telling has been, through the ages, both a serious business and a lighthearted diversion. Year in, year out, tales are conceived, committed to writing, devoured, forgotten. What becomes of them? A few survive, and these, like a scattering of seeds, are blown across the generations, propagating new tales and furnishing spiritual nourishment to many peoples. Most of our own literary inheritance has come to us in this way, from remote epochs, from distant, strange corners of the world. Each new poet adds something of the substance of his own imagination, and the seeds are nourished back to life. Their germinative power is perennial, only waiting to be touched. And so, though from time to time varieties may seem to have died out, one day they reappear, putting forth their characteristic shoots again, as fresh and green as before.

The traditional tale and the subjects akin to it have been discussed exhaustively from the points of view of the anthropologist, historian, literary scholar, and poet, but the psychologist has had surprisingly little to say—though he has his own valid claim to a voice in this symposium. Psychology throws an X-ray into the symbolic images of the folk tradition, bringing vital structural elements to light that were formerly in darkness. The only difficulty is that the interpretation of the disclosed forms cannot be reduced to a dependable system. For true symbols have something illimitable about them. They are inexhaustible in their

Psychology throws an X-ray into the symbolic structures of stories

1

suggestive and instructive power. Hence the scientist, the scientific psychologist, feels himself on very dangerous, very uncertain and ambiguous ground when he ventures into the field of folklore interpretation. The discoverable contents of the widely distributed images keep changing before his eyes in unceasing permutations, as the cultural settings change throughout the world and in the course of history. The meanings have to be constantly reread, understood afresh. And it is anything but an orderly work—this affair of interpreting the always unpredicted and astonishing metamorphoses. No systematist who greatly valued his reputation would willingly throw himself open to the risk of the adventure. It must, therefore, remain to the reckless dilettante. Hence the following book.

The dilettante—Italian *dilettante* (present participle of the verb *dilettare*, " to take delight in")—is one who takes delight (*diletto*) in something. The following essays are for those who take delight in symbols, like conversing with them, and enjoy living with them continually in mind.

The moment we abandon this dilettante attitude toward the images of folklore and myth and begin to feel certain about their proper interpretation (as professional comprehenders, handling the tool of an infallible method), we deprive ourselves of the quickening contact, the demonic and inspiring assault that is the effect of their intrinsic virtue. We forfeit our proper humility and open-mindedness before the unknown, and refuse to be instructed—refuse to be shown what has never yet quite been told either to us or to anybody else. And we attempt, instead, to classify the contents of the dark message under heads and categories already known. This prevents the emergence of any new meaning or fresh understanding. The fairy tale, the childlike legend (i.e., the message bearer) is methodically regarded as too lowly to merit our submission, both the tale itself and those zones of our nature that respond to it being comparatively unadult.

2

Yet it would have been through the interaction of that outer and this inner innocence that the fertilizing power of the symbol might have been activated and the hidden content disclosed.

The method—or, rather, habit—of reducing the unfamiliar to the well-known is an old, old way to intellectual frustration. Sterilizing dogmatism is the result, tightly enwrapped in a mental self-satisfaction, a secure conviction of superiority. Whenever we refuse to be knocked off our feet (either violently or gently) by some telling new conception precipitated from the depths of our imagination by the impact of an ageless symbol, we are cheating ourselves of the fruit of an encounter with the wisdom of the millenniums. Failing in the attitude of acceptance, we do not receive; the boon of converse with the gods is denied us. We are not to be flooded, like the soil of Egypt, by the divine, fructifying waters of the Nile.

It is because they are alive, potent to revive themselves, and capable of an ever-renewed, unpredictable yet self-consistent effectiveness in the range of human destiny, that the images of folklore and myth defy every attempt we make at systematization. They are not corpselike, but implike. With a sudden laugh and quick shift of place they mock the specialist who imagines he has got them pinned to his chart. What they demand of us is not the monologue of a coroner's report, but the dialogue of a living conversation. And just as the hero of the key story of the following series (a noble and brave king who finds himself conversing with the implike inhabitant of what he had taken to be a mere dead body hanging from a tree) is brought to a heightened consciousness of himself through his humiliating exchange of words and rescued from a disgraceful, completely odious death, so too may we be instructed, rescued perhaps, and even spiritually transformed, if we will but humble ourselves enough to converse on equal terms with the apparently moribund di-

3

vinities and folk-figures that are hanging, multitudinous, from the prodigious tree of the past.

The psychological approach to the enigma of the symbol, the design to extract from it the secret of its depth, cannot but fail, if the searching intelligence refuses to acquiesce to the chance of being taught something by the living aspect of the object under its attention. Anatomization, systematization, and classification are all well enough, but these do not elicit conversation from the specimen. The psychological investigator must be ready to set his method aside and sit down for an extended chat. Then, perhaps, he will find that he has no further taste or use for his method. This is the mode of the dilettante, as distinguished from the technique of the more stately gentleman of scientific decorum.

What characterizes the dilettante is his delight in the always preliminary nature of his never-to-be-culminated understanding. But this, finally, is the only proper attitude before the figures that have come down to us from the remote past, whether in the monumental epics of Homer and Vyāsa or in the charming little wonder stories of the folk tradition. They are the everlasting oracles of life. They have to be questioned and consulted anew, with every age, each age approaching them with its own variety of ignorance and understanding, its own set of problems, and its own inevitable questions. For the life patterns that we of today have to weave are not the same as those of any other day; the threads to be manipulated and the knots to be disentangled differ greatly from those of the past. The replies already given, therefore, cannot be made to serve us. The powers have to be consulted again directly—again, again, and again. Our primary task is to learn, not so much what they are said to have said, as how to approach them, evoke fresh speech from them, and understand that speech.

In the face of such an assignment, we must all remain dilet-

4

tantes, whether we like it or not. Some of us—scholarly specialists
—tend to favor certain very definite, and consequently limited,
methods of interpretation, admitting only these within the pale
of our authoritative influence. Other interpreters champion zeal-
ously this or that esoteric line of tradition, regarding it as the
one true clue, and its special cluster of symbols as the unique, all-
comprehensive, and self-sufficient oracle of being. But such rigid-
ities can only bind us to what we already know and are, rivet
us to a single aspect of the symbolization. By such stern and constant faiths we cut ourselves off from the infinitudes of inspiration that are alive within the symbolic forms. And so, even the
methodical interpreters are no more than amateurs in the end.
Whether relying, as scientists, upon strict philological, historical,
and comparative methods, or piously following, as initiates, the
secret, oracular teachings of some self-styled esoteric tradition,
they must remain, ultimately, mere beginners, hardly beyond the
starting point in the unending task of fathoming the dark pool
of meaning.

Delight, on the other hand, sets free in us the creative intuition, permits it to be stirred to life by contact with the fascinating
script of the old symbolic tales and figures. Undaunted then by
the criticism of the methodologists (whose censure is largely inspired by what amounts to a chronic agoraphobia: morbid dread
before the virtual infinity that is continually opening out from
the cryptic traits of the expressive picture writing which it is
their profession to regard) we may permit ourselves to give vent
to whatever series of creative reactions happens to be suggested
to our imaginative understanding. We can never exhaust the
depths—of that we may be certain; but then neither can anyone
else. And a cupped handful of the fresh waters of life is sweeter
than a whole reservoir of dogma, piped and guaranteed.

"Abundance is scooped from abundance, yet abundance remains." So runs a fine old saying of the Upanishads of India. The

5

original reference was to the idea that the fullness of our universe —vast in space, and with its myriad of whirling, glowing spheres, teeming with the hosts of living things—proceeds from a superabundant source of transcendent substance and potential energy: the abundance of this world is scooped from that abundance of eternal being, and yet, since the supernatural potential cannot be diminished, no matter how great the donation it pours forth, abundance remains. But all true symbols, all mythical images, refer to this idea, one way or another, and are themselves endowed with the miraculous property of that inexhaustibility. With every draft drawn from them by our imaginative understanding, a universe of meaning is disclosed to the mind; and this is a fullness indeed, yet further fullnesses remain. No matter what the reading accessible to our present vision, it cannot be final. It can be only a preliminary glimpse. And we should regard it as an inspiration and a stimulation, not as a final definition precluding further insights and differing approaches.

The following essays, therefore, do not pretend to be more than examples of how to converse with the fascinating figures of folklore and myth. The book is a conversation primer, a reader for beginners, an introduction to the grammar of a cryptic but readily enjoyed, pictorial script. And since, with respect to this science of interpreting symbols, even the advanced reader must inevitably discover, time and again, that he is still but a beginner, the following essays are intended also for him. The *diletto*, the delight, that he can experience in rereading the well-known symbols of life (the proportion of his delight to his quarrelsome righteousness) will represent the degree to which his lifelong contact with them has imbued him with their abundances of nature and the spirit. The true *dilettante* will be always ready to begin anew. And it will be in him that the wonderful seeds from the past will strike their roots and marvelously grow.

6

PART I

ABU KASEM'S SLIPPERS

W<small>HO</small> knows the story of Abu Kasem and his slippers? The slip- ⌐ B.OS.
pers were as famous—yea, proverbial—in the Bagdad of his time
as the great miser and money-grubber himself. Everybody regarded them as the visible sign of his unpalatable greed. For
Abu Kasem was rich and tried to hide the fact; and even the
shabbiest beggar in town would have been ashamed to be
caught dead in such slippers as he wore—they were so shingled
with bits and pieces. A thorn in the flesh and an old story to
every cobbler in Bagdad, they became at last a byword on the
tongues of the populace. Anybody wishing a term to express the
preposterous would bring them in.

Attired in these miserable things—which were inseparable
from his public character—the celebrated businessman would
go shuffling through the bazaar. One day he struck a singularly
fortunate bargain: a huge consignment of little crystal bottles
that he managed to buy for a song. Then a few days later he
capped the deal by purchasing a large supply of attar of roses
from a bankrupt perfume merchant. The combination made a
really good business stroke, and was much discussed in the
bazaar. Anybody else would have celebrated the occasion in
the usual way, with a little banquet for a few business acquaint-
ances. Abu Kasem, however, was prompted to do something
for himself. He decided to pay a visit to the public baths, a place
where he had not been seen for quite some time.

In the anteroom, where the clothes and shoes are left, he met

9

an acquaintance, who took him aside and delivered him a lecture on the state of his slippers. He had just set these down, and everyone could see how impossible they were. His friend spoke with great concern about making himself the laughingstock of the town; such a clever businessman should be able to afford a pair of decent slippers. Abu Kasem studied the monstrosities of which he had grown so fond. Then he said: "I have been considering the matter for many years; but they are really not so worn that I cannot use them." Whereupon the two, undressed as they were, went in to bathe.

While the miser was enjoying his rare treat, the Cadi of Bagdad also arrived to take a bath. Abu Kasem finished before the exalted one, and returned to the changing room to dress. But where were his slippers? They had disappeared, and in their place, or almost in their place, was a different pair—beautiful, shiny, apparently brand-new. Might these be a surprise present from that friend, who could no longer bear to see his wealthier acquaintance going around in worn-out shreds, and wished to ingratiate himself with a prosperous man by a delicate attention? Whatever the explanation, Abu Kasem drew them on. They would save him the trouble of shopping and bargaining for a new pair. Reflecting thus, and with conscience clear, he quit the baths.

When the judge returned, there was a scene. His slaves hunted high and low, but could not find his slippers. In their place was a disgusting pair of tattered objects, which everyone immediately recognized as the well-known footgear of Abu Kasem. The judge breathed out fire and brimstone, sent for the culprit and locked him up—the court servant actually found the missing property on the miser's feet. And it cost the old fellow plenty to pry himself loose from the clutches of the law; for the court knew as well as everyone else how rich he was. But at least he got his dear old slippers back again.

10

Sad and sorry, Abu Kasem returned home, and in a fit of temper threw his treasures out of the window. They fell with a splash into the Tigris, which crept muddily past his house. A few days later, a group of river fishermen thought they had caught a particularly heavy fish, but when they hauled in, what did they behold but the celebrated slippers of the miser? The hobnails (one of Abu Kasem's ideas on economy) had ripped several gaps in the net, and the men were, of course, enraged. They hurled the muddy, soggy objects through an open window. The window happened to be Abu Kasem's. Sailing through the air, his returning possessions landed with a crash on the table where he had set out in rows those precious crystal bottles, so cheaply bought—still more precious now because of the valuable attar of roses with which he had filled them, ready for sale. The glittering, perfumed magnificence was swept to the floor, and lay there, a dripping mass of glassy fragments, mixed with mud.

The narrator from whom we receive the story could not bring himself to describe the extent of the miser's grief . "Those wretched slippers," Abu Kasem cried (and this is all that we are told), "they shall do me no further harm." And so saying, he took up a shovel, went quickly and quietly into his garden, and dug a hole there in order to bury the things. But it so happened that Abu Kasem's neighbor was watching—naturally deeply interested in all that went on in the rich man's house next door; and he, as so often is the case with neighbors, had no particular reason to wish him well. "That old miser has servants enough," he said to himself, "yet he goes out and personally digs a hole. He must have a treasure buried there. Why, of course! It's obvious!" And so the neighbor hustled off to the governor's palace and informed against Abu Kasem; because anything that a treasure seeker finds belongs by law to the Caliph, the earth and all that is hidden in it being the property

11

of the ruler of the faithful. Abu Kasem, therefore, was called up before the governor, and his story, that he had only dug up the earth to bury an old pair of slippers, made everybody laugh uproariously. Had a guilty man ever accused himself more glaringly? The more the notorious miser insisted, the more incredible his story became and the guiltier he seemed. In sentencing him, the governor took the buried treasure into account, and, thunderstruck, Abu Kasem heard the amount of his fine.

He was desperate. He cursed the wretched slippers up and down. But how was he to get rid of them? The only thing was to get them somehow out of town. So he made a pilgrimage into the country and dropped them into a pond, far away. When they sank into its mirrored depths he took a deep breath. At last they were gone. But surely the devil must have had a hand in it; for the pond was a reservoir that fed the town's water supply, and the slippers swirled to the mouth of the pipe and stopped it up. The guards came to repair the damage, found the slippers, and recognizing them—as indeed who would not?—reported Abu Kasem to the governor for befouling the town's water supply; and so there he sat in jail again. He was punished with a fine far greater than the last. What could he do? He paid. And he got his dear old slippers back; for the tax collector wants nothing that does not belong to him.

They had done enough damage. This time he was going to get even with them, so that they should play him no more tricks. He decided to burn them. But they were still wet, so he put them out on the balcony to dry. A dog on the balcony next door saw the funny-looking things, became interested, jumped over, and snatched a slipper. But while he was playing with it, he let it fall down to the street. The wretched thing spun through the air from a considerable height and landed on the head of a woman who was passing by. She, as it happened, was pregnant. The sudden shock and the force of the blow brought on a miscarriage,

12

Her husband ran to the judge and demanded damages from the rich old miser. Abu Kasem was almost out of his mind, but he was forced to pay.

Before he tottered home from the court, a broken man, he raised the unlucky slippers solemnly aloft, and cried with an earnestness that all but reduced the judge to hysterics: "My lord, these slippers are the fateful cause of all my sufferings. These cursed things have reduced me to beggary. Deign to command that I shall never again be held responsible for the evils they will most certainly continue to bring upon my head." And the Oriental narrator closes with the following moral: The Cadi could not reject the plea, and Abu Kasem had learned, at enormous cost, the evil that can come of not changing one's slippers often enough.[1]

But now, is that really the one thought to be gleaned from this celebrated tale? It is certainly a trivial counsel—not to become a slave to avarice. Should not something have been said about the mysterious vagaries of the fate that always brought the slippers back to their rightful owner? Some point would seem to lie in this malicious repetition of the same event, and in the crescendo with which the fiendish articles affect the whole nature of their bewitched owner. And is there not some point, also, in the remarkable intertwining of all the people and things that play into the hands of chance in this affair—neighbors, dog, officials and regulations of all kinds, public baths and water systems —making it possible for chance to do its work, and tie more

[1] From the *Thamarat ul-Awrak* (Fruits of Leaves) of Ibn Hijjat al-Hamawi. Another rendering into English will be found in H. I. Katibah, *Other Arabian Nights,* Charles Scribner's Sons, New York, 1928, "The Shoes of Abu Kasim." Richard F. Burton gives a very much abridged and greatly differing variant of the tale in his *Supplemental Nights to the Book of the Thousand Nights and a Night,* vol. IV, Benares, 1887, pp. 209–217, "How Drummer Abu Kasim became a Kazi," and "The Story of the Kazi and his Slipper." Here we find that, having won release from his slippers, Abu Kasem fared to foreign parts and became himself a Cadi.

tightly the knot of destiny? The moralist has considered only the miser who received his just deserts and the vice that developed into the fate of one who practiced it. He has treated the story as an example of the manner in which one may punish oneself by means of one's favorite bent. But to have made this point, the tale need not have been anywhere near so witty, so profound; there is nothing mysterious about morality. Abu Kasem's relationship to his slippers and his experiences with them are actually very mysterious—as dark, as fateful and full of meaning, as the ring of Polycrates.[1]

A chain of malicious accidents, but taken together they combine to form a strange configuration, just right for story-making, and the result is a tale not easily forgotten. This annoyance of the indestructible slippers that cost their owner many times their value, worth nothing in themselves, yet draining him of his fortune, this theme, with its variations, grows to the proportions of a great hieroglyph, or symbol, for which there should be possible many and various interpretations.

Out of a series of mere chances a destiny is spun. Every effort the victim makes to put an end to his difficulty only serves to increase the snowball, until it swells to an avalanche that buries him under its weight. A jokester mixes up the slippers, probably for no better reason than to gloat over the embarrassment of the miser. Chance brings them back under the house from which they had been thrown into the river. Chance hurls them into the midst of the precious bottles. Chance calls the attention of a neighbor to the miser's activity in his garden. Chance swirls the slippers into the water pipe. Chance calls the dog up onto

---

[1] While King Polycrates, the ruler of Samos, was entertaining the King of Egypt, evidence of his extraordinary good fortune continually came pouring in. The King of Egypt was alarmed and begged Polycrates to sacrifice some valuable thing voluntarily in order to avert the envy of the gods. Polycrates threw his ring into the sea. The next day it was found by the cook in a fish being prepared for the royal dinner. The King of Egypt, terrified, left for home.

the next-door balcony, and drops one of the slippers on the head of the pregnant woman who happens to be walking past. But what is it that makes these accidents so fateful? Pregnant women are always walking down the street, other people's dogs always love to snatch other people's belongings, water is continually running through pipes, and now and then the pipes get stopped. Mislaid rubbers, exchanged umbrellas: that kind of thing happens every day without any meaningful story growing out of the harmless events. The air is filled with such minute dust particles of fate; they form the atmosphere of life and all its events. Those that made for the calamity of Abu Kasem were a mere handful among thousands.

With Abu Kasem's slippers we walk right into one of the most far-reaching of all questions concerning human life and destiny, one which India was looking straight in the face when she formulated such conceptions as "Karma" and "Māyā." Whatever a human being brings into direct contact with himself out of the mass of whirling atoms of possibilities fuses into a pattern with his own being. In so far as he admits that a thing concerns him it does concern him, and if related to his deepest aims and desires, his fears and the cloudy fabric of his thoughts, it can become an important part of his destiny. And, finally, if he senses it as striking at the roots of his life, that very fact itself is his point of vulnerability. But on the other hand, and by the same token, in so far as one can break loose from one's passions and ideas and thereby become free of oneself, one is released automatically from all the things that appear to be accidental. They are sometimes too meaningful, and at other times have too much the tinge of pertinent wit about them, to deserve the hackneyed name of mere "accident." They are the stuff of fate. And it would constitute a lofty, serene freedom to be released from the natural compulsion to choose from among them—to choose, from among the whirling atoms of mere possibility, something that should

15

become involved with one as a possible destiny, and even strike perhaps at the root of one's being. There are two mirror worlds, and the human being is between them: the world outside and the one within. They are like two Magdeburg hemispheres, between which the air has been pumped out and whose edges cling together by suction, so that all the king's horses cannot pry them apart. What binds the two externally—inclination, repulsion, intellectual interest—is the reflection of an inner tension, of which we are not readily aware because we are ourselves within ourselves, whether we will or no.

Abu Kasem has worked on his slippers as grimly and obstinately as on his business and his fortune. He is as attached to their poverty as to his riches. They are the all-concealing mask of his prosperity, its other face. Most significant is the fact that he himself has to take all the necessary steps to get rid of them; he can leave nothing to his servants. That is to say, he cannot be parted from them; they are a fetish, soaked with his demonic possession. They have drawn into themselves all the passion of his life, and that passion is the secret thing from which he cannot break away. Even while he is bent on destroying them, he is passionately bound to them. There is something of the *crime passionnel* about the fierce joy he takes in being alone with them as he puts them to death.

And this passion is mutual; that is the great point of the story. These impish slippers are like two dogs turned loose, who, after a lifetime of companionship with their master, return to him again and again. He thrusts them from him, but they become independent only to find their way back to him. And their very faithfulness develops into a kind of innocent maliciousness. Their spurned devotion takes its revenge for the treachery of Abu Kasem's attempt to divorce himself from them, the faithful guardians of his ruling passion. However one looks at it, such inanimate objects have a living rôle to play. Gradually, and with-

The slippers are a demonic possession —
He is passionately bound to them

The slippers share the same passion for him

out our knowing it, they become charged with our own tensions, until finally they become magnetic and set up fields of influence that attract and hold us.

The life accomplishment of a man, his social personality, the contoured mask shielding his inner character: that is the shoes of Abu Kasem. They are the fabric of their owner's conscious personality. More, they are the tangible impulses of his unconscious: the sum total of those desires and achievements in which he parades before himself and the world, and by virtue of which he has become a social personage. They are the life sum for which he has struggled. If they have no such secret meaning, why then are they so motley, so uniquely recognizable; why have they become proverbial and such old and trusted friends? Just as they represent to the world the whole personality of Abu Kasem and his miserliness, so they mean unconsciously to himself his greatest, most consciously cultivated virtue, his merchant's avarice. And all of this has brought the man a long way, but holds more power over him than he supposes. It is not so much that Abu Kasem possesses the virtue (or vice), as that the vice (or virtue) possesses him. It has become a sovereign motive of his being, holding him under its spell. Suddenly his shoes begin to play tricks on him—maliciously, so he thinks. But is it not he who is playing the tricks on himself?

Abu Kasem's mortification is the natural consequence of being forced to drag around with him something that he refused to relinquish at the proper time, a mask, an idea about himself, that should have been shed. He is one of those who will not let themselves pass with the passing of time, but clutch themselves to their own bosom and hoard the self which they themselves have made. They shudder at the thought of the consecutive, periodic deaths that open out, threshold after threshold, as one passes through the rooms of life, and which are life's secret. They cling avidly to what they are—what they were. And then, at last, the

17

worn-out personality, which should have been molted like the annual plumage of a bird, so adheres that they cannot shake it off, even when it has become for them an exasperation. Their ears were deaf to the hour when it struck, and that was long ago.

In some cultures there are sacramental formulas for putting off the old Adam—initiations, demanding and causing a complete breakup of the existing mold that has bewitched and bound its wearer. He is invested with an entirely new costume, which brings him under the spell of a new magic and opens to him new paths. India, for example, has, at least as an ideal formula, the four sacred ages or stages of life: that of the student or neophyte, that of the householder, that of the hermit, and that of the pilgrim—each with its characteristic costume, means of livelihood, and system of rights and duties. The neophyte, as boy and youth, lives in chastity, submissively follows the guidance of his teacher, and begs his bread. Then, sacramentally advanced into his own household, the man takes a wife and devotes himself to the duty of bringing sons into the world; he works, earns money, governs his household and provides his dependents with food and shelter. Next, he retires to the forest, subsists on the wild food of the wilderness, no longer works, has no domestic ties or duties, and directs his whole attention inward to himself—whereas formerly his duty had been to give of himself for the good of the family, the village, and the guild. Finally, as pilgrim, he quits the forest hermitage and, free from any habitation, homeless, begs his bread as in the days of his youth—but now imparting wisdom, whereas then he received it. Nothing that he ever had, either human companionship or worldly possessions, remains to him any more. All has gone from his hands, as though only loaned to him for a while.

Civilizations like that of India, founded on a cornerstone of magic, help their children through those necessary transformations that men find it so hard to accomplish from within. This they do by means of undisputed sacraments. The bestowal of the special vestments, implements, signet rings, and crowns, actually re-creates the individual. Changes of food and the reorganization of the outer ceremonial of life make possible certain new things, certain actions and feelings, and prohibit others. They are much like commands issued to a hypnotic subject. The unconscious no longer finds in the external world the thing to which it had so long reacted, but something else; and this rouses within it new responses, so that it breaks from the hardened patterns of its past.

Therein lies the great value of magic areas of life for the guidance of the soul. The spiritual powers being symbolized as gods and demons, or as images and holy places, the individual is brought into relationship with them through the procedures of the investiture, and then held to them by the new ritual routines. A perfected, unmarred sacramental system of this kind is a mirror world, which catches all of the rays sent up from the depths of the unconscious and presents them as an external reality susceptible to manipulation. The two hemispheres, the inner and the outer, then fit together perfectly. And any considered change of scenery in the tangible sacramental mirror sphere brings about, almost automatically, a corresponding shift in the interior field and point of view.

The gain which the rejection of this magic conditioning has brought to the modern man—our exorcism of all the demons and gods from the world, and the increase therewith in our rationally directed power over the material forces of the earth—is paid for by the loss of this mirror control over the forces of the soul. The man of today is helpless before the magic of his own invisible psyche. It drives him whither it will. And from among the many possibilities of events, it perversely conjures up for him the mirage of a diabolical external reality, without furnishing him with any counter magic, or any real understanding of the spell that has befooled him. We are hampered on every hand by insufficient solutions of the great life questions. The result is a no man's land of physical and spiritual suffering, caused by the insoluble in many forms, and made excruciating by the absence of a way out. This, to unsympathetic eyes, can seem amusing, and, in the realm of art, is what produces comedy—works of the kind of our present comedy of Abu Kasem.

Fairy tales and myths usually have a happy ending: the hero slays the dragon, frees the maiden, tames the winged horse, and wins the magic weapon. But in life such heroes are rare. The daily conversations in the bazaar, the gossip of the market place and the law courts, tell us a different tale: in place of the rare miracle of success, there is the common comedy of failure; instead of Perseus conquering the Medusa and saving Andromeda from the sea monster, we have Abu coming along in his miserable slippers. Abu Kasem is certainly the more frequent type in the everyday world. Here there is much more of tragicomedy than of mythological opera. And such gossip as surrounded Abu Kasem all his life, and made him immortal as a comic figure, is the mythology of the everyday. The anecdote as the finished product of gossip corresponds to the myth, even though it never reaches such lofty heights. It shows the comedy of the Gordian knot which only the magic sword of the mythical hero can cleave.

And so—let us change our shoes. If it were only as simple as that! Unfortunately, the old shoes, cherished and lovingly patched for a lifetime, always come back—so the story teaches us—obstinately and persistently, even after we have finally made up our minds to discard them. And even if we take the wings of the morning and fly unto the uttermost parts of the sea, they are there with us. The elements will not accept them, the sea spews them out, the earth refuses to receive them, and before they can be destroyed by fire, they fall through the air to com-

20

plete our ruin. Not even the tax collector wants them. Why should anything in the world burden itself with the full-fledged demons of our ego, just because we have at last become uneasy in their presence?

Who is to deliver Abu Kasem from himself? The way he sought deliverance was obviously futile: one does not get rid of one's beloved ego simply by throwing it out of the window when it has begun to play one tricks. In the end, Abu Kasem conjured the judge at least not to hold him responsible for any future deviltries his slippers might play. But the judge only laughed at him. And will not our judge, too, laugh at us? We alone are responsible for this innocent lifelong process of building our own ego. Involuntarily and lovingly we have patched together the shoes that carry us through life; and we shall remain subject, in the end, to their uncontrollable compulsion.

Something of this we already know from having observed the uncontrollable compulsion at work in others—for example, when we have read their unintentional gestures. It is a force that is made manifest all around us, in all kinds of spontaneous expressions: people's handwriting, failures, dreams, and unconscious images. And it has more control over a man than he himself realizes or would have anyone believe—infinitely more than his conscious will. Its ungovernable drives are the demonic horses harnessed to the chariot of our life, the conscious ego being only the driver. So that there is nothing for it but to resign oneself, like Goethe's Egmont, "to hold fast the reins and to steer the wheels clear, now to the left, now to the right, here from a stone, there from a precipice."

Our fate first deposits itself in our lives through our innumerable tiny movements, the scarcely conscious actions and neglects of everyday life; then, through our choices and rejections it gradually thickens, until the solution reaches a saturation point and

21

is ripe for crystallization. A slight jar, finally, is enough, and what has long been forming as a cloudy liquid, something indefinite, merely holding itself in readiness, is precipitated as a destiny, crystal-clear and hard. In the case of Abu Kasem, it was the genial mood following his successful business deal, a dizziness at the marvelous double stroke by which he had acquired the little crystal bottles and the attar of roses, that raised his opinion of himself and set the wheel of his fate in motion. He felt that things should continue in this way, with little gifts from fortune, pleasant little returns such as his thrifty and industrious life had earned for him. "Look, another one! Why, Abu Kasem, you lucky dog, these luxurious slippers, and brand-new, in place of the old! Perhaps they have come from that critical friend, who could no longer bear to see you going around in your old tatters."

Abu Kasem's avarice, puffed up by his momentary good fortune, kicked over the traces a little. It would have insulted his feeling of triumph, and dissipated his lofty mood, to have had to come down to the idea of really putting his hand in his pocket to buy himself a new pair of shoes. He would have been able to find the old slippers in the dressing room, just as the judge's slaves soon found them, had he only troubled to hunt around a little, in the sober but annoying suspicion that someone might have been trying to make a fool of him. Instead, he flattered himself by taking the new ones, a little dizzied and blinded by the beautiful things; for they really satisfied his unsuspected unconscious impulses. It was a childish act of sweet self-forgetfulness, a momentary lack of self-control; but something was given expression through it, which for a long time had been disregarded. Something that had been quietly growing overwhelmingly powerful was at last given its play, and the particle that swells to an avalanche was set in motion.

The very same net with which Abu Kasem had fished up his

shady gains in the bazaar he had now unconsciously snarled about himself, a net spun of the threads of his own avarice. And so he found himself in a pretty predicament, caught fast in the mesh of himself. What for a long time had been building within, a slowly growing, threatening tension, had unpredictably unloaded itself into the outer world and carried him into the clutches of the law, where he was now left to lash helplessly in a tangle of public mortification, neighborly blackmail, and trouble with the authorities. Abu Kasem's own behavior, his greedy prosperity and his avid hoarding of himself, had long been sharpening the teeth of this machinery and fitting them into place.

According to the Indian formula, man sows his seed and pays no attention to its growth. It sprouts and ripens, and then each must eat of the fruit of his own field. Not only our actions, but also our omissions, become our destiny. Even the things that we have failed to will are reckoned among our intentions and accomplishments, and may develop into events of grave concern. This is the law of Karma. Each becomes his own executioner, each his own victim, and, precisely as in the case of Abu Kasem, each his own fool. The laughter of the judge is the laughter of the devils in hell at the damned, who have uttered their own sentence and burn in their own flames.

The story of Abu Kasem shows how finely woven is the net of Karma, and how tough its delicate threads. Can his ego, whose demons now have him fast in their clutches, free him; can it put itself to death? In his despair, is he not already on the very verge of the recognition that no one can relieve him of his slippers, no power on earth destroy them, but that he must in some way go about getting rid of them nevertheless? If they could only become unessential to him, piece by piece, as they became more valuable to him with every mending! If he could only free

23

himself from their motley, patch by patch, until they were nothing but a pair of indifferent rags! [1]

It is told in the tale that the judge could not refuse Abu Kasem his boon, which means that he was no longer to be haunted by his dreadful slippers. The light of his new day, in other words, had begun to dawn. But that light could be rising, ultimately, from no other place but the deep crater of his own interior, which up to now had been shrouding his vision with its cloudy distillations. *Nemo contra diabolum nisi deus ipse.* The far-spun mysterious ego, which he had so painfully woven around himself as his world—the judge, the neighbors, the fishermen, the elements (for even these took part in the play of his secretly beloved ego), the filthy slippers, and his wealth—had been sending him hint after hint. What more could he ask from his external mirror sphere? It had spoken to him in its own way, blow upon blow. The final release, now, would have to come from himself, from within. But how?

It is at such a moment that the hint of a dream can be helpful, or an inkling of insight in response to the oracle of some timeless

---

[1] Strindberg conceived this way back, in his *inferno* period. He discovered in Swedenborg the conception of the punishment that a man hangs around his own neck, having produced it from his own unconscious, and he knew from experience how uncannily inanimate objects can play their fatal tricks—strange articles, indifferent houses and streets, institutions, and all the rags and tags of the everyday.

As an old man, very tired, Strindberg wrote a fairy story based on the old tale of Abu Kasem's slippers ("Abu Casems Toffler," *Samlade Skrifter*, Del. 51, Stockholm, 1919). But his version does not fulfill the promise of the title. Many essential points have been changed and much that is unessential has crept in. The tattered slippers are not Abu Kasem's own lifework, but were only given to him by the Caliph to prove his avarice. In some of his earlier writings, on the other hand, he had dealt more successfully with this question of the self-engendered destiny—the self-built theater of life, which then comes alive and begins to play with us because its wings and props are expressions of our own inner being. He had presented it as a phase of his own journey into hell in *To Damascus* (1898), where he showed how our material world is produced from the stuff of our own involuntary compulsions—both the fiendish compulsions and the silently helpful.

tale. For the hidden magician who projects both the ego and its mirror world can do more than any exterior force to unravel by night the web that has been spun by day. He can whisper: "Change your shoes." And therewith we have only to look and see of what our slippers have been made.

A PAGAN HERO AND A
CHRISTIAN SAINT

1

ONCE upon a time there lived a mythical king and his queen—
King Conn of Ireland and Queen Eda of Brittany; and their marriage was a union so perfect that it equaled that of Heaven and
Earth, which is the macrocosmic archetype of all weddings. The
historians declare that the perfection of their character and conduct was reflected in the blessings of their reign: "the earth
produced exuberant crops and the trees ninefold fruit; rivers,
lakes, and the sea teemed with choice fish; the herds and the
flocks were unusually prolific."

Such descriptions of natural abundance are not unusual in the
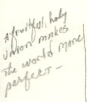 legends of beneficent reigns; for when two faultless rulers con-
form to the divine law of the universe and guide their people by
their own model conduct, they bring into operation the quickening power of perfection. The consummate king and queen make
manifest together what the Chinese term *Toa:* the virtue of the
universal order. They make *Tao* manifest as *Teh:* the virtue of
their own proper nature. And this virtue is self-effulgent. Its influence penetrates like magic into the vital centers of everything
around them, so that even the spirit of the land appears to be
affected. Harmony and beatitude go out from it. The fields produce, the herds multiply, and the cities thrive, as in a Golden
Age.

Now this King Conn and Queen Eda had a son, and since the

druids foretold at his birth that he should inherit the good qualities of both his parents, he was given both their names and called
Conn-eda. And, indeed, he was an extraordinary child. He grew
up to be the idol of the king and queen, and the pride of his
people. He was greatly honored and beloved.

But sad to relate, during the years of his youth the high
promise of Conn-eda's career was abruptly darkened; for his
mother died, and his father, on the advice of the druids, took another wife. She was the daughter of the king's arch-druid, had
children of her own, foresaw that Conn-eda would succeed to
the throne, and out of jealousy and hatred began to seek his ruin.
She desired his death, or at the very least his exile from the
land, and to bring her evil purpose to pass began to circulate
calumnious reports. But the youth was above suspicion. And so,
presently, she resorted to supernatural devices and betook herself to a celebrated witch.

The wicked queen was obliged to fulfill a number of odd and
very costly requirements, but in the end was supplied with a
miraculous chessboard, so charmed that its owner should always
win the first game. She was to challenge the unsuspecting prince
with the suggestion that the winner of a game might impose
whatever *geis*, or "condition," he liked and, when she then had
won, was to pledge him, under penalty of exile, to procure within
a year certain mythical trophies: three golden apples from the
fairy realm, as well as the black steed and the hound of supernatural powers belonging to the fairy king. So precious and well
guarded were these that should the prince attempt to procure
them he would undoubtedly meet his death.

The game was arranged. The prince had no suspicion of evil,
and the queen won. But she was so keen to have him completely
in her power that she challenged him to a second try, and this
time, to her astonishment and mortification, lost. She was unwilling to play again. She announced her *geis*, and when Conn-

27

eda heard it, he realized that he had been betrayed. But the second *geis* was his to name. He decided to keep the queen immobile while he was gone. So he required that she should sit upon the pinnacle of the castle tower and there remain, exposed to sun and storm and subsisting on the most meager fare, until his return—or until the expiration of the stipulated year and a day.

Conn-eda now was in desperate need of advice. He resorted to a puissant druid; but when the sage consulted the particular divinity he worshiped, it was revealed that neither the druid nor his god had any power to help. There existed, however— so the druid suggested—a certain Bird of the Human Head, a peculiar creature fabled for its knowledge of the past, present, and future, which lived concealed in a dangerous wilderness and even if found would be difficult to cajole. It was the druid's belief that, if induced to speak, that bird might be of valuable assistance. "Take yonder little shaggy horse," he said, "and mount him immediately; for in three days the bird will make himself visible and the little shaggy steed will conduct you to his abode. But lest the bird should refuse to reply to your queries, take this precious stone and present it to him, and then little danger and doubt exist but that he will give you a ready answer."

Conn-eda mounted the unimpressive steed, and let the reins fall loose on its neck so that the animal might take whatever road it chose. It was a magical horse, possessed of the gift of speech, and it carried its rider safely through a series of adventures. In due time the prince came to the hiding place of the strange bird, presented the stone, and posed his question concerning the quest. Whereupon the creature, in response, flew to an inaccessible rock at some distance, and from that perch commanded in a loud, croaking, human voice: "Conn-eda, son of the King of Cruachan, remove the stone just under your right foot and take the ball of iron and the cup you will find under it;

28

then mount your horse, cast the ball before you, and having so done, your horse will tell you all the other things you will need to know."

Removing the stone, Conn-eda took the iron ball and the cup, mounted the horse, and cast the ball before him. It rolled on ahead at a regular rate, and the shaggy horse began to follow its lead. They arrived, in this fashion, at the shore of Loch Erne. But the ball did not stop; it rolled into the water and disappeared.

At this juncture the horse gave its first piece of advice. "Alight now," it said, "and put your hand into my ear; take from thence the small bottle of 'All-heal' and the little basket that you will find there, and remount with speed; for just now your great dangers and difficulties begin."

They went into the water, following the way taken by the iron ball, and the lake lay only as an atmosphere above their heads. The ball was rediscovered rolling quietly along. It came to a broad river, traversed by a ford, but defended by three terrible serpents with yawning, frightfully hissing mouths and formidable fangs.

"Now," said the shaggy horse, "open the basket and cast from it a piece of the meat into the mouth of each serpent; when you have done this, secure yourself in your saddle so that we may make all due arrangements to pass. If you cast the pieces of meat into the mouth of each serpent unerringly, we shall pass them safely; otherwise we are lost."

Conn-eda flung the pieces with unerring aim. "Bear a benison and victory," said the little horse, "for you are a youth who will win and prosper." Then it gave a leap and with a single mighty bound cleared both the river and the ford. "Are you still mounted, Prince Conn-eda?"

"It has taken only half my strength to remain so," Conn-eda replied.

They proceeded, following the ball, until they came in view

of a great mountain flaming with fire. "Hold yourself in readiness," warned the horse, "for another dangerous leap." And he sprang from the earth and flew like an arrow over the burning mountain. "Are you still alive, Conn-eda, son of the king?"

"I am just alive and no more, for I am greatly scorched," the prince replied.

"If you are alive at all," the little horse said, "I feel assured that you are a young man destined to meet supernatural success and benisons. Our greatest dangers are over, and there is hope that we shall overcome the next and last."

Conn-eda, on the advice of the druidic steed, applied the elixir "All-heal" to his burns and was made as whole and fresh as ever. Then they set out once again along the track of the iron ball, and at last arrived at the fortress of the fairies—a vast city, surrounded by high walls, and defended not by arms, but by two towers of flame.

"Alight on this plain," the horse said, "and take a small knife from my other ear, and with this knife you shall kill me and flay me. When you have done this, envelop yourself in my hide and you can pass the gate unscathed and unmolested. When you get inside you can come out at pleasure, because, when once you enter, there is no danger, and you can pass and repass whenever you wish; and let me tell you that all I have to ask of you in return is that, once inside the gate, you will immediately come back and drive away the birds of prey that may be fluttering round to feed on my carcass—and more, that you will pour any drop of that powerful 'All-heal,' if such still remains in the bottle, upon my flesh to preserve it from corruption."

The prince was deeply shocked. "Well, my noblest steed," he said, "because you have been so faithful to me hitherto, and because you still would have rendered me further service, I consider such a proposal insulting to my feelings as a man and totally at variance with the spirit which can feel the value of

30

gratitude, not to speak of my feelings as a prince. But as a prince I am able to say: Come what may—come death itself in its most hideous forms and terrors—I will never sacrifice friendship to personal interest. Hence I am, I swear by my arms of valor, prepared to meet the worst—even death itself—sooner than violate the principles of humanity, honor, and friendship!"

The animal insisted in its demand. "Never, never!" repeated the gentle prince.

"Well, then, son of the great western monarch," said the horse in a tone of sorrow, "if you refuse to follow my advice on this occasion, I tell you that both you and I shall perish and shall never meet again; but, if you act as I have instructed you, matters will assume a happier and more pleasing aspect than you can imagine. I have not misled you heretofore, and if I have not, what need have you to doubt the most important portion of my counsel? Do exactly as I have directed you, else you will cause a worse fate than death to befall me. And moreover, I can tell you that if you persist in your resolution, I have done with you forever."

The prince, in the end, reluctantly took the knife out of the horse's ear and, with trembling hand, experimentally pointed the weapon at its throat. Whereupon, as if impelled by some magic power, the blade struck suddenly of itself deep into the neck, and the work of death was done. The distracted youth cast himself beside the carcass on the ground and cried aloud until his consciousness was gone.

When he recovered, he assured himself that the little steed was dead, and then, though with misgivings and abundant tears, essayed the task of flaying. This done, he enveloped himself in the hide and in a half-demented state passed through the gate. He was neither molested nor opposed. But the splendor of the fairy city had no charm for him; he was moving in a daze, absorbed entirely in his grief.

When the last request of the horse forced itself upon his mind,

31

he returned to the carcass, put the birds of prey to flight, and with the precious ointment embalmed the now mangled remains. To his surprise, the inanimate flesh commenced to undergo some strange change, and in a few minutes, to his unspeakable joy, it assumed the form of the handsomest and noblest young man imaginable and came to life. The two embraced in an ecstasy of delight.

"Most noble and puissant prince," the new youth declared, "you are the best sight I ever saw with my eyes, and I am the most fortunate being in existence for having met you! Behold in my person, changed to the natural shape, your little shaggy horse. I am the brother of the king of the fairy city, and it was the wicked druid who kept me so long in bondage; but he was to give me up when you came to consult him, because the condition, the *geis* of my bondage, was then broken. Nevertheless I could not recover my pristine shape and appearance unless you acted as you have kindly done. It was my own sister who urged the queen, your stepmother, to send you in quest of the apples, the steed, and the powerful puppy hound, which my brother has now in his keeping. My sister, rest assured, had no thought of doing you the least injury, but much good, as you will find hereafter, because, if she were maliciously inclined toward you, she could have accomplished her end without any trouble. In short, she only wanted to free you from all future danger and disaster and recover me from my relentless enemies through your aid. Come with me, my friend and deliverer, and the steed and the puppy hound of extraordinary powers and the golden apples shall be yours, and a cordial welcome shall greet you in my brother's abode."

The happy ending is quickly told. Conn-eda obtained the three trophies and was urged to spend the remainder of his period of trial in the fairy realm as the guest of the king. When the time for his departure came, he was besought to return at least once every year. On the journey home no difficulties presented themselves, and in due time he came in sight of the wicked queen. She was still perching on her uncomfortable pinnacle, but full of hope, for the last day of the ordeal had dawned. The prince, surely, would fail to arrive and therewith would forfeit all of his rights to the kingdom.

But lo! Behold! She thought she spied him. He was returning, mounted on a black charger and leading a hound by a silver chain. The queen cast herself from the tower in a fit of despair and was dashed to bits. And when the king was apprised of her base conduct, he ordered that her remains should be burned.

The prince planted his three golden apples in the garden. Instantly a magnificent tree sprang up, bearing golden fruit, which caused all the realm to produce exuberant crops. If the years of Conn-eda's father had been great, his own were greater, and the long reign is famous to this day for its abundance. The kingdom that Conn-eda governed still bears his name: it is the western Irish province of Connacht.[1]

So runs the ancient pagan myth, as it has come down to us in the simple speech of the nineteenth-century peasant cottage; and though it has survived many centuries of change, its images still carry the force of their primitive, pre-Christian lore of the soul. They follow patterns well known from many other myths and tales of wonder, patterns adapted from the rich world treasury of symbolic forms, and like the shaggy horse himself, when dissected and sympathetically regarded, they undergo a remarkable transfiguration.

[1] "The Story of Conn-eda; or the Golden Apples of Lough Erne," translated by Nicholas O'Kearney from the original Irish of the story-teller, Abraham McCoy, and published by W. B. Yeats, *Irish Fairy and Folk Tales*, New York, Modern Library, no date. The tale was first printed in the *Cambrian Journal*, 1855.

A parallel romance, dealing with a prince of Ireland and a shaggy horse, will be found in Jeremiah Curtin, *Myths and Folk-lore of Ireland*, Boston, Little, Brown and Co., 1890: "The King of Ireland and the Queen of the Lonesome Island,"

The young prince Conn-eda is the faultless offspring of the ideal mythical male and female, incorporating the virtues of both his parents; this fact is represented in his twofold name. He is hailed as the perfect successor of his father, because he is virtually the consummate human embodiment of *Tao*. The energies of life, both in man and in nature, should function harmoniously and produce abundantly under his influence; an ideal conjunction of cosmic and human processes should make itself everywhere manifest in the conditions of his realm. He should be the perfect ruler, at once beneficent and forceful, checking, balancing, and co-ordinating all of the mutually antagonistic elements that make for life, both the creative and the destructive, the evil and the good.

However, though no one is aware of the fact (Conn-eda least of all), he is not yet really fit; for though faultless in the virtues of youth, he is still ignorant of the possibilities of evil which are present everywhere in his realm and in the world—in human nature as well as in the subhuman, elemental forces of the cosmos. The purity and radiance of the boy's nature have preserved his heart from all the darker motives of existence. He knows nothing of the sinister other half, nothing of the ruthless, destructive powers that counterbalance virtue—the selfish, disruptive, fiendish violences of ambition and aggression. These, under his benign rule, would have emerged to wreck the harmony of the realm. So guileless is he, indeed, that he is not even aware of the malice of the stepmother under his own roof.

Conn-eda, that is to say, has everything to learn. Before he can cope with the multiplicity of life's forces, he must be introduced to the universal law of coexisting opposites. He has to realize that completeness consists in opposites co-operating through conflict, and that harmony is essentially a resolution of irreducible tensions. For he does not yet understand that the pattern of existence is woven of antagonistic co-operation, al-

34

ternations of ascendancy and decline, that it is built of bright *and* dark, day *and* night—*Yang* and *Yin,* in the Chinese formulation. To become the perfect king, therefore, he must make himself complete, and, to do this, must confront and integrate the reality most contrary and antagonistic to his own character. He must come to grips with the forces of evil, hence the necessity to follow the hidden road of the dolorous quest. His myth, his wonder tale, is an allegory of the agony of self-completion through the mastery and assimilation of conflicting opposites. The process is described in the typical symbolic terms of encounters, perils, feats, and trials.

Conn-eda first confronts the contradictory principle in the form of the self-will and lust for power of the ruthless stepmother, who drives him out of the realm, that is, out of the kingdom of the living. Her earlier intrigue and calumnies should have warned him, but in his boyish good faith he falls into the trap of the friendly game.[1] Thus proven incapable of recognizing and matching evil on the plane of human life, he is compelled to face it in the much cruder, undisguised, subhuman form of the destructive elements of nature. This is the sense of his descent into the miraculous lake. There he endures the blind fury of the powers of life in their unpacified, sheerly destructive aspect, the aspect exactly opposite to that of their harmonious co-operation in the terrestrial kingdom of his father, where they were tempered by the magic influence of human virtue. The interaction of the conflicting opposites under the masterly control of the perfect king was not disastrous at all, but wholly creative, manifesting the contrarieties of *Yang* and *Yin* as integrated in the wholeness of the order of *Tao.*

The powers on the infrahuman level are represented by the

---

[1] For chess in its original aspect of a conflict in which the players stake *themselves,* cf. Otto Rank, *Art and Artist,* New York, 1932, Chapter X, "Game and Destiny."

elements of water and fire. These are indispensable and useful when harnessed to human need and subjected to intelligent control, but blind and wrathfully indifferent in and of themselves. Water and fire, mutually antagonistic energies of nature, are both conspicuous for their ambivalent effects. At once life-sustaining and destructive (much more obviously so than the two other elements, air and earth), they represent the whole realm and force of the extrahuman world and its creating and dissolving, at once propitious and disastrous, character. They represent the totality of life energy and the whole of the life process, the constant action and interaction of conflicting opposites.

Conn-eda, then, has to make his way through the wrath and dread of water and fire as an initiation into the chaotic, inhuman side of life. Similarly, in the ancient mysteries of Isis and Osiris the initiate was required to pass through water, had to pass, that is to say, through the threat and experience of death, whence he would emerge reborn as a "Knower," a "Comprehender," beyond fear and released from all attachment to the perishable ego personality. This is the traditional way of initiation—a way attested abundantly in the mythologies and folk literatures of the world.[1]

Conn-eda escapes destruction as much through his own valor and virtue as through the support and advice of miraculous helpers. The deadly powers of the water are represented most appropriately in his story (as quite commonly in mythology) by the gigantic serpents. He propitiates these by executing—fearlessly, dexterously, carefully—a ritual of offerings; as sacrificial substitutes for his own flesh and life he tosses pieces of meat into their jaws. This amounts to a recognition of the reality of the chaotic powers, an acceptance of their *divine* character as

[1] Mozart presents an allegory of this same way of initiation in *The Magic Flute,* a work inspired by the description of the mysteries of Isis and Osiris in the Latin novel of Apuleius, *The Golden Ass.*

The hero affirms — the evil — worships it → Does not flee from it —

demonic presences entitled to worship. Instead of resisting, fighting, or bolting, the hero affirms. He confronts and deals with their tremendous reality, thus becoming a Knower, not shrinking from their fiendishness, but paying due heed to them in their ambivalent nature; for they are merciless, yet susceptible to propitiation, devilish, yet to be understood and treated as divine.

Conn-eda is thus outgrowing his innocence. Such a childlike state of grace has to be surpassed through experience, and experience precisely of the intrinsically twofold, ambivalent character of everything that forms life's warp and woof. Such an awakening entails the peril of a loss of all faith in virtue and in the values of the good—the peril of indifference or callousness to the distinction between good and evil and to their unending strife; or it may entail the opposite spiritual disaster—impotent despair, absolute disillusionment in man's capacity to realize the everlasting, great ideals. Conn-eda, however, is superior to these two perils; for he is, by birth, by nature, the hero elect, preordained to the life-revivifying quest. He is "a young man destined to meet supernatural success and benisons."

Nevertheless, it is only "just alive" and "greatly scorched" that he escapes the flames of the fiery mountain, his second trial. It is himself this time, who, in a symbolic way, is offered to the powers; but he passes through, and emerges to be anointed with the magic balm. "All-heal" is the same elixir as the Greek "Ambrosia," the Vedic "Amrita." It is the liquor of life, the drink and fare of eternity, which the gods enjoy in their abode: they are sustained by it in their immortality and bestow it on the heroes of their choice, whom it comforts and restores. It has been held in reserve for Conn-eda by the miraculous force that is conducting and supporting him, and when he is anointed with it he is symbolically reborn "of water and of the spirit." The death of the old Adam and the resurrection of the new is brought to pass, and the chosen one becomes the "Twice-born." His eyes having

37

been washed in death, he is made fit to see the fairy city—that is, the kingdom of God, which is within all men and things.

During the trials, Conn-eda is assisted by miraculous beings who come to his rescue and guide him, under the mask of animals. We have here an example of the ever-recurrent folk tale and myth motif of the "helpful animals." These symbolic figures embody and represent the instinctive forces of our nature, as distinguished from the higher human qualities of intellect, reason, will power, and good will. And it is already a sign that the hero is fit to conquer when these queer and unlikely helpmates appear and he submits to their advice. The higher human faculties would have been inadequate to conduct and support Conn-eda through his trials, which are of a character essentially incompatible with either the credence or the judgment powers of the conscious human intellect. He has, however, humility and faith; and it is precisely because of this disposition of his heart that those "other forces" embodied in the "helpful animals" are at his disposal. The young prince places implicit trust in the cryptic, not too encouraging suggestions of the old druid, and has humble faith in the shaggy unprepossessing horse. With these odd, unreasonable talismans and riding the shaggy little mount, he triumphs where a more prepossessingly and rationally equipped hero would have failed. No knightly charger this, no such brilliant stallion as would have befitted Conn-eda's princely valor; yet he trusts implicitly its sagacity and strength.

In the picture language of folklore and myth, the symbolic figure of mount and rider represents the centauric character of man, fatefully compounded of animal instinct and human virtue. The horse is the "lower," purely instinctive and intuitive aspect of the human being, the mounted knight the "higher" portion: conscious valor, the moral sense, will power, and reason. Normally, the rider is regarded as the guiding, goal-determining, dis-

38

criminating member of the fellowship and the steed as merely the servile, though not undignified, vehicle. Here, however, in this pagan Irish myth, it is the knight who submits, humbly, faithfully, letting his reins lie loose on the animal's neck.[1] Conn-eda, this hero of heroes, in his trial-beset passage through the unpredictable realm of nature's chaotic forces (the passage of his initiation into the dark secrets of the foundation of both the cosmic and the human-social worlds of forms), follows without qualm the lead of his "lower" wisdom, the inferior and despised aspect of his centauric nature, the unreasonable, instinctive impulses of his composite being. And this advice comes to him, not only through his mount, but also through the Bird of the Human Head and the rolling iron ball.

The druid to whom Conn-eda first betook himself was wise beyond the wisdom of his knowing, because he knew precisely what it was that he did not know. And it is indeed very wise to be clear about the limits of one's information; wise to know where, and from whom, the missing knowledge may be obtained; and wise to know what rituals, what requirements of approach, must be satisfied before the desired intelligence can be made one's own. Such wisdom was the wisdom of the druid, the Wise Old Man, the archetypal teacher, Conn-eda's *guru* and friend.

The Bird of the Human Head is to be understood as the animal aspect of the knowledge of the wholly human druid—just as, in the symbol of the horse and rider, the animal is the "lower" aspect of the knight. This oracular "rare bird" is more knowing than the Wise Old Man, because it is directly a part of nature,

---

[1] ["Now the Gods, ascending, knew not the way to the heavenly world, but the horse knew it" (*Śatapatha Brāhmaṇa* 13.2.8.1). Cf. René Guénon, *Aperçus sur l'initiation*, Paris, 1946.—AKC.]

EDITOR'S NOTE: Dr. Ananda K. Coomaraswamy has kindly supplied a few footnotes to supplement the material left by Dr. Zimmer. These are introduced in square brackets, and initialed AKC.

the voice of the wilderness untouched by human culture, the lord of the secret of the forest in which it dwells.[1] A human head poised on an airborne body, very difficult to deal with, elusive, hardly to be met, propitiable by a gift, yet swift to withdraw, this queerly embodied semihuman voice, croaking measured, peremptory advice, demands submission—blind and absolute submission—to the mutest forces: Conn-eda is assigned by it to the guardianship of a rolling iron ball.[2]

The ball follows gravity and so rolls to the center of all things, to the fairy realm of the universal forces, to God's bosom. It follows, and in following makes visible, the most general of all laws, the law that controls the movements of the heavenly bodies, the law that directs the orbit of each sphere in exact accordance with the weight of its mass, and in such a manner that the earth unfailingly encircles the sun, and the moon the earth. The ball opens the way directly by gravitation to the Unmoved Mover— that First Principle dealt with by Giordano Bruno in his *Della Causa Principio e Uno*—the center out of which everything proceeds, around which everything revolves, and back into which everything must in the end return.

To be able, like the hero Conn-eda, to let oneself go, yielding trustingly to the ground law that is the secret sense of one's own weightiness, and which, nevertheless, is singing everywhere— in the harmony of spheres, the primeval melody of the All, the "singing-match of the planet-brothers," the "thunder-passage" of the sun, in the hymn everlasting of the innermost heartbeat and circulation of the world organism—is to solve absolutely everything at a stroke. For this is to fall in with the vast rhythm of the universe and to move with it. This is to follow the blindest,

[1] [One must remember that "the speech of birds" is the language of angelic communication.—AKC.]

[2] This rolling ball reminds one of the wheel and rolling apple that the Irish epic hero Cuchullin follows on his way to Scathach's realm beyond the "bridge." Cf. Eleanor Hull, *The Cuchullin Saga in Irish Literature*, London, 1898, pp. 57-84.

dullest, mutest impulse—sheer gravity—yet thereby to plumb to the center of all things: that point where the greatest quiet abides; that point around which everything must circulate, simply because it holds its peace.[1]

Conn-eda consents at every turn to the dictates of nature's wisdom. He recognizes and accepts instinctual guidance under whatever mask, whatever garb, it may come to him: speaking horse, speaking bird, or rolling iron ball. And it is because of this openness to the nonrational that he is competent to follow the difficult path. Being an Irishman—and, moreover, one of the early period—he is spared the characteristic fault of modern man, the too exclusive reliance on intellect, reasoning, and consciously directed will power. As far as Conn-eda is concerned, the basis for the modern problem does not exist; he offers no resistance whatsoever to the guidance of the unconscious. Spontaneously and wholeheartedly, he submits to all the inscrutable commands and outlandish agents that steer him on.

But he shrinks from a deed of thanklessness and cruelty. Among his virtues is a trait of human gentleness, which must be counteracted if it is not to destroy both himself and his realm; for every impulse to violence is so alien to his nature, every motive of injustice so far from his comprehension, that he is defenseless against them. They have already caught him totally unprepared. His ultimate test, therefore—the supreme, most necessary test—will require him to slay, with a cold, inhuman thanklessness, his closest friend, this shaggy little mount and faithful guide, through

[1] This is the secret of the Chinese formula of *Wu Wei:* the avoidance of resistance and self-assertion. All stars have to circle around the Pole Star, because it remains still. All vassals and creatures in their respective circles move spontaneously in submission to the emperor, because he understands how to make his heart empty and motionless while sitting in perfect self-collection on his throne. He commits no act of interference. He knows nothing of management or plan. His serene countenance is directed southward, and he radiates to mankind and the whole world of nature the virtue of his own harmonization with the law of the circling play of heaven and earth.

41

whom he has achieved what his human powers of action and understanding never could have won for him.

The tests have been increasing toward this climax. At the first, the serpents were appeased by a substitute offering; at the second, the hero himself became the symbolic victim and was dangerously burned. But at this last, death is not to be mocked, and Conn-eda himself, moreover, is to be made its agent. Conn-eda is required to be ungrateful, merciless, and inhuman, required to violate his knightly virtue—that knightly, human virtue for which, during his model youth and boyhood, he was so greatly praised. He is required, that is to say, to be not only the sacrificer but the victim; for what he must annihilate is his own cherished character, and there is no self-conquest more arduous for the truly virtuous than this one of recreancy to the higher nature, sacrifice of the ideal, denial of the model role that one has striven always to represent.

Conn-eda must come to terms with the necessity to be ruthless. For how could the prince ever become the perfect king without understanding, from within, crime and the quality of the inhuman? How could the king preside as a supreme judge unless capable of surmounting his most cherished personal feelings, his propensity for indiscriminate mercy and compassion? The innocent youth must consummate his initiation into the wisdom of evil through the enactment of a crime; and this symbolic, sacramental act will fit him to dispense not only mercy but justice—make him a real Knower, capable of controlling the forces of darkness. Lacking this, he would never have been competent to establish, preserve, or himself represent, the harmony of *Tao*. Ignorant of the dark, the young king would never have understood the interaction of darkness against light, the co-operative mutual antagonism of the two, which is universal in the cosmos as well as in society: the reciprocal play of day and night, growth and decay. And in token of his transformation, his

42

attainment through crime to a new and superhuman stature and power, the innocent youth is finally compelled even to don the blood-dripping hide of his blameless victim. With this then as a protective garment, he is able to pass unharmed between the blazing towers, the towers of nature's wrath, the towers that guard the entrance to the fairy realm, where the all-supporting, all-dissolving, eternal energies of existence have their source.[1]

But this is not the whole of the meaning of the sacrifice. In doing away with the druidic horse, Conn-eda is annihilating not only his human virtue, but also that instinctive, intuitive power which up to this moment has been his indispensable guide —the wise and gentle animal nature represented in the rider's mount. The brave beast, with its all-knowing resourcefulness and supernatural strength, has borne him through two terrific trials. It jumped the abyss of water, passing fearlessly within reach of the serpents, and it soared like a rocket through the flames of the blazing crater, all with the marvelous felicity of a dream. Yet now, at the ultimate bound, the animal demands its own immolation.

Conn-eda will never achieve perfection, that is to say, unless the instinctive portion of his centauric character is radically changed. There must be a critical separation of the responsible, reasoning *I* from the unconscious, instinctual part. Up to the present, the guidance of the deep unconscious has been without moral counterpoise—the conscious, moral personality having played no role, either in the formulation or in the judgment of the hero's acts. There must now, therefore, be a momentary disintegration of the unitive companionship of the ideal friends, a decisive putting asunder of the rational and the instinctual aspects of this single human nature. That is why the gentle guide

---

[1] For the flaying motif, cf. Ananda K. Coomaraswamy, "Sir Gawayne and the Green Knight," *Speculum* XIX, Jan. 1944, p. 108, note 3; also, Paul Radin, *The Road of Life and Death*, The Bollingen Series V, 1945, p. 112.

demands its own cold immolation. That is why Conn-eda must become the sacrificial hand, hot with the blood of the creature he has loved and to whom he is indebted for his life. Stabbing the shaggy throat, he annihilates not his human virtue only, but his animal wisdom and support. However criminal, heartless, irrevocable, and unreasonable the sacrifice, nevertheless it effects a miraculous transformation and rebirth.

He kills his Animal wisdom + support -

Nothing dies, nothing perishes, nothing suffers annihilation utterly. No virtue, no energy is lost. Destruction—death—is but an outer mask of transformation into something better or something worse, higher or lower.

Destruction; Death is an outer mark of transformation

The miraculous sacrifice is performed upon a willing victim who has asked for it, and who submits to it as a supreme service. And the work is performed with deep regret and awe: this is the important detail. Though apparently heartless, selfish, and ungrateful, the act is counterbalanced by diametrically opposite, compensating deeds and dispositions: contrition and mercy, and the sprinkling of the precious elixir "All-heal." The prince brings to pass an integration of antitheses. Having conquered his own gentleness, he has nevertheless not lost it. Counteracting it, he has not permitted it to die. And it is precisely this—this ambilaterality—that has brought the miracle to pass.

Resuscitated, the guide assumes the appearance of a fairy prince very like Conn-eda himself—heir apparent to the throne of the fairy realm of life. And in so far as he is of human figure, this prince is the equal of Conn-eda, but in so far as he is of supernatural character, the superior. On the other hand, the little mount was inferior as to figure, though superior in its instinctive wisdom, untiring strength, and cheerfulness in trial, as well as in the possession of the implements of healing and salvation, which it carried in its ears. What the auspicious transformation signifies is the integration of this superiority on a higher plane.

While still in its animal form, the guiding principle was com-

44

pelled to operate on the unconscious level—clear-sighted, yet
mute and instinctive, like the wit of a sleepwalker balancing along
the edge of a roof. Dark, possibly demonic, irresponsible, indifferent (though not so when serving the elect rider), it was subdued in its potential splendor. With death and disenchantment,
however, the "sub" becomes immediately "super" consciousness.
No longer animal, but human in character and expression, the
fairy power is restored to the fullness of its glory. Nature discloses the muffled presence at the root of it. And Conn-eda is
greeted by a comely brother as conscious as himself, but superior
still in power and in wisdom.

The moral of the story, at this point, is one generally voiced
by Irish myths and fairy tales: follow your unconscious intuitive
forces blindly and with confident faith; they will carry you
through your perilous trials. Cherish them; believe in them; do
not frustrate them with intellectual distrust and criticism; but
permit them to move and sustain you. They will bear you through
the barriers, across thresholds and beyond dangers that could not
be met with any other guide, surpassed on any other mount.
And until they ask you of themselves to consummate what will
be felt as a painful parting, do not kill them. When the time
comes, they will mark the moment and indicate the way; for,
better than the rider, these mute forces understand that death,
the dolorous sundering, is a prelude to rebirth, transmutation
and reunion, and they know when the possibility for the miracle
is present. They know what our ego, conscious and rational,
never will comprehend, must not even try to comprehend before
the instant of the event itself: they know, namely, that there
is no death.

Death, annihilation: this is one of those basic, limited, and
delimiting conceptions that circumscribe our consciousness,
constitute the foundation of our ego world, and supply the
motivation for the organization of our personality. Personality,

consciousness, and the ego world arise and grow in time and space; they are liable to destruction, and consequently are right in dreading death. But if we assume that what they are and comprehend constitutes the whole of our existence, we are wrong. Their self-awareness and scope of operation are only one phase, one expression, reflex, or manifestation, of life's energy within the compound of the individual.

There is within us yet another being, underneath the born and perishable ego, which, knowing nothing of annihilation, feels perfectly secure in the valley of the serpents and the leap across the perilous stream. This is the presence that in its gentle, casual way, asks of the clinging rider, even in the moment of soaring over the terrifying obstacles: "Are you still in the saddle? . . . Are you still alive?" Undaunted by the perils of the elements, unscorched by the flames of the mountain, sacrificed, reborn, virtually imperishable, this priceless creature partakes of the virtue of the immortal. It holds the greatest expectations for its rider: "You are a youth that will win and prosper . . . a young man destined to meet with supernatural success and benisons." But the rider's fulfillment will depend on the sacrificial deed. Our unconscious life energy, subsisting apart from ego consciousness, unfailingly instinctive, reflects the divine portion of our human nature; but only by transmuting it through our conscious work into the higher form of intuitive superconsciousness shall we ever attain to those magic gifts that are the prizes of the quest.

The golden apples, the puppy hound of extraordinary powers, and the black steed are the gifts and tokens of the virtues of the fairy realm of undying life. The apples are identical with the Nordic apples of Freya's garden, the classical apples of the Hesperides, and the biblical fruit of the tree of everlasting life, which our first parents neglected to pluck.[1] Aphrodite, the

[1] Genesis 3:22.

Goddess of Love, the Golden-Throned, gave three such talismans from her gardens in the sacred isle of Cyprus to the young Hippomenes, when he had staked his life on his race with the maid, Atalanta. Whenever the miraculously fleet girl, scornful and chaste as the virgin goddess Artemis, drew a little ahead in their race, the youth tossed these golden, irresistible charms, one by one, before her, and she stooped to pick them up. That was how he won, and the girl lost, her wild maidenhood. For the golden apples break the spell of the fear of death—the fear of passing with the passage of time—and unite the will with its proper aim. They are the fare that sloughs away mortality. They are the sustenance of the immortals. Those who taste become identified with the imperishable portion of their nature and are as gods.

The puppy hound of extraordinary powers, scenting out, pursuing, never off the trail, and infallibly attaining its aim, is the ideal pointer, an embodiment of instinctive wisdom and awareness, its quarry being any sort of deer in the wild wood of life and the unconscious. It is another embodiment of the instinct and intuition of the shaggy horse. And the black steed too, a magnificent charger, is still another embodiment: a high, knightly transfiguration of the formerly very modest mount. This is the proper form for the steed and companion of the hero king.[1]

Thus Conn-eda has forfeited nothing by departing from the fairy lake and its prince; for there is no parting, no death, no loss, on the higher plane of superpersonal existence. Under the form of the apples, the dog, and the black charger, he keeps with him the powers that formerly, through the humble service of the shaggy horse, had supported and guided him. They represent that other "lower" aspect of his centauric nature, which

[1] "There is no horse so tough as a black horse," says the grandmother of the hero Finn McCool, when she is fleeing with him from a charge of knights. "A white horse has no endurance; . . . there is never a brown horse but it is giddy." Jeremiah Curtin, *op. cit.*, pp. 208-209.

now has revealed itself in its pre-eminent form. They make known the lofty meaning of the former guide, the shaggy horse, that had been neither black, nor white, nor brown, but the perfect union of all qualities and contrarieties—the more modest vehicle of the same life force that has now revealed its might.

On his quest to the higher realm the hero spends the ritualistic period of one year, which is the symbol of one life or incarnation, one complete cycle of existence—spring to winter, birth to death. During this eon he shares the life of the immortals. He is accepted by them as of their kin through the holy rite of hospitality, and this makes him, finally, one of their kind. He becomes established in, and imbued with, the qualities of their higher mode of being. The formerly dormant, divine essence within him thus being quickened, he acquires a dual character and is made an inhabitant of the two spheres, the mortal and the divine.[1] Such is the twofold character and double citizenship conferred on the perfected initiate by the ultimate sacrament of Assumption, or Transfiguration, which both symbolizes and brings to pass the Apotheosis of Man.

When the man-god at last returns, reborn and bearing the tokens of his wisdom and power, the forces of evil collapse automatically and of themselves. The queen stepmother dashes herself to the ground. Such an end is the only real defeat there can ever be for the forces of evil: self-dissolution, self-annihilation, before a qualitative (not quantitative) superiority—a superiority that has been achieved through self-sacrifice, self-conquest, and an effective integration, in a reconciled and reconcilable form, of the essence of the power of evil itself. For every lack of integration in the human sphere simply asks for the appearance, somewhere in space and time, of the missing opposite. And the

[1] ["This self gives itself to that self, that self gives itself to this self. Thus they gain each other. In this form he gains yonder world, in that form he experiences this world" (*Aitareya Āranyaka* II. 3.7).—AKC.]

48

personification, the embodiment, of that predestined antagonist will inevitably show its face.

This is the manner of the dragon's service to life. It brings into undeniable statement the power of the missing, not-yet-integrated factor, and compels the warders of society to take that factor into account. This is the manner of the dragon's "antagonistic co-operation." Before it can be undone, the hero himself, the hero-society, must undergo a transformation, a crisis of disintegration and then reintegration on a broader base, whereupon the *raison d'être* of the dragon will have been surpassed, and in despair of its now vain, purely destructive nothingness, it will evanesce, burst and disappear. But, on the other hand, if conquered merely by a weight of arms, the necessity for its reappearance will not have been eliminated, and after a time of recuperation, it will throw off the fetters of whatever underworld dungeon it may have been assigned to, come breaking through the fault in the walls of the current system, and precipitate "another war."

Those who are innocent always strive to exclude from themselves and to negate in the world the possibilities of evil. This is the reason for the persistence of evil—and this is evil's secret. The function of evil is to keep in operation the dynamics of change. Co-operating with the beneficent forces, though antagonistically, those of evil thus assist in the weaving of the tapestry of life; hence the experience of evil, and to some extent this experience alone, produces maturity, real life, real command of the powers and tasks of life. The forbidden fruit—the fruit of guilt through experience, knowledge through experience—had to be swallowed in the Garden of Innocence before human history could begin. Evil had to be accepted and assimilated, not avoided. And that is the second great lesson of this pagan tale.

A very deep meaning attaches, finally, to the notion that the fairy kingdom requires the deed of the perfect human hero if

49

it is to regain its lost prince and be rescued from distress—if it is to regain, that is to say, the fullness of its splendor. Through an earlier mythological disaster, not fully recounted in our tale, the brother of the king of the realm of the fairy powers, the king himself in duplicate as it were, became estranged from his transcendental home and condemned to the inferior existence-form of the shaggy horse. His domain was rendered somehow kingless thereby (though ruled, still, by its king), powerless, invalidated, and bereft.

The fairy prince desires deliverance from this exile, and his kingdom awaits his return; yet he is permitted to make the necessary journey only when bearing the human rider on his back. Only by assisting the mortal hero to immortal life can the superhuman prince effect his own salvation. The human being attains also thereby salvation, completeness, and the power to overcome distress, while the fairy realm, receiving back its prince, reintegrating the lost one into its system, is healed of its affliction, restored to perfection, and flooded with joy.

The meaning is, as we have already seen, that a co-operation between the conscious and unconscious forces is necessary if the state of superconscious perfection is to be known. In the perilous quest for the divine symbols of life, the mute, instinctive faculties of the psyche co-operate with the conscious personality. Of themselves they already tend to return to the higher, superhuman sphere from which they sprang; they are hoping for, expecting, and striving for, their own long-postponed restoration. Nevertheless, they require the deed of the human being. As the animal warns: "If you do not follow my advice, both you and I shall perish." All action rests with the hero. As protagonist of the conscious principle, it is he who has to perform the decisive acts. Conn-eda must discover and appease the speaking bird, unearth the talismans, make use of the magic implements in the horse's ears. Yet he is not the directing principle. His role is to

50

be only an instrument. His destiny is to save and redeem those very powers of the divine kingdom that guide and save himself.

This paradoxical motif opens a tremendous vista, revealing one of the major problems of mythology and theology. It is, in fact, identical with the fundamental theme of our Jewish-Christian belief: that of the human savior's redemption of the god. Jesus Christ, the Messiah, the second and human person of the Trinity, brings redemption by appeasing the vengeful Father God, Jehovah, who has become absorbed in a strictly negative attitude toward mankind, his chosen people. The universal hero submits to his own immolation, dies, but rises transfigured from the tomb. And by virtue of the all-healing blood of that Lamb, the Father himself becomes transformed. The Jewish tribal Jehovah, liberated from the spell of his wrath, becomes the universal Holy Ghost, and the Christian benison goes out to all the world, quickening human life for the new dispensation.

Richard Wagner presents and develops this same theme as the pivotal problem of his later works. And what we find is that the savior, Jesus Christ of the New Testament, has now to be saved himself: Parsifal restores to power the divine principle of Christ's blood in the vessel of the Grail. What had become dormant and ineffectual he brings to effusion, and the chorus of angels rejoices. *Erlösung dem Erlöser!* "Redemption to the Redeemer!" These are the last words of the mystical work. The hero in human form has quickened the quickening essence of the Holy Spirit. The human has restored once again the power of the divine.

Wagner's Brünnhilde likewise—symbolic of humanity incarnate, "the fallen goddess," suffering and compassionate—redeems All-Father Wotan from the spell of his spiritual impotence. Self-renouncing, self-immolating, she leaps into the purifying flame, and, before her act of self-extinction, sings her final song: *Ruhe,*

51

ruhe, du Gott! "Rest thou, rest, thou God!"—words at once of requiem and of liberating conjuration.

The fierce tribal divinity, Jehovah, was the archetypal projection of the paternal urge-for-offspring of Abraham himself, patriarch of patriarchs, who yearned to beget a multitude of descendants, numerous as the sands of the sea. This was perhaps a compensatory desire that took possession of him when Sarah, his wife, remained for so many decades barren. Abraham's very personal and particular, indeed exclusively familial, Jehovah—jealous, touchy, irascible, punctilious and revengeful—had to be metamorphosed into the universal, superpersonal Holy Ghost, beyond all the bounds of race and language, in order that the sweet dew of heaven should be dispensed to all. The progression was from a tribal, national, chauvinistic religion, full of self-pride (as if any people were the chosen folk; as if all were not chosen by Providence to fulfill their singular tasks in accordance with their particular virtues!) to a religion that should be universal: a transformation comparable to that effected in India with the development from Hinduism to Mahāyāna Buddhism. This wonderful miracle of metamorphosis has been consummated for us on the spiritual plane by the mediation of Jesus Christ. On the physical plane of the nations of our Christian civilization, however, the effects are hardly yet perceptible—even in spite of Easter, weekly communion, "Onward, Christain Soldiers," and Wagner's redemption of the redeemer.

2

The problem of our redemption through the integration of evil is illuminated from another and surprising angle by a medieval German legend of the fifteenth century, a dark, uncanny version of the life of Saint John Chrysostom, "John Golden-

Mouth," the celebrated bishop of Constantinople who was born at Antioch about A.D. 345. He won the love of his people by his gift of eloquence, and the hatred of many of the court and cloister by his zeal for ascetic reform. Having brought synods, emperors and popes to heel, he died in exile at the age of sixty-two.

The strange story goes that there was once in Rome a pope who used to ride abroad on horseback with his knights. And it was his custom, during these excursions, to draw away from his suite, and, while remaining in the saddle, recite his prayers alone. On one of these pious occasions he heard a voice crying and he thought: "What a pitiable voice!" He rode in its direction. But when he heard it again and looked about, there was no one to be seen.

The pope realized that he must have been overhearing the lamentations of a ghost. So he bade the spirit, in the name of God, to declare itself. "I am a miserable soul," the voice answered mournfully, "suffering in the flames of hell."

In pity, the pope inquired how the poor thing might be relieved of its pain. "You cannot help," came the reply. "But there is in Rome a certain pious man, married to a virtuous wife, and I know that she has conceived by him a child that is to be a blessed man, called John, and he will become a priest. Now if that priest will say sixteen masses on my behalf, I shall be released from these fires of hell." The soul then told in what street the parents would be found and what their names were, and with a final, bloodcurdling scream, was gone.

The pope returned to the city and inquired after the pious couple. When they were found, he begged them to tell him when their child was to be born. He had the infant carried to his court, where he christened it John and took it into his protection, caring for it as though it were his son.

John at the age of seven was sent to school, but was conspic-

53

uously poor in his studies. The other boys began to make mock of him, and he was ashamed. So when he went to church every morning he prayed before the image of Our Lady that she should help him in his work. One day the lips of the image moved and the Virgin spoke. "John, kiss my mouth," she said, "and you shall be filled with knowledge and become the master of all arts. You shall become more learned than any man on earth." The boy was afraid, but the image gave him courage. "Kiss me, John. Come! Do not be afraid." He pressed his trembling mouth to the lips of the Blessed Lady, kissed her, and by that kiss drew into himself wisdom and a miraculous knowledge of the arts.

John returned to the school, and he settled down to listen and learn. But it transpired that he knew more than all the others together and no longer required to be taught. There was a golden circlet around his mouth, and it shone like a star. His companions were astonished. "How does it happen that you now know everything?" they demanded. "Only yesterday, not even a flogging could teach you!" He described to them the miracle by which he had acquired his golden sign, and they called him Golden-Mouth. "You deserve this title," they said, "for the words from your mouth are as gold." And thereafter it was John Golden-Mouth who did all the teaching in the school.

The good pope entertained a great love for John Golden-Mouth and, since he was impatient to release the suffering soul from hell, had the boy ordained as soon as possible. John celebrated his first mass at the age of sixteen. But while he was at the altar a disquieting thought occurred to him: "O Lord, I am as yet too young. To become a priest and commune with God before being really prepared must be contrary to the heavenly will. I am going to rue this day forever." He continued saying the mass, but a resolution was taking shape in his mind. "Temporal possessions are bad for the soul; I therefore pledge myself to be poor, for the sake of God. When the banquet in honor of

54

my first mass is over, I shall withdraw to the wilderness and remain there as a hermit as long as I live. Would that this mass were over!" he thought. "Oh, but it is long!"

The pope, full of joy, held a banquet for John Golden-Mouth and everybody rejoiced at the early ordination, but the young priest remained firm in his resolve. When the company had dispersed, he stole away, clad in poor clothes and carrying scarcely a loaf of bread.

When the pope learned of this event he was greatly troubled, and together with his suite searched everywhere for the vanished prodigy. But John had built himself a hut of bark and leaves in a hidden fastness of the wilderness, beside a spring and at the edge of a cliff. The hermitage was not discovered. Subsisting on roots and herbs, he remained there and he served God day and night. He prayed, he fasted, and he kept himself continuously awake, steadfast in devotion.

Now not far from the forest in which John had built his hermitage there lived an emperor in a castle, and one day the daughter of this emperor went with the maidens of her suite to gather flowers. A sudden gale arose, swept the country, and was so terribly strong that it lifted all the frightened maidens high into the air. When they were set down again, they discovered that the princess was no longer among them, nor could they imagine in what direction she might have been blown. The emperor, of course, was distracted when he was told, and searched diligently and extensively. But the beautiful royal maid could not be found.

Actually, she had been set down by the gale precisely at the door of John's hermitage, quite unhurt. She was lost and bewildered, but seeing the little hut—and John within it, who was kneeling at his prayers—felt reassured. She called. Hearing the clear voice, the saintly youth turned his head, and when he perceived her, was alarmed. The apparition implored him not to

55

leave her outside to die of hunger or to fall prey to the animals of the forest, and at last he was persuaded to admit her to the cell; for he considered that he should be guilty before God if he permitted her to die.

John took his staff, however, and drawing a line across the floor of the cell, divided it in two. One side he assigned to the girl. And he commanded her not to cross the line, but to lead, in her part of the cell, such a life as should befit a proper recluse. They continued for a while, side by side in this way, praying, fasting, and serving God, but the Tempter envied them their life in sanctity. He succeeded one night in provoking John to cross the line and take the girl in his arms, whereupon they fell into sin. And after that they were smitten with remorse.

John was afraid that if the girl should remain with him he would fall again, so he conducted her to the edge of the cliff and pushed her over. But the moment he had done this, he understood that he had sinned even worse than before. "Oh, wretched, accursed creature that I am!" he cried. "Now I have murdered this innocent girl. She would never have thought of sin had I not seduced her. And I have deprived her now of her life. God certainly will avenge this terrible sin on me forever."

John quit his hermitage in despair and left the wilderness. "Lord, my God," he lamented, "Thou hast forsaken me." After a time he felt a little hope. "I shall confess," he decided; and so he proceeded to the pope, confessed his sin, and professed repentance, but his godfather, who did not recognize him, turned him away in a terrible storm of indignation. "Depart from my sight, you have dealt bestially with this innocent girl," said the pope, "and the sin is on your head."

"I shall not doubt God," John thought; and he returned, deeply afflicted, to his hut, where he knelt and made this solemn prayer and vow: "May God, whose mercy is greater than my sin, accept graciously the penance I am about to impose upon myself. I vow to walk on all fours, like a beast, until I shall have earned God's grace. God, in His mercy, will let me know when I have atoned."

And he went down on his hands and moved about on all fours; and when he grew tired, he would creep into the hut and lie down there like a beast. He existed in this manner many years, never drawing his body up to standing posture. His garment rotted and fell away, his skin grew rough and hairy, and he became unrecognizable as a human being.

Meanwhile, it so happened that the wife of the emperor gave birth to another child, and the pope was asked to baptize it. He came and took the infant in his arms, but it cried out, loudly: "You are not the one to baptize me." The pope was astonished and afraid and tried to quiet the babe, but it persisted in its resistance, and when its will was sought, it replied: "Saint John, the holy man, is the one who is going to baptize me. God will send him to me from the wilderness." The pope returned the child to the nurse, and, going to the empress, inquired: "Who is this Saint John that is to baptize the babe?" But no one knew.

About this time, the hounds of the huntsmen of the emperor ran down a very curious beast. The men could not imagine what it was. But since it gave no resistance, they readily captured it, and, throwing a cloak around it, bound its legs. Then they brought it to the emperor's castle, and the rumor went out and many people came to look at it, but the animal crept under a bench and tried to hide.

The nurse with the child was among the visitors, and there were present at the time many knights and ladies. The child commanded: "Show me the beast." A servant stirred it from its hiding place, and twice it made its way back, but the third time it remained in view.

Then the newborn infant addressed it. "John, dear lord," it

said with a firm, clear voice, "I am to receive baptism by your hand."

The uncouth creature on all fours, hairy, weird, lifted a voice that was firm and clear and made reply: "If your words be true and this is the will of God, speak once again."

The newborn infant answered: "Dear father, why do you tarry? I am to be baptized by your hand."

Whereupon John called aloud to God: "O Lord, let me know by the voice of this child if my sins be atoned."

And the child continued: "Dear John, rejoice, for God has forgiven you all your sins. Arise, therefore, and, in the name of God, baptize me."

John lifted his body from the ground and rose up like a human being. The filth and dirt that clung to his skin fell away immediately, like withered bark, and his body became clean again, bright and smooth. They brought him clothing. The pope and nobles bade him welcome. When John had baptized the babe, the pope invited him to sit down.

"Dear father," John asked, "do you not know me?"

"No," the pope replied, "I do not."

John said: "I am your godchild. You baptized me with your own hands, sent me to school, and, while I was still a very young lad, ordained me. But while celebrating my first mass, I thought it unseemly to take the Host in my unready hands, and so, after the mass and the following banquet, I stole away to the wilderness, where I have prayed, suffered, sinned, and repented, these many years." John described in all candor how he had seduced the maid and murdered her, and confessed his sin to the pope himself.

The emperor was informed of the story, and his heart grew heavy. "That was my beloved daughter," he thought; and he prayed John to conduct him to the cliff where the girl had been killed. They might recover her bones, he said, and accord them decent, Christian burial. So John guided the huntsmen to the hut where they had captured him, and then rode with them through the forest to the cliff. When they peered over the brink they beheld a young woman quietly sitting below.

John called to the solitary figure: "Why are you sitting like this, alone at the base of the cliff?"

She answered: "Do you not see who I am?"

"No," said John, "I do not."

"I am the one who came to your cell," she said, "and you thrust me over the brink."

John was amazed.

"God bore me up," said she, "so that I came to no harm." And by a great miracle, she was as beautiful there as she had ever been, and she was clothed in royal garments.

The emperor and empress took her to their hearts, giving thanks to God for her recovery, and the pope then departed for Rome, requiring John to go with him.

"How many masses have you said, dear son?" the pope asked.

"Not more than that one," John replied.

"Alas!" said the pope.

"What is it, my dear father?"

"I am filled with woe at the thought of that poor soul still suffering in the fires of hell."

John said: "O my holy father, what do you mean?"

Then his godfather described to him the encounter with the suffering voice, and John learned that he could redeem the soul by the saying of sixteen masses. "That," said the pope, "is why I brought you up to be a priest."

John offered up one mass a day for sixteen days, and the suffering soul was rescued from its pain. The pope in due time made John a bishop, and he filled the office with humility, serving God with the utmost devotion. His sermons were like chaplets of gold, and he was called again "John Golden-Mouth." And he

59

wrote many books about God. When his ink ran out, he would go on writing from his mouth, and the letters that then flowed from his pen were of purest gold.[1]

This is a very German tale (like many of the fairy tales of the Grimm collection), sinister, yet filled with a profoundly comforting import. Its first appearance in print was in 1471, eighteen years before the birth of Martin Luther, yet it already voices certain Lutheran motifs. These were in the air at that time, broadcast by the spirit of the age. And Martin Luther was the mastermind, the glowing heart, the great individual, who tuned in,

---

[1] Richard Benz, ed., *Alte deutsche Legenden*, Jena, 1922. This collection is based on a medieval source, a popular collection of legends current in MSS. in numerous editions since 1471, augmented by pieces from *The Lives of the Fathers (Vitae Patrum)* and *The Lives of the Saints (Heiligenleben)*, compiled by Hermann of Fritzlar.

A different version of the biography and legend of Saint John Chrysostom appears in the *Golden Legend* by Jacobus de Voragine (Jacobi a Voragine), Cap. cxxxviii, "De Sancto Johanne Chrysostomo," *Legenda Aurea, vulgo Historica Lombardica dicta*, Th. Graesse, ed., Breslau, 1890, pp. 611-620. Cf., also, "St. John Chrysostom," *The Golden Legend of Jacobus de Voragine*, translated and adapted from the Latin by Granger Ryan and Helmut Ripperberger, New York, Longmans, Green and Co., 1941, vol. i, pp. 137-145. The saint as described here lacks the one thing to make him fascinating, namely, an inner biography, an evolution of character through trials and triumphs, temptation, downfall, and final redemption by divine grace. He is but an ideal soldier of the church militant, Christianity having already won the battle for an earthly empire, and his "life" is merely the history of a clerical officer amidst the clash and clamor of forgotten party feuds, revealing no secret of the human soul. The Christian heyday of the early martyrs was over. The new Christian order having prevailed, aggressive idealism and holy fury were now turned inward, zealous churchmen denouncing and purging each other for heresy. Among these wranglers Saint John Chrysostom contended valiantly, accepting every challenge from adversaries without the fold, as well as from his own intriguing, jealous rivals, within. Altogether, he was but a highly successful dignitary, stern and uncompromising, meddlesome and aggressive, troublesome, and of one ilk with his scheming rivals. For the lover of strange stories, such as recount experiences of the soul on its everlasting quest and tell of exemplary lives full of purport, the figure of this haughty, forbidding and fighting churchman is altogether devoid of interest. John's biography in *The Golden Legend* suggests nothing of the ominous line of the Gradual: "Blessed the man that endureth temptation; for when he is tried, he shall receive the crown of life which the Lord has promised them that love him."

amplified, and projected these ideas into the future. His teaching is one of the earliest, most significant, and explosive of the historical expressions through which modern Western man has asserted and discovered himself: a radical discrediting of the *charisma* of the traditional, inherited religion, as represented by the Roman Catholic sacerdotal system—that automatic, magical transference of the priestly power to absolve sin, communicate grace, and release souls from purgatorial flame.

The pope in the present tale is incapable of either rescuing the poor soul or baptizing the infant; the institutionalized, channelized magic of the sacraments, even when administered by the highest representative of the ecclesiastical routine—the benign, good-willed high priest of Rome—fails to operate in the great emergencies of life. Saint John, the hero, prefigures the bold and paradoxical word of Martin Luther: *Fortiter pecca!* "Sin bravely." No one but the sinner can become a saint; for it is only through individual experience, a process of personal sin, suffering, and repentance, that the power can be acquired to dispense the grace of God, to conjure with the blessed water of the Holy Ghost and the blood of the Lamb. Grace has to be won. And the very potentialities of our human nature that we term "devilish" are the eagle's beating wings that carry us aloft toward the supernatural kingdom of grace.

John of the legend had been hurried too quickly along the path of saintly perfection; the powers of heaven and hell had collaborated with the authorities of the earth to work miraculously in his favor, but in such a manner that neither temptation nor experience was entailed. His way was opened for him by the urgent cry of the poor soul in hell; learning and churchly wisdom were bestowed on him by the bounty of Mary; the pope adopted him as a spiritual son, with the ready consent of his parents, supervised his progress, and at the earliest possible moment ordained him priest. Nevertheless these authorities were not quite in the right, and John himself could not but feel it. He comprehended that the highest human office—that of communing with God and dispensing God's grace in the form of the Eucharist—was meant to be held not by an "innocent," but by one who had had "experience." "I am as yet too young! This must be very much against the heavenly will." That is to say, it must be against the laws of life—the rules of this game to which we have been challenged by inscrutable powers. And the required experience, as John subsequently learned, was of those dark and evil forces which it is the virtue of the Holy Sacrament to overcome. The young priest's feeling of unworthiness sent him to the wilderness—but it was the wilderness of life.

John Golden-Mouth, the Christian saint, is superior to Conneda because, whereas the pagan hero was sent on the path of adventure accidentally, in ignorance and by inadvertence, John has been moved by his own conscious sense of a personal insufficiency. Officially, the sacrament is valid when dispensed by any priest properly ordained in the orthodox line of the apostolic succession—no matter what his personal character may be, whether he be worthy or unworthy, knowing or ignorant. But John feels that the priest of God should be a Knower, and that he himself, in spite of the anointment of his hands, is inadequate. He is supposed to absolve from sin; yet he does not know what sin is—he has never sinned. In spite of the approbation of the world, he is really ineligible. This is what he feels. And the feeling saves him from the common fate of the usual incumbent of the clerical office, the mere dignitary of the church; his feeling rescues him and opens for him the path to sainthood.

Though the favor of the pope and the popular admiration which his learning and power of speech have aroused might well have fostered in him flattering illusions, John's intuitive realization of his actual spiritual state and the sincere humility of his character prevent his seduction. His genius knows how important

62

it is to integrate the wisdom of the dark powers from which he
has been defended both by his clerical upbringing and by the
innocence of his unassuming nature. Yet he cannot anticipate
the humiliations, sufferings, and iniquities that the rugged path
of integration through experience is going to entail. Nobody can
ever anticipate such things. And in this respect he is as ignorant
as the pagan prince, Conn-eda, who simply entrusted his fate
to the mute iron ball and relied without question on the advice of
the shaggy horse. Such ignorance is basic—not only basic, actually salutary; for without it there can be no fructifying impact
of experience, no "new thing," to take root, grow up, and mature
through life into wisdom. Only he who is honestly ignorant
can grow really wise.

John is more advanced than Conn-eda, however, in so far as
it is he himself who prescribes the treatment of which he stands
in need. Stumbling along his path of peril he is protected by the
moral, irrational qualities of humility, sincerity, honesty, and un-
selfishness. Thanks to these, the directions of his intuition can be
heard, and the instinct of his heart can grope along, devising self-
inflicted punishment and atonement for its own healing. John
dispatches himself on the indispensably necessary quest for experience by fleeing into the wilderness of life. Then, having followed the impulse of the beast that was lurking beneath his garb
of innocence, he invents his own atoning cure. He enacts literally
the very semblance of that beast, until told to stop by the word
of God. Thus the guiding forces, which in the pagan myth were
wholly externalized under various masks, are in this Christian
legend merged with the actor in whom they work. His instinct,
intuition, moral reactions, and the forces of his feeling, all proceed from a single, profound, and interior root.

Conn-eda accepted and assumed his animal aspect by don-
ning the blood-dripping hide of the innocent and gentle horse,
and by this significant symbolic gesture of assent and identifica-

63

tion the divine virtues of his human animal nature were un-
bound from darkness. The wisdom of the pagan doctrine represented in this image was founded on an intimacy with man's
instinctual, subhuman virtues, and out of this intimacy had proceeded sympathy and faith. But for the Christian saint there
could be no possibility of such direct acceptance. The elementary
forces of nature had been long and deliberately excluded from
his system of integration, never invited to participate as respected
guides. John took his start from the top rung of the ladder of
spiritual evolution, where he stood (thanks to the co-operation
on his behalf of both human and superhuman favor) in a role of
the highest human dignity, that of priest. He found himself dispensing the grace of the Almighty, renewing the sacrifice of the
Redeemer, by virtue of the magic power laid upon him at his
ordination. And this power was out of all proportion to his
individual attainment. Derived from the treasury of the superabundant merit of the Savior himself, Jesus Christ, and chan-
neled through the centuries by the apostolic succession of the
bishops of the Roman Catholic Church, it had simply been
brought to him and thrust upon him. But, intrinsically, who was
he, to contain and dispense this tremendous mystery of the grace
that conquers sin? Who precisely was he, to bring to pass with
his word the alchemical transmutation of base matter into the
Most Exalted, and to bring man thereby out of the abyss of
exile into the immediate presence of the Lord his God? Though
endowed with a gift of mellifluous speech and blessed with all
clerical wisdom, John knew in his candid soul that he, nevertheless, knew nothing. And he was perfectly right; for wisdom really
commensurate to the operation of the sacrament certainly is not
to be gained in a monastic, celibaterian avoidance of the impact
of the powers of life, but through a courageous coming to terms
with the created world, an adventure into the wilderness of life,
a descent into the hell pits of the soul.

64

John descends, therefore, from the golden rung, goes down into the subregions, puts off his unsubstantial mask of saintliness, and becomes a beast. And there the primary forces of existence, unknown to his former attitude of innocence, break upon him with an irresistible fury. Knowing that he will sin, and sin again, if he does not put the maiden away from him, he solves his problem in the crudest manner possible: he throws her out of his life sphere physically, in a brutal gesture of helpless despair, thus simply removing the object of allurement, the immediate occasion of temptation, and effecting a kind of self-castration. He fares, after that, even worse than before, experiences the full impact of the elementary, discovers the ultimate depths of the devilishness within him, and dons the mask of the loathsome beast that he has found himself to be. The priestly habit rots, the saintly hermitage becomes a weird monster's den. John keeps to the filthy, brute existence until the higher forces speak to him once more with a convincingness equal to that of the revelation at the time of his first mass.

John had been hailed at his conception as a redeemer yet to be born, but had to *become* something before he could fulfill his mission. He had to pass through an irrational, mad, vile and subhuman initiation of defeat. The higher forces did not abandon him. They announced themselves the second time through the voice of an unchristened infant, as yet, so to speak, not fully humanized, and the priest was released from the self-prescribed, cleansing penance of his foul animal incarnation, to become reborn the saint.[1]

[1] John Chrysostom brought about consciously the crisis of transformation that overcame King Nebuchadnezzar in the Book of Daniel. "The King spake and said, Is not this great Babylon, that I have built for the house of the kingdom by the might of my power, and for the honour of my majesty? While the word was in the king's mouth, there fell a voice from heaven, saying: O King Nebuchadnezzar, to thee it is spoken; The Kingdom is departed from thee. And they shall drive thee from men, and thy dwelling shall be with the beasts of the field: they shall make thee to eat grass as oxen, and seven times shall pass over thee, until thou

know that the most High ruleth in the kingdom of men and giveth it to whomsoever he will. The same hour was the thing fulfilled upon Nebuchadnezzar: and he was driven from men, and did eat grass as oxen, and his body was wet with the dew of heaven, till his hairs were grown like eagles' feathers, and his nails like birds' claws. And at the end of the days I Nebuchadnezzar lifted up mine eyes unto heaven, and mine understanding returned unto me, and I blessed the most High, and I praised and honoured Him that liveth for ever, whose dominion is an everlasting dominion, and his kingdom is from generation to generation; . . . and none can stay his hand and say unto him, What doest thou? At the same time my reason returned unto me; and for the glory of my kingdom, mine honour and brightness returned unto me; and my counselors and my lords sought unto me; and I was established in my kingdom, and excellent majesty was added unto me" (Daniel 4:30-36). Such metamorphoses and temporary eclipses always threaten the great in the moments of their overconfidence. Compare also, Apuleius, *The Golden Ass.*

FOUR ROMANCES FROM THE CYCLE OF KING ARTHUR

1

ON NEW YEAR'S EVE, when the old year takes to its deathbed and life, having passed through its longest night, begins to disentangle itself from the grip of wintry death, during that spell between the feasts of Christmas and Epiphany when ghosts and specters are supposed to be abroad, the Green Knight made his unheralded appearance at King Arthur's court. He rode directly into the hall, and was a man of gigantic stature; his armor and horse, his face and weapon, were green, and what he carried was not a sword but an archaic battle-ax. He uttered a challenge to the assembled knights of the Round Table, to meet him on his own terms or else be disgraced in the eyes of the world.

But the terms were very strange. The knight who would dare to arise and champion the reputation of King Arthur's court should take the ax of the apparition and try to decapitate him with a single stroke. In return, on the following New Year's Eve, the selfsame champion should appear at the "Green Chapel" and there encounter the challenger again, but that time it should be he, and not the Green Knight, who would offer his neck to the ax.

The giant stated his terms, and the whole circle of the Round Table sat amazed. The amazement was succeeded by a general uneasiness, for not one of the knights had arisen to accept. Then

67

King Arthur himself made a move to save the honor of his court, but his nephew, Sir Gawain, quickly interposed. The young man strode to confront the unnatural visitant and pledged himself to fulfill the stipulations. The Green Knight dismounted, handed Sir Gawain his ax, bent and readied his neck, and waited. Gawain gripped and weighed the mighty weapon, then, finally, with a single prodigious stroke, severed the head, so that it dropped, rolled a little, and lay still. But the Green Knight behaved as though nothing had happened. Calmly stooping, he retrieved the head, clasping it by the loose hair, and, taking his ax again from the other's unresisting hands, easily mounted his large green horse. The head, dripping blood, slowly moved its lips, and the voice was heard again, bidding Gawain not to fail next year in his appearance at the chapel. Then the decapitated giant tucked the head under his arm and rode away.

When the year was again drawing to its close, shortly following Halloween, Sir Gawain was prepared to set forth for the unknown Green Chapel. He mounted his steed amid the lamentations of the court, for no one expected him ever to return. Nevertheless the young knight himself was sufficiently cheerful. "What should I fear?" he demanded. "What else can befall a man except that he should go to meet his destiny?" And so he rode away.

Gawain rode alone. He proceeded northward through the wilderness and the winter. No one in the desolate countryside could point the way for him or tell him anything about the chapel. It had never been seen or heard of. He was compelled to follow his own inner voice. The adventure was long and the cold increasingly severe, so that Gawain was presently in great want and riding hopelessly astray.

On Christmas eve, when he was lost in a somber forest, he prayed to Christ and the Virgin to reveal to him some shelter where he might celebrate the birth of his Savior. Then he came unexpectedly upon a mighty castle, deep within the wilderness, and there he was made welcome with a most hospitable reception. The host, a man of towering stature and sinister countenance, was solicitous to make him comfortable; and the wife, a lady of dazzling charm, as well as an imposing older matron who resided with them in the castle, seemed equally delighted to entertain as their guest such a celebrated knight. His anxiety to know the way to the Green Chapel was allayed, for he was told that the place was near at hand, in a narrow and forlorn valley that could be easily reached. If he started New Year's morning, he would arrive in plenty of time for the appointment; meanwhile, it was urged, he should remain at the castle. And so, he stayed, and was honored, and pleasantly entertained.

Three days before the morning of Gawain's departure, his host set forth at dawn for a day of hunting. The two had good-heartedly agreed the night before, while drinking together at the hearth, that whatever game should fall to the hunter during his day should belong to the guest, and in exchange the host was to receive whatever booty Gawain might win by taking his ease at home. That had been a rather amusing pact, and they had had a good laugh.

The departure at dawn was made clamorous by the yelping of the hounds, clatter of the horses, trumpeting of the hunting horns, and shouts of the considerable retinue. Whereafter, the castle, deserted of its inmates, became still. Gawain rolled over. But he was gently roused, presently, by the realization that someone was sitting on the edge of his bed. It was the wife of his host. When the castle had been cleared, the beautiful woman had stealthily entered the chamber and settled herself on Gawain's bed, inside the curtains.

She was talking to him in a low, gentle, rich and beautiful voice, and Gawain felt himself irresistibly moved. Being the knight he was, however, he also felt himself immovably bound in duty to his host. With an almost superhuman command of his impulses, he resisted the irresistible, and the magnificent woman had to content herself with the bestowal of a helpless kiss.

The lord of the castle returned at dusk, and his men were laden heavily with the quarry. The animals were deposited on the floor of the hall in rows, and the host then presented them to Gawain, who, in keeping with the pact, rendered to the towering hunter the kiss that he had received. And then, again, the two had their hearty laugh. How trifling this booty of the stay-at-home in contrast with the hunting catch of the day!

Next morning, the lord of the castle went off again, and again the lady came inside the curtains. She was more urgent than the day before, and Gawain's self-mastery became more precariously balanced. But the knight was skillful; not only did he withstand his pressing hostess, but he also comforted and assuaged her, so that, though dismissed, she was not humbled—and she gave him two kisses, this time, before she took her leave.

The host returned a little late that day, having killed a mighty boar, which he presented. And when he received the two pecks on the cheek in return, the men again had their laugh.

The third and final morning before Gawain's departure, things went a little less urbanely inside the curtains of the bed. The woman insisted with a desperation that made the celebrated guest's continued chivalry seem oddly arbitrary. The case was rendered the more acute by the fact that this young and handsome Gawain had a considerable reputation as a lover. "Tell me at least," the woman implored, "that you are in love with some other lady, and that you have sworn to her to remain faithful." But the youth replied that there was no such special mistress in his life.

Then the woman seemed to cast about for some token, something that in some manner, even some intangible manner, should make him somehow her own; and she drew from her finger a

heavy ring, which she pressed him to receive. But again he resisted—for a ring is a symbol of the personality, and to bestow a
ring implies the surrender of one's being. To bestow one's ring
is to bestow a power, the authority to speak or act in one's name.
Thus a king will commit his ring to the officer empowered to issue
commands and to seal acts in his stead, and a lady will give her
ring to the knight who is *her* knight. To accept such a token implies a troth, some sort of bond; and Sir Gawain, in keeping
with his character as knight of King Arthur's Round Table, was
very strict with himself about such binding implications.

The young man, in these last hours of his life, was being subjected, it would appear, to a very delicate and telling test. The
following dawn he was to proceed to meet the Green Knight and
submit to the loss of his head. Meanwhile he had one day—one
day in this prematurely glowing sunset moment of his precious
youth. And could his young body have created a living answer
to its own now furiously heightened wish for life, it would have
conjured up nothing more desirable than this beautiful and
gentle, urgent woman who had come to him. One last time the
glamour of the world was now before him, offering to his lips one
ultimate, comparatively brief yet sumptuous taste of the life he
would too quickly lose. Nevertheless the knight—this practiced
lover of noble and beautiful ladies, not at all unsusceptible to
their charms and claims—was refusing the boon, this cup of
pleasure filled to the brim.

Sir Gawain's professed and actual grounds for the unnatural
act were his chivalric obligations to the absent host, and if we
are to appreciate the symbolism of his predicament we must
try to understand these as he did himself. He was being tempted
to renounce for one moment of self-indulgence his life dedication to the perfection of chivalry. Were he to yield, his fault
would be not carnal license (that, we may believe, he would
not have eschewed) but insincerity and infidelity, and this

71

would have signified the disintegration of the self-consistency of his being. For Sir Gawain was an initiate—one of the leading initiates—to the sacred circle of the Round Table, dedicated solemnly and seriously to the model life of the chivalric ideal. To have succumbed to the allure of an episodical love adventure at the cost of the consequentiality of his career would have been to betray not his host only, but himself. His life was destined soon to end; let it then continue to the end. Let it not collapse in a transitory hour of luxurious chance.

But for the thwarted woman there was a contrary problem of honor now in play, and she would not be denied entirely in her requirement that some slight concession at least should be made to her undisguised advance. Gawain would not accept her person. Gawain would not accept her ring. Was there not then, perhaps, something still less binding that he might deign to receive from her, some trifle, less than a gift, a mere nothing, yet a particle of her existence, that should constitute a secret link between them? When she dropped her eyes, her glance fell upon a small green girdle, a mere bit of lace, that she was wearing about her waist. The trembling hands unclasped it, and, pressing it upon the reluctant hero in the bed, she whispered as though the walls might overhear: "Please take it. It is a mere nothing, but it possesses a miraculous power." Gawain had not yet permitted the temptress to close his hand. "Whosoever carries this bit of lace on his person," she told him, "cannot be harmed."

That was a telling thrust. Gawain's resistance, for a moment, somewhat relented, and the persistent woman began to press down his fingers. Stooping to conquer, she had brought forth a bribe, an appeal to whatever minute particle of fear might yet reside within the heart of this very brave young man who had traveled far to meet death face to face. There would be little, perhaps even nothing, contrary to the interests of his host in the acceptance of such a timely talisman. The woman pleaded with an air of loving thoughtfulness, anxious for the youth's security—farsighted, unselfish, motherly, no longer seeking to win her point by allure. And Gawain was caught by the strategy unawares. The fingers began to close of themselves on the frail green girdle. Then he suddenly clasped it and took it, and the woman in the warmth of her gratitude and satisfaction roundly kissed him thrice. The young knight was going to ride more confidently on his quest the next morning, a little less frank and bright, less conscious of his valor, less forthright than he would have been had he not withheld one little thing from the host at the ceremonial of their daily exchange, but nevertheless an extraordinarily heroic horseman.

The hunter returned even later than the day before, and could show as booty only one lean and smelly fox. His bag had been declining day by day, while that of the guest within the castle walls had been increasing. At the moment of the exchange, the host, with an apologetic shrug, presented his miserable offering, and the guest, with just a trace of awkwardness, three kisses. The bit of green lace did not appear, and the woman, who had been standing, anxiously watching, relaxed with a look of grateful joy.

Next morning a squire conducted Sir Gawain to the forlorn valley, and when he pointed out the path to the Green Chapel, offered an earnest warning to turn back. No one, said he, had ever returned after proceeding to that chapel. "Therefore, good Sir Gawain," he said, "let the man alone. Go away in some other direction and I swear to keep your secret." But the young knight was not afraid, and with the green girdle about him he would no doubt survive where the others had failed.

He went on alone, and in due course arrived at a gloomy vault, sunk into the ground, battered with age, and coated with moss, a ghostly trysting place, desolate and silent. Drawing rein before it, he listened; and he had not been listening long when he heard a grinding noise, as if someone were whetting an ax, coming through the wintry air from the wooded slope on the other side of the stream. Gawain called out his name and announced his coming. A voice replied that he should wait, and then again there was that gruesome noise of an ax being sharpened. The sound abruptly ceased, and in an instant the great Green Knight came out of a cave and could be seen descending the slope.

The greeting was brief and businesslike. Gawain was conducted to the place of execution. Imitating his model of the year before, he stood quietly with bent and readied neck, but at the moment of the rushing ax instinctively "shrank a little with his shoulders." One might say that this was a second symptom of the trait that had compelled him to accept the bit of lace, and it is interesting to note that even though (or perhaps precisely because) he was now protected by the talisman, he could not quite accept the threatened blow.

The Green Knight, seeing him flinch, checked the stroke and rebuked Gawain for cowardice. The youth protested. He was not in the fortunate position, he declared, of being able to snatch up his head the moment it fell. Nevertheless he readied himself again, with the promise that this time he would not quail.

The Green Knight again lifted the ax. The downstroke had already begun, when the towering executioner, perceiving that the knight was standing firm this time, again interrupted himself, arresting the swing of his two great arms, and remarked approvingly: "Thus I like you. Now I will deliver the blow. But first take off that cap King Arthur gave you, so that I may catch your neck in just the proper way."

Gawain was exasperated. "Hit hard," he cried, "or I shall think you do not dare to deal the blow."

"Forsooth," said the Green Knight, "your quest will soon have found its reward."

He lifted the ax for the third time, swung it high, poised it, and brought it down; but in such a manner that it nearly missed, only slitting the skin with the edge, just marking the neck with a tiny bleeding streak.

Gawain, having felt that, leapt aside, quickly grabbed his weapons, and prepared himself to fight. "I withstood you!" he shouted. "One stroke was the pledge, and no more!"

The Green Knight was smiling, calmly leaning on the ax. "Do not be excited," he said, "you have received the blow you deserved. I shall do nothing more to hurt you. Twice I checked myself. Those strokes were harmless because twice you kept your pledge to me and gave me back the kisses you had accepted from my wife. The third time, however, you failed. And so I have marked you with my ax. That green girdle you are wearing belongs to me; it was made by my wife for me. It was I who sent her to you with her blandishments, her kisses, and the green temptation. I know everything that came to pass. And amongst the knights of the world Sir Gawain is like a pearl among white peas. You failed, just a little, when you were put to trial for the third time; not, however, out of lust for self-indulgence, but because you loved your life and felt unhappy to lose it."

Sir Gawain had flushed with shame. "Curses on the two of you," he shouted. "Fear and Desire! You are the destroyers of manly valor and heroship." Taking off the girdle, he handed it back, but the Green Knight refused to receive it. He comforted the young hero, bidding him retain the green lace as a gift, then invited him to share again the hospitality of the castle.

Gawain refused to go with him, but consented to keep the girdle, which he tied with a hidden knot beneath his arm. It should remind him forever of how he had failed. And thus he returned uninjured to the Round Table of King Arthur's court, where he told his tale. The knights made little of the failure but much of the heroism of the victory. And in memory of the remarkable event, all agreed that they should wear, forever after, a bit of green lace.[1]

2

Thus concludes the tale; but we are left with a question. Who, namely, was that weird, imperious being, qualified to challenge, test, unmask, and pass sentence? The Green Knight who could tuck his head under his arm and appear with it in place again, whose wife was the fairest temptress in the world, and whose Green Chapel was a kind of eerie crypt, "the cursedest kirk," as Gawain judged it, "that e'er I came in!"—who is he and what is his name?

In folklore and fairy tale the dead not uncommonly carry their heads under their arms to frighten the people they meet. They toss their heads up into the air and play ninepins with their skulls. Pale green, furthermore, is the color of livid corpses: the paintings of the Buddhist art of Tibet, which adhere in their color symbolism to a very definitely prescribed tradition, employ such a green to denote whatever appertains to the kingdom of King

[1] *Gawain and the Green Knight* comes to us in a single manuscript of the late fourteenth century (Cotton MS. Nero A.x., fols. 91-124 v⁰, in the British Museum), which contains three other celebrated medieval poems: *The Pearl, Cleanness,* and *Patience. Gawain* was first edited by Sir Frederic Madden, *Syr Gawayne,* The Bannatyne Club, London, 1839, then by Richard Morris for the Early English Text Society, in 1864. It has been translated into modern English by Miss Jessie L. Weston, London, 1898 (New York, 1905); the Rev. E. J. B. Kirtlan, London, 1912; and K. G. T. Webster (W. A. Neilson and K. G. T. Webster, editors, *The Chief British Poets of the Fourteenth and Fifteenth Centuries*), Boston, 1916. An important study of the sources and variants appears in George Lyman Kittredge's *A Study of Gawain and the Green Knight,* Harvard University Press, Cambridge, Mass., 1916. See also Ananda K. Coomaraswamy, "Sir Gawain and the Green Knight" in *Speculum* XXI, pp. 104-125,—a study of the decapitation motive with Oriental parallels.

Death.[1] We may safely assume that the death-green, towering apparition out of the forlorn valley of the "cursedest kirk," carrying an archaic ax over his shoulder instead of a contemporary, chivalric Christian sword and mounted on a steed as remarkable both for color and for size as himself, was the great reaper, Death. And the dazzlingly beautiful woman, embodying and representing the glamour of the world, offering the cup of desire, tempting to enjoy, is Life, Death's bride.[2]

The legend of the Buddha contains a celebrated instance of this ancient and apparently universal mythological theme of the testing of the hero by the personifications of death and life. During the epochal night when the Savior was in meditation under the Bo-tree, on the Immovable Spot, and on the brink of realization, he was approached by the supreme tempter Māra, "he who kills," "he who puts to death." Māra came in the guise of an attractive youth, carrying a lute; Māra's other name is Kāma, "desire," "lust." And he paraded three voluptuous damsels before the Buddha's eyes (they are termed Māra's daughters in the legend) who attempted to display themselves; but the hero was unmoved. Then the tempter, assuming his furious aspect,

---

[1] In the early Irish epics, which apparently were the sources for the medieval English romance of *Gawain and the Green Knight*, the giant is not green but black, or rather, he is dressed in black (*Fled Bricrend* 16:91-102. Cf. G. L. Kittredge, *op. cit.*, pp. 10-15). It has been suggested that the color green came into the legend through the fault of a mistranslation of the Irish word *glas*, which can mean either "gray" or "green" (cf. Roger S. Loomis, *Celtic Myth and Arthurian Romance*, Columbia University Press, 1927, p. 59). Yet even though it is a late element in the story, the color was appropriate to the original character of the Challenger, and must have been regarded as such by both the narrator and his audience. The Irish original of the figure of the uncanny Challenger was the god and gatekeeper of the Other World, Curoi Mac Daire (Roger S. Loomis, *op. cit.*, Chapter XI; see also, A. C. L. Brown, *Origin of the Grail Legend*, Harvard University Press, Cambridge, Mass., 1943, pp. 71, 357, 378). In one of his apparitions Curoi was known as "Terror, the son of Great Fear" (*Fled Bricrend* 14:75-78; G. L. Kittredge, *op. cit.*, pp. 17-18).

[2] ["Life" and "Death" are equally *nomina Dei*. "Green" stands for either or both.—AKC.]

amassed his demon army so that—as in the temptation of Sir Gawain—the lure of life and the terror of annihilation should assault the hero simultaneously. Devils in battle gear surrounded and stormed the solitary, silent figure. And just as Gawain was tempted thrice by the woman, so was the Buddha by the three daughters; as Gawain faced the threat of the ax, so the Buddha faced the hurled missiles of the horde. The devils menaced his meditation by the very terror of their faces—many of them the visages of beasts and birds of prey. They flung burning trees, rocks, flaming mountains, but the Savior remained unmoved; for he knew that the tumult all around him, the fury of the army, and the allure of Māra's daughters represented no more than a mirror reflection of the inner, elementary forces of his own primitive human nature, which were clinging still to phenomenal existence, clamoring for carnal assuagement, and dreading the destruction of the physical frame. By the act of comprehending the terror and allure as the two manners of deportment of a single master tempter, the World Savior released himself from the cosmic enthrallment of his longing and fearing ego. Recognizing that the opposites, though contrary in apparent form, were the paired manifestations of a unique reality, he remained steadfast between. The last fitful flame of personal feeling was made extinct in him. (As "The Buddha," i.e., "The Enlightened One," he was "The Extinct One," the one who had passed into Nirvāna.) And so the damsels paraded their charms before empty eyes and the hurled missiles were transformed into flowers of adoration. The antagonist, with all his devils and daughters, had at last to withdraw.

The correspondences between these temptations of Gautama, which, according to the Buddhist tradition, represented the final step in his initiation to "The Kingly Lion Throne of the Teacher of Gods and Men," and those of Sir Gawain are obvious. In both cases death incarnate functions as the master of initiation.[1] The champion of the Round Table fares less gloriously than Gautama, for, after all, he is not a world savior but only "the best of knights"; nevertheless, his romance is a version of the same universal mystery. Through the valley of death he is conducted to the aloof and lonely sanctuary of life renewed, and there, having withstood the trial, is reborn. This is a chivalric medieval version of the mystery of dying to the transient individuality— which is compounded of desire and fear—and gaining resurrection in the higher life immortal.

The gift bestowed on the initiate, the green girdle of the color of death—who but Death himself could have bestowed this boon? It confers immortality, releases the bearer from the power of death, and is the talisman of rebirth.[2] Gawain's manner of receiving it was undoubtedly questionable. He accepted it with a pang of shame, surreptitiously, as booty snatched in secrecy and concealed. Had he been able to return it at the moment of the evening exchange, his initiation might have taken some less frightful form; he might have been spared the encounter at the Green Chapel. Nevertheless, after the completion of the trial there can be no doubt that he merits the trophy, and so Death settles it upon him as a legitimate gift.

In this late chivalric adventure Death plays the same role as in the ancient myths and epics of Gilgamesh, Herakles, Theseus and Orpheus. Those earlier heroes, too, went into the netherworld (or into far-off, forbidden or unknown lands) to gain through death's mystery the treasure of everlasting life. But in the present version the point of the challenge, temptation,

[1] ["What is 'beheading'? Slaying the carnal-soul (nafs=Heb. nefesh) in the Holy War" (Rūmī, Mathnawī 2.2525).—AKC.]

[2] The paramount hero of the Irish epic cycle from which the romances of the Round Table largely derive, Cuchullin, the prototype of Sir Gawain, is likewise reported to have been the wearer of a magic belt that rendered him invulnerable.

and trial, is not made quite clear. The romance seems to miss
something of its own suggested depth. It does not insist upon its
meaning. One cannot even be sure that the thirteenth and
fourteenth century French and English poets, who constructed
this romance out of earlier materials, consciously intended the
reading that inevitably emerges when the traditional episodes
which they successfully synthesized are comparatively con-
strued.[1] The Green Knight, for example, before dismissing
Gawain, opens his visor and discloses his true face, his hidden
character and significance; yet the name that he announces is
not his true *nomen*. He introduces himself merely as *Bernlak de
Hautdesert*, "Bernlak of the Lofty Desert." Still another joke of
disguise, played this time not on the hero alone but on the read-
ers and the poets too.[2]

The imposing older matron within the castle is revealed to be
Morgan the Fay, once the mistress of the wise and powerful
Merlin, whose wizardry she learned and whom she then conjured into a living grave.[3] It is declared that she was the one
who had sent the Green Knight on his mission to King Arthur's
court and by her magic had given him the power to play that
trick with his head. One of her sons, it seems, had been refused
admission to the exclusive circle of the Round Table, and being
a revengeful woman she had wished to discredit the valor of the
knights. She had also hoped that Queen Guinevere might drop

[1] Their case resembles that of the dreamer not understanding the symbols
presented to him by the creative genius of his own interior. They knew how to
gather, combine, and modify traditional motifs according to the traditional
spirit and laws of their inherited story art, but it does not follow that they altogether understood what the combinations signified.

[2] For a discussion of this name, cf. Roger S. Loomis, *Romanic Review*, xv. p.
275 f.

[3] The Gawain-poet here identifies Morgan le Fay (Fata Morgana), King
Arthur's half-sister, with Niniane, the mistress of Merlin; elsewhere in the
Arthurian romances the two are kept distinct. The story of Niniane and Merlin
will be found *infra*, pp. 181-201.

dead of the fright and shame. She herself is the king's half-sister and therefore an aunt of Sir Gawain, who is King Arthur's nephew, etc., etc. It is apparent that the interest of the adventure has degenerated to the purely social and genealogical level. Themes that must once have been enacted on a higher mythical stage now appear obscured and encumbered with the trappings of chivalric pride and family intrigue. Indeed, such is the case with the whole cycle of Sir Gawain—not alone with this present encounter of the Green Knight. Gawain's numerous legends are alive with wonderful mythological images, adventures in lonely enchanted castles and on lovely far-off fairy isles, but all the mythology has become transformed according to the social formulae of medieval amour and knightly tournament. A watchful eye, nevertheless, can detect and read again the older symbolism with its timeless meaning.

We hear, for example, of the Marvelous Castle, *Le Château Merveil:* [1] a place full of frightening trials and amazing experiences, comparable to Merlin's "Valley of No Return." Three queens and countless maidens are its prisoners; the mistress is a lady of superhuman beauty; the Château is a veritable "isle of women." Like the netherworld of antiquity, it is approached in a little boat, under the guardianship of a ferryman, or, according to another version, by a tiny floating island. [2] The surrounding waters are difficult to traverse; not everyone can attain the other shore; and the boatman gives a warning to the hero who confronts him with the demand to be taken over. "Whoever ferries across," says he, "must remain in yonder realm forever." Like the island of the Phaeacians visited by Ulysses (which, fundamentally, was an enchanted land of the blessed departed),

[1] Chrétien de Troyes, *Conte del Graal,* and Wolfram von Eschenbach, *Parzival,* supply the principal versions, but a number of lesser texts contribute also to our knowledge of the legend of *Le Château Merveil.* Cf. Jessie L. Weston, *The Legend of Sir Gawain,* London, 1897, pp. 27-28.

[2] Heinrich von dem Türlin, *Diu Krône.*

Gawain's castle of women can be reached only with divine help, or by virtue of some charm. The one who enters and survives the trials demonstrates himself to be the hero elect, effects the release of all the women from their spell of bondage, and becomes the lord consort of the queen. He becomes, in fact, the lord and husband of all the women and maidens of the blessed realm.

According to one of the versions of the adventure,[1] three stately queens of differing age, whom Gawain encounters on the enchanted island, reveal themselves to be his grandmother, mother, and sister; that is, the realm he has discovered is that of the "Mothers," the mysterious shadow zone into which Faust was later to descend with his magic key to discover and deliver the shade of Helen of Troy.[2] This is the everlasting sphere of womanhood, representative of the timeless abode of inexhaustible life, the well of death from which life pours forth in perennial rebirth. It is a mysterious locality that has been visited by numberless legendary and romantic heroes of the world, can be recognized under many historical transformations, and belongs to our universal treasure store of archetypal symbolic images. The representations that have come down to us in Celtic fairy tale and Arthurian romance disclose features deriving from the primitive matriarchal civilization that flourished throughout western France and in the British Isles in pre-Celtic times. Among the multitudinous females of the ageless lineage of motherhood, descending age by age from the primordial great-great-grandmother of the matrilineal clan, the knight, the manly youth, the boy hero (*puer aeternus*),[3] being wearied of his long

---

[1] Chrétien's *Conte del Graal.*
[2] Goethe, *Faust* II. 1. vv. 6213 et seq.,
    Göttinnen thronen hehr in Einsamkeit,
    Um sie kein Ort, noch weniger eine Zeit;
    Von ihnen sprechen ist Verlegenheit.
    Die *Mütter* sind es!
[3] Sanskrit: *Sanatkumāra.*

82

adventure, discovers at last his rest. Hither he has come—to this hidden sanctuary of the fountainhead—for a solution of the riddle of life and death. And here he shall win the long-desired and withheld reply. His oracle shall be maternal womanhood, the unspoken intuitive wisdom of the life force which, by its living presence, shall make intelligible to him the mystery of its own repeated rebirth through the transient generations.

The realm, however, as described in the romances, is not precisely one of happiness. It is a region of a certain bliss, but destitute of action and adventure, a world of the departed, a sort of exile, beyond struggle and strife. King Arthur and his knights, we are told, mourned the disappearance of Gawain as though he had been dead; and shortly before his own death the king, in a vision, beheld the hero as a kind of specter surrounded by the women of the court of the miragelike, enchanted realm.[1] That miraculous land, though idyllic, is, to use Nietzsche's phrase, *tot vor Unsterblichkeit,* "dead for sheer immortality": the women there, as well as their male consort, dwell in the melancholy of the mood of the dead. They yearn to be back in the world of man and common life, but can never leave the island. The ferryman, like the Charon of antiquity who steered the barge of the departed souls, transports his voyagers in only one direction. And in that place there is neither night nor day. It is the "realm from which no wanderer returns," *li reaume don nus éstranges ne retorne.*[2]

This hopeless formula, the "Land of No Return" (Hamlet's

[1] Malory, *Morte d'Arthur* xxi, 3.

[2] Chrétien de Troyes, *Le chevalier de la charrette,* vv. 644-645 (Foerster's edition, Halle, 1899, p. 25).

[Contrast the point of view of *Jaimīniya Upanishad Brāhmana* 3.28.5: "Who having cast off this world would desire to return again? He would be only *there!*" The Hero's return to the cave (as in Plato's *Republic*) is a deliberate descent, a voluntary *sacrifice;* it does not mean that he would prefer "to be only *there.*" The Land of No Return = Brahmaloka (*Upanishads, passim*). As Dante says, however, we must die to live up there.—AKC.]

"undiscovered country from whose bourn no traveler returns") [1] is of very ancient standing as a term for the kingdom of the dead. It derives from the Mesopotamian tradition, first appearing, as far as the extant records are concerned, on a greatly damaged series of cuneiform tablets (c. 2000 B.C.) recounting the descent of the Sumerian goddess Inanna (= Babylonian Ishtar) to the netherworld.[2] That dim domain has been for millenniums the holy goal of all the great questing heroes, from Gilgamesh to Faust, for it is the repository of the spiritual treasure of the mystic wisdom of rebirth. The keys that unlock the tabernacle of life unending are to be discovered there, and the boon of immortality itself. But the hero discovers then that he is bound (as all mankind is bound) to the maternal principle of Mother Earth, Mother Life, bound to the ever-revolving wheel of life-through-death; and he becomes enwrapped therewith in the heroic melancholy that was known to all the valiant seekers of yore who descended into the abyss of the domain beyond. Gawain is such a hero. Gawain is shrouded in the composed sadness of Gilgamesh and Aeneas. He is the hero pilgrim eternal who has come to the source of life through the disillusioning initiation of rebirth in death.

But there is still another version:[3] Gawain, the hero, may return; Death cannot retain him; he may reappear from the enchanted realm. He then brings back with him—with the rise of the New Year reborn—a magical balsam of invulnerable life. But in order to have won this, he must have resisted the blandishments of the mistress of the realm of death. As in the castle of the Green Knight, so also in the miragelike enchanted isle, Sir Gawain, by refusing to become the lord consort of the dazzlingly

---

[1] *Hamlet* III, i, 79-80.

[2] S. N. Kramer, *Sumerian Mythology*, Memoirs of the American Philosophical Society, vol. xxi, 1944, p. 90.

[3] *Diu Krône*, vv. 17329 ff.

beautiful shadow-queen, withstands the temptation that would transform him into a fairy-bound, divine, everlasting specter. By not capitulating to the generating principle of the life that is bound with death, the hero disengages himself from the self-consuming cycle. And he becomes competent and eligible to carry back with him the mystical trophy (corresponding to the green girdle of the Green Knight) that grants release.

Birth and death and rebirth in unending cycle is the permanent character of the process of life. It is illustrated in the cycles of the year and day, as well as in the passage of the generations and in the metamorphoses of the individual during the course of a lifetime. This, the oldest romance of the soul, is what is rendered by the mythical element preserved in the knightly narratives of King Arthur's court. And this precisely is what gives to the old stories (watered down though they be, and spiced to the taste of a comparatively modern, though now already outmoded, chivalry) the power to strike our intuition with a wonderful meaning. Their quests are man's millennial quest for breath-taking answers to the abiding enigmas of his existence in the world.

The antiquity of the mythical element in these chivalric, twelfth to fourteenth century narratives of the poets of the medieval courts is suggested by the curious weapon that Death carries in his character as the Green Knight: He appears before the champions of the Round Table, whose fashionable tournaments and battles were conducted with swords and lances, bearing over his shoulder a large, archaic battle-ax, a clumsy weapon, reminiscent of the long-forgotten Age of Stone. Death, caring absolutely nothing about progress and the developments of human invention, remains unalterable, and, despite everything man can do to change him, sticks to his tradition.

But Gawain, too, betrays unmistakable symptoms of a derivation from the remote past. His strength, for example, increases

85

until noon, and then declines. Indeed, out of deference to Sir
Gawain, it was for a while the custom at King Arthur's court to
schedule all tournaments for the morning hours of the day.
Apparently the knight was a solar god, masquerading under
medieval armament, doomed, as ever, to expire every twilight
and pass into the "Land of No Return." Like Osiris, he there became the king, the sun, of the netherworld, but, like the rolling
solar disk, traversed and broke free from the "great below," to
reappear reborn in the east as the orb of the new day. Gringalet,
Gawain's stallion, had shining red ears, and his sword, Escalibor,
threw a blaze of light.[1]

In the *Château Merveil* Gawain was subjected to tests more
bizarre than those in the castle of the Green Knight. His principal encounter was with a certain perilous bed, *Liz de la
Mervoille*, "The Marvel Bed"—no pleasant piece of furniture.
Though at first glance it looked like any other bed, peaceful and
inviting to the hero after the long and venturesome journey, the
instant he lay down to sleep, it went raving mad. It galloped to
and fro across the room, bolted against the walls, bucked and
quaked, as though it could not bear to be possessed by the
cavalier who had taken the liberty to put his trust in its appearance of quiet willingness. It behaved like a reluctant bride in
rebellion against the embrace being forced upon her. It kicked
about and ricocheted, until, conquered by the patient firmness
of the hero, at last it quieted down. This, however, was not the
end. Peace had by no means been established. Through the curtains of the bed came pelting a hail of stones, then a shower of

---

[1] Weston, *op. cit.*, pp. 12-17. Like the animals of the sun-gods in other
mythologies (the Cattle of the Sun, for instance, in the Greek and Hindu) Gringalet was very precious to possess and in constant danger of being stolen or going
astray. The sword Escalibor (Excalibur) was assigned by the romances also
to King Arthur. In the old French *Roman de Merlin*, chapter XXI, Sommer's
edition, p. 270, it is declared that Arthur presented Escalibor to his nephew when
he dubbed him a knight.

arrows from countless invisible crossbows. Happily, Sir Gawain had taken to heart a bit of advice from the ferryman and had not removed his armor when committing his weary bones to the soft couch, for hell was now loose all around him. He saved himself beneath his shield.

Having withstood these severe preliminary tests of his constancy and forbearance (indispensable virtues for one who would get along with the feminine principle, win its esteem, and constrain its compliance), the hero was put through a third exercise by the chary femininity of the invaded castle. The door of the room flew open and a mighty lion, giving a terrific roar, burst in upon the already battered adventurer. The kingly animal, valor incarnate, put Gawain's intrepidity to a fearful proof. Mauled and slashed, bleeding from many wounds, the valorous knight eventually mastered the beast, killed it, and then collapsed across the carcass in a deathlike sleep. He could not know that he had satisfied and quelled, at last, the recalcitrant feminine element of the castle. He had carried his suit to a successful close. The feminine presence, which before yielding had been earnest to test the newcomer by every means, now made its appearance. The queens and all the damosels entered the chamber and approached the unconscious figure of the elect sprawled helpless over their lion, tended him with balsam, soothed and healed the wounds, and presently restored him to his strength. The numerous ladies, younger and older, formerly so haughty, now served and comforted him; for they had been released from their spell of amazonian superiority and seclusion by his patient valor. They now recognized him willingly as their master and lord.

In this charming and entertaining pictograph, the conquest of womankind represents, and is represented as, the fulfillment of the task of life. The male hero's compassing of the feminine principle (aloof, and contrary to manhood) by recognizing and acquiescing to its intrinsic features, signifies a reconciliation and union in him of opposites; and this eventuates in his release from every onesidedness, as well as from all the consequent fears and desires. The victory amounts to an accession to the wholeness of human consciousness, the winning of a maturity that balances the terms of life-death, male-female, and the other contrarieties that split our common expression and experience of the single reality that is life. The very virtues that have here enabled Gawain to redeem woman from the spell of her own nature— patience, constancy, intrepidity, self-abnegation—lead also to the sanctuary of death, unbolt its gate, and open its treasury of enlightenment. They are the keys to the wisdom beyond the terminals of temporal life and death, keys to the understanding of life eternal. By acknowledging the hidden identity of opposites and disregarding the conflicting appearances that normally beset the mind and excite the worries of our unenlightened, everyday reactions, the tested hero finds himself delivered from the natural terror of extinction in change. He is made whole. He is united with the permanence of being. He is flooded with an unbounded knowledge and imperturbable wisdom. Thus this pictographic romance brings together and identifies, in a most simple and mystic manner, the two—usually separated—deeds of the conquest of woman and the realization of immortality.

3

There is another remarkable chivalric tale of Sir Gawain which achieves an even closer fusion of the two initiations. It is a rather puzzling and humorous adventure in which a share of the exploit falls to King Arthur. But the paramount deed is that of Sir Gawain. He is the king's youthful alter ego, and, as such, the active agent in the mystical act of disenchantment. Loyal and cou-

Sir Gawain is the King's youthful alter Ego –

rageous, upon him devolves the critical and most difficult task.

The king had gone with a small company of his young knights for a day of hunting in the forest; Sir Gawain was among them. They were familiar with the country and had no expectation of any miraculous event. Then the king spurred a little ahead of the others and suddenly started a great hart. He took after it and had ridden scarcely half a mile before he brought it down. He dismounted, hitched his horse to a tree, drew his hunting knife, and proceeded to the dressing of the kill. But as he was stooping over his quarry in a little patch of fern, he became aware that there was somebody watching; and when he lifted his eyes he beheld before him a well-armed knight of forbidding aspect, "fulle strong and of greatt myghte."

"Welle i-met, kyng Arthour!" said the big man. "Thou hast done me wrong many a yere, and wofully I shalle quytte the here; I hold thy lyfe days nyghe done."

Thus threatened with immediate death, the king was quick to respond with the reproach that there would be little honor for the other in such a deed: "Thou armyd and I clothyd butt in grene." He asked to know the quarreler's name.

"My name," said the man, "is Gromer Somer Joure." The name meant nothing to the king.

The king's argument, however, had touched a delicate point of knightly honor, and so the big man in armor was forced to relent a little—not entirely, but a little. And the condition that he proposed for the king's escape constitutes the theme and thread of this grotesque romance.

Sir Gromer Somer Joure required that his defenseless victim should swear to return to this same spot the same day the following year, unarmed as now—clothed in but his hunter's green—and bring as quittance for his life the answer to the following riddle: What is it that a woman most desires in all the world?

The king gave his pledge and returned in great dejection to

the company of his knights. Sir Gawain, his nephew, noted the sorrow of his countenance and drew him aside to ask what had taken place. The king explained in secrecy. The two deliberated together, riding a little apart from the others of the company, and presently Gawain came forth with an excellent suggestion.

"Let your horse be made ready to ride into strange lands, and wherever ye meet either man or woman, ask of them what they say to the riddle. And I shall ride another way and enquire of every man and woman and get what I may, and I shall write down all the answers in a book."

> The kyng rode on way, and Gawen a-noder,
> And euere enquyred of man, woman, and other,
> Whate wemen desyred moste dere.
> Somme sayd they lovyd to be welle arayd,
> Somme sayd they lovyd to be fayre prayed;
> Somme sayd they lovyd a lusty man,
> That in theyr armys can clypp them and kysse them than;
> Somme sayd one; somme sayd other;
> And so had Gawen getyn many an answere.
>
> Syr Gawen had goten answerys so many,
> That he made a buke greatt, wytterly;
> To the courte he cam agayn.
> By that was the kyng comyn withe hys boke,
> And eyther on others pamplett dyd loke.
> "Thys may nott ffaylle," sayd Gawen.
> "By God," sayd the kyng, "I drede me sore,
> I cast me to seke a lytelle more."

One month remained. The king, being uneasy in spite of the number of the collected answers, spurred again, and he adventured into the forest of Inglewood, and there he met with the most ugly hag mankind had ever seen: face red, nose snotted withal, mouth wide, teeth yellow and hanging down over the lip, a long thick neck, and hanging heavy paps. A lute she bore upon her back, and she was riding a richly saddled palfrey. It was an unseemly sight to see so foul a creature ride so gaily.

She rode directly to the king, gave him greeting, and told him, without ado, that none of the answers he and Gawain had found would be a bit of good to him. "If I help thee not, thou art but dead," she said. "Grant me, Sir King, but one thing, and I shall make warranting for thy life; or else thou shalt lose thy head." "What mean you, Lady," asked the king. "Tell me what is your meaning and why my life is in your hand, and I shall promise you anything you ask." "Forsooth," the hideous old creature replied, "thou must grant me a knight to wed; his name is Sir Gawain. I will make thee such a covenant that, if thy life be not saved by my answer, my desire shall be in vain; but if my answer shall save thee, thou wilt grant me to be Gawain's wife. Choose now, and quickly, for it must be so, or thou art but dead." "Mary!" said the king, "I may not grant thee to make warrant Sir Gawain to wed thee. All lieth in him alone." "Well," said she, "now go home again and speak fair words to Sir Gawain. Though I be foul, yet am I gay." "Alas!" he said. "Now woe is me!"

King Arthur returned to the castle; and his nephew, Gawain, responded courteously. "Nay," said Gawain, "I had liefer myself be dead than thee. I shall wed her and wed her again, though she were a fiend as foul as Beelzebub; or else I were not your friend." "Gramercy, Gawain," then said King Arthur; "of all knights that ever yet I found, thou bearest the flower."

Dame Ragnell was the name of the hag. When King Arthur, returning, gave her his promise and that of his nephew, she replied, "Sir, now shalt thou know what women desire most of high and low. There is one thing in all our fantasy, and that now shall ye know: We desire of men, above all manner of thing, to have the sovereignty."

And then she told the king that the big knight would be wroth when he heard this. "And he will curse her fast that taught it thee, for his labor is lost."

King Arthur galloped through mire, moor, and fen to his appointment with Sir Gromer Somer Joure; and the moment he arrived at the place assigned he found the other there before him.

"Come, Sir King," said the armed challenger, "now let us see what shall be thine answer."

King Arthur pulled his two books out and presented them, with the hope that some one of the earlier answers might be sufficient, and himself and his nephew thus be released from the unpleasant bond.

Sir Gromer looked on the answers—every one. "Nay, nay, Sir King," he said, "thou art but a dead man."

"Abide, Sir Gromer," said the king, "I have one answer more." Sir Gromer paused to hear. "Above all things," the king said, "women desire sovereignty, for that is their liking, and that is their most desire."

"And she that told thee now, Sir Arthur, I pray to God I may see her burn in a fire, for that was my sister, Dame Ragnell, that old scott, God give her shame—else I had made thee full tame. . . . Now have good day." The crotchety knight had long been harboring this grudge against King Arthur, because the king had once deprived him of his lands and given them "withe greatte wrong" to Sir Gawain. But now the opportunity for his revenge was lost, so he stormed away; for he would never again have the luck to encounter his life enemy unarmed.

King Arthur turned his horse into the plain, and soon met again with Dame Ragnell. "Sir King," she said, "I am glad that you have sped well; I told you how it would be. And now, since I have saved your life, Gawain must wed me. That is a full gentle knight. Openly I would be wed and before I allow you to part from me. Ride before, and I will come after, unto thy court, King Arthur."

And the king had great shame of her; but when they arrived in the court and all were wondering greatly whence so foul a thing had come, the knight, Sir Gawain, stepped forth without sign of reluctance and manfully pledged his troth.

> "Godhauemercy," sayd Dame Ragnelle then,
> "Ffor thy sake I wold I were a fayre woman,
> Ffor thou art of so good wylle."

All the ladies of the court and the knights were in great sorrow for Sir Gawain; and the ladies wept in their bowers that ever he should wed such a wight; she was so foul and horrible. She had two teeth, like boar's tusks, on either side, of length a large handful, the one tusk going up and the other down; and she had a mouth full wide and foully begrown with many hairs. Nor would she be put off with a little, quiet wedding (which was the desire of the queen), but insisted upon a high mass and a banquet in the open hall with everybody there. At the feast she tucked three capons away, as many curlews, and a number of various roasts of meat, tearing at it all with her long tusks and fingernails till only the bones remained. Sir Kay, Gawain's companion, but a brash, discourteous fellow, shook his head. "Whosoever kisses this lady," he said, "of his kiss he stands in fear." And so the bride kept gobbling away, till meat was done.

That night, in the bed, Sir Gawain could not at first bring himself to turn and face her unappetizing snout. After a little time, however, she said to him: "Ah, Sir Gawain, since I have wed you, show me your courtesy in bed. It may not be rightfully denied. If I were fair, you would not behave this way; you are taking no heed of wedlock. For Arthur's sake do kiss me at least; I pray you, do this at my request. Come, let us see how quick you can be!"

The knight and loyal nephew of the king collected every bit of his courage and kindness. "I will do more," he said in all gentleness, "I will do more than simply kiss, before God!" And he turned around to her. And he saw her to be the fairest creature that ever he had seen without measure.

She said: "What is your will?"

"Ah, Jesu!" he said, "what are ye?"

"Sir, I am your wife, securely; why are ye so unkind?"

"Ah, lady, I am to blame; I did not know. You are beautiful in my sight—whereas today you were the foulest wight my eye had ever seen! To have you thus, my lady, pleases me well." And he braced her in his arms and began kissing her, and they made great joy.

"Sir," she said, "my beauty will not hold. You may have me thus, but only for half the day. And so it is a question, and you must choose whether you would have me fair at night and foul by day before all men's eyes, or beautiful by day and foul at night."

"Alas," replied Gawain, "the choice is hard. To have you fair at night and no more, that would grieve my heart; but if I should decide to have you fair by day, then at night I should have a scabrous bed. Fain would I choose the best, yet know not what in this world I shall say. My dear lady, let it be as you would desire it; I rest the choice in your hand. My body and goods, my heart and all, is yours to buy and sell; that I avow before God."

"Ah, gramercy, courteous knight!" said the lady. "Mayst thou be blessed above all knights in the world, for now I am released from the enchantment and thou shalt have me fair and bright both night and day."

And then she recounted to her delighted husband how her stepmother (God have mercy on her soul!) had by necromancy enchanted her; and she was condemned to remain under that loathsome shape until the best knight of England should wed her and yield to her the sovereignty of all his body and goods. "Thus was I deformed," she said. "And thou, Sir Knight, courteous Gawain, hast given me the sovereignty for certain. Kiss me, Sir Knight, even now and here, I pray thee; be glad and make good cheer." And there they made joy out of mind.

> Thus itt passyd forth tylle mid-daye.
> "Syrs," quod the kyng, "lett vs go and assaye,
> Yf Sir Gawen be on lyve;
> I am fulle ferd of Sir Gawen,
> Nowe lest the fende haue hym slayn,
> Nowe wold I fayn preve.
> Go we nowe," sayd Arthoure the kyng.
> "We wolle go se theyr vprysyng,
> Howe welle that he hathe sped."
> They cam to the chambre, alle in certeyn.
> "Aryse," sayd the kyng to Sir Gawen,
> "Why slepyst thou so long in bed?"
> "Mary," quod Gawen, "Sir kyng, sicurly,
> I wold be glad, and ye wold lett me be,
> Ffor I am fulle welle att eas;
> Abyde, ye shalle se the dore vndone,
> I trowe that ye wolle say I am welle goon,
> I am fulle lothe to ryse."
> Sir Gawen rose, and in his hand he toke
> His fayr lady, and to the dore he shoke,
> She stod in her smok alle by that fyre,
> Her her was to her knees so red as gold wyre,
> "Lo! this is my repayre,
> Lo!" sayd Gawen Arthoure vntille,
> "Syre, this is my wyfe, Dame Ragnelle,
> That sauyd onys your lyfe." [1]

[1] From *The Weddynge of Sir Gawen and Dame Ragnell*, a fifteenth-century poem preserved in a manuscript of the early sixteenth (Rawlinson C 86). The same story is told, with variations, in the ballad, *The Marriage of Sir Gawaine* (preserved in Bishop Percy's folio manuscript, mid-seventeenth century), where

II. THE KNIGHT WITH THE LION

The romances of the Round Table have for hundreds of years laid their spell over the soul of Europe. Wrought by the twelfth and thirteenth century poets of France, Germany, and Britain, from materials deriving largely from the ancient treasuries of the Celts, these legends of faërie, quest, and disenchantment have deeply impressed themselves on the consciousness (and also upon the unconscious) of the descendants of those who first enjoyed them. We shall not dwell on the circumstances that induced me to glance from my special field of ancient Hindu mythology to this tradition belonging to the most distant corner of ancient Europe, nor pause to justify and elaborate upon the technique of comparative interpretation that is carrying us along on this dilettant adventure of tentative elucidation. The method is not intended, or expected, to yield results of philological importance; the indicated parallels are not presented as evidence for a comparative history of motifs and versions. The aim of this re-creation is simply to let the old symbolical personages and adventures again work upon and stimulate the living imagination, to revive them, and to awaken in ourselves the old ability to read with intuitive understanding this pictorial script that at

---

the challenging knight is described as "a bold barron . . . with a great club vpon his backe, standing stiffe and strong," and the first encounter takes place at Christmastide, with the second fixed for New Year's Day. Cf. Gower's *Tale of Florent* (*Confessio amantis* i, 1396-1861), and Chaucer's *Tale of the Wyf of Bathe.*

A convenient assemblage of these materials will be found in Bartlett J. Whiting's "The Wife of Bath's Tale," published in W. F. Bryan and Germaine Dempster's *Sources and Analogues of Chaucer's Canterbury Tales,* The University of Chicago Press, Chicago, 1941, pp. 223-264. The verses in the above account are quoted from this presentation of the text. For a study of the Irish sources and background of the Gawain cycle, see G. H. Maynadier, *The Wife of Bath's Tale,* London, 1901, Jessie L. Weston, *op. cit.,* and Roger S. Loomis, *Celtic Myth and Arthurian Romance,* New York, 1927. See also, Ananda K. Coomaraswamy, "C. the Loathly Bride," *Speculum* XX, Oct. 1945, pp. 391-404.

one time was the bearer of the spiritual sustenance of our own ancestors. The answers to the riddles of existence that the tales incorporate—whether we are aware of the fact or not—are still shaping our lives.

But centuries have passed; and, though in the profoundest sense it is certainly true that the messages of these old romances are very close to us, in another way they are remote. Most of us enjoyed them during childhood in one or another of those lovely, colorfully illustrated editions intended for the very young, and some of us have delved into works of the authentic tradition: Malory's *Morte d'Arthur*, for example. But, on the whole, we can find little or nothing of contemporary moment in these often interminable documents of a departed age. The medieval poets dwelt so persistently on the specific social and psychological problems of their own feudal society that they seem now rather quaint and boring, very much of the past. And so, although they charmed for a moment our childhood and the formative centuries of our civilization, we are glad to leave them (as adult reading fare) to the philologists and those unfortunate students who have to train their minds on dead languages and their ears on the intricacies of meters that have lost their ring. Chrétien de Troyes, Wolfram von Eschenbach, and the Gawain-poet have found their resting place in a dusty corner of the modern attic, along with the rest of the bric-a-brac that we modern Occidentals piously stored out of the way when we outgrew the chivalric conventions of the medieval world.

And yet the generations that fashioned these romances are not merely our spiritual ancestors, but to some extent our physical as well. They are inside our bones—unknown to us; and when we listen, they are listening too. As we read, some dim ancestral ego of which we are unaware may be nodding approvingly on hearing again its own old tale, rejoicing to recognize again what once was a part of its own old wisdom. And if we heed, this inner presence may teach us, also, how to listen, how to react to these romances, how to understand them and put them to use in the world of everyday.

One of the most popular of the tales was that of Owain, or Yvain, "The Knight with the Lion, and the Lady of the Fountain,"[1] a really wonderful story of how a young and heroic adventurer made his way to the fountain of life and conquered it, won the Lady of the Fountain and lost her again, but then, after madness and misery, trials and triumphs, rediscovered her and became, this time forever, the lord of both the fountain and its queen. The adventures apparently represent some sort of initiation to maturity—the way of a single-hearted hero endowed with intuitive powers, but blind with unconsciousness.

B.0S.

"King Arthur was at Caerleon upon Usk, and one day he sat in his chamber, and with him were Owain the son of Urien, and Kynon the son of Clydno, and Kai the son of Kyner, and Guinevere and her handmaidens at needlework by the window. And if it should be said that there was a porter at Arthur's palace,

---

[1] Chrétien de Troyes, *trouvère* at the fashionable court of the Countess Marie de Champagne (daughter of Eleanor of Aquitaine and King Louis VII of France), produced his version of the romance about 1173 (the date is not exactly known). Chrétien seems to have been the first to recount in French most of the adventures of the knights of the Round Table. About 1300 his *Yvain, ou Le Chevalier au Lion* was translated into German by Hartmann von Aue, the most prominent of the German poet-novelists of the time, a little later into English (under the title *Yvain and Gawain*) by an anonymous North-country poet of outstanding talent, and during the fifteenth century into German again, by the Bavarian, Ulrich Furterer. Swedish, Danish, and Icelandic translations are also known.

The following account will not be based, however, on Chrétien or any of his translators, but on the Welsh version, as preserved in the fourteenth-century *Red Book of Hergest*. Although the Continental tradition of the knights of the Round Table reacted on the little mountain country of King Arthur's origin and modified there the native legends, nevertheless the original Celtic quality and spirit maintains itself in this tale, and the adventures are rendered with a vigorous will and understanding. The romances of the *Red Book of Hergest* were translated early in the last century by Lady Charlotte Guest, and published under the title *The Mabinogion* (1838-49); now available in Everyman's Library No. 97. The story of Owain there appears as "The Lady of the Fountain."

there was none. Glewlwyd Gavaelvawr was there, acting as porter, to welcome guests and strangers and to receive them with honor, and to inform them of the manners and customs of the court; and to direct those who came to the hall or to the presence chamber, and those who came to take up their lodging.

"In the center of the chamber King Arthur sat upon a seat of green rushes, over which was spread a covering of flame-colored satin, and a cushion of red satin was under his elbow.

"Then Arthur spoke. 'If I thought you would not disparage me,' said he, 'I would sleep while I wait for my repast; and you could entertain one another with relating tales, and obtain a flagon of mead and some meat from Kai.' And the king went to sleep."

Kai went to the kitchen and to the mead cellar, and returned bearing a flagon of mead and a golden goblet, and a handful of skewers, upon which were broiled collops of meat. Then they ate the collops and began to drink the mead. And presently, the young knight Kynon was persuaded to tell a story. And it was the tale of how he had attempted a certain quest and failed.

Kynon had equipped himself and set forth to travel through deserts and distant regions; and at length he attained to the summit of a steep, where he found an open space, and in the midst of it a tall tree, under the tree a fountain, and by the side of the fountain a marble slab with a silver bowl attached by a chain of silver. Kynon took the bowl and cast a bowlful of water upon the slab; whereupon, immediately, a mighty thunder shook the air, a terrific storm broke, and a shower of hailstones jeopardized the hero's life. He defended both his horse's head and his own with his shield. And when the shower had passed he perceived that every leaf on the tree had been carried away. But then the sky became clear and the dreadful devastation was succeeded by a kind of new spring that more than compensated for the fear. Great flocks of multicolored birds lighted upon the tree and sang, covering its bare branches, a melodious foliage. "And truly, Kai," Kynon declared, "I never heard any melody equal to that, either before or since."

But when Kynon was most charmed with listening to the birds, lo, a murmuring voice was heard through the valley, approaching him, and it was saying, "O knight, what has brought thee hither? What evil have I done to thee, that thou shouldst act toward me and my possessions as thou hast done this day? Dost thou not know that the shower today has left in my dominions neither man nor beast alive that was exposed to it?" And thereupon, behold, a knight on a black horse appeared, clothed in jet-black velvet, and with a tabard of black linen about him. And they charged each other; the onset was furious, and Kynon was overthrown. Then the knight passed the shaft of his lance through the bridle rein of the other's horse and rode off with the two horses, leaving Kynon where he was. And so the young, overbold champion from the court of King Arthur returned along the road by which he came.

The young Owain, while listening to this tale of his friend, determined in his heart to attempt the remarkable adventure. On the morrow, with the dawn of day, he put on his armor and mounted his charger, and traveled through distant lands and over desert mountains. And at length he arrived at the first adventure of the way, which was precisely as Kynon had described it: the fairest valley in the world, wherein were trees of equal growth, and a river through the valley with a path beside it; finally, a large castle, at the foot of which was a torrent. And the lord of the castle accorded the errant young knight a generous welcome. Maidens were there, working at satin embroidery, seated on chairs of gold; and they rose to wait upon Owain; they took off his soiled garments and placed others upon him; and the meal that they set before him was of every sort of meat and liquor that he had ever seen. When the host learned of his guest's des-

100

tination, he gently smiled, and said: "If I did not fear to distress thee too much, I would show thee that which thou seekest. But if thou wouldst rather that I should show thee thy disadvantage than thine advantage, I will do so." And he described to Owain the manner of the adventure. After a night's sleep, Owain found his horse made ready for him by the damsels, and he departed.

The temptation to remain and idle his life away at the sumptuous table among the beguiling daughters of the lord of the Castle of Abundance ("the least fair of them was fairer than the fairest maid thou hast ever beheld in the Island of Britain") lay behind him, but a second temptation, namely that of fear, lay soon before. Following the road described by both Kynon and the host, he went into the wilderness and came to a large glade where he saw sitting a black man of great stature on the top of a mound. He was not smaller in size than two men of this world. And he was exceedingly ill-favored, having but one foot, and one eye in the middle of his forehead. He carried a club of iron of prodigious size. And he was the Woodward of the Wood, the master and the lord of the wilderness. Owain beheld a thousand wild animals grazing around him. And when he struck a stag so great a blow with his club that it brayed vehemently, all the animals came together, as numerous as the stars in the sky, so that it was difficult to find room in the glade to stand among them. And there were serpents and dragons and divers sorts of animals. However, Owain did not shrink from this terrifying circumstance, but went up to the giant and asked of him his road. And perceiving the young man to be dauntless, the lord of the wilderness pointed out the way. And so the knight proceeded, with that temptation too behind him: the temptation of fear before the terror of the wilderness and the ruthless forces of the animal realm.

Owain attained the marvelous fountain, and, following all instructions, took up the silver bowl and poured the water on the slab. And lo, the thunder was heard immediately, and then the shower broke, more violent than Kynon had described it. When the sky again grew bright, the tree at the well stood bare of foliage, but the birds arrived and settled down upon the tree, and they sang their celestial song.

Dipping up and pouring out the waters of life, the hero had brought about an augmentation of life, but of death also; for the two counterbalance each other in mysterious proportion. The fury of the tempest had transformed the tree of life into the condition of winter, but it had been followed by a miraculous spring, with feathered blossoms that could sing and fly. Now, however, the Black Knight would appear, the lord of the Lady of the Fountain. Clothed in the black of death, he would charge with the power of the storm of death itself; and the one who had presumed to approach, he would overthrow.

Owain heard and beheld the Black Knight coming toward him through the valley, prepared to receive him, and encountered him violently. Both their lances broke; they drew their swords and fought blade to blade. Then Owain struck a blow through the helmet, headpiece, and visor of the knight, and through the skin and the flesh and the bone into the very brain. The Black Knight felt that he had received a mortal wound, upon which he turned his horse's head and fled. And Owain pursued him. Following upon him close, he descried a castle, resplendent and vast, into the gate of which the Black Knight was allowed to enter, but the portcullis was let fall upon Owain. It struck his horse behind the saddle and cut him in two, and carried away the rowels of the spurs that were upon Owain's heels. The portcullis descended to the floor.[1] And the rowels of the spurs and part of

[1] Cf. Ananda K. Coomaraswamy, "Symplegades," in *Studies and Essays in the History of Science and Learning offered in Homage to George Sarton on the Occasion of his Sixtieth Birthday*, ed. M. F. Ashley Montague, New York, 1947, pp. 463-488.

the horse were left without, while Owain with the other part of the horse remained between the two gates; and the inner gate was closed, so that Owain could not go thence, and he was in a perplexing situation.

He could see, through an aperture in the gate, a street facing him, with a row of houses on each side. And he beheld a maiden, with yellow curling hair, and a frontlet of gold upon her head; and she was clad in a dress of yellow satin, and on her feet were shoes of variegated leather. And she approached the gate and desired that it should be opened. "Heaven knows, lady," said Owain, "it is no more possible for me to open it from hence than it is for thee to set me free." She spoke him fair and flattered him as a singularly faithful knight in the service of ladies; and then she handed in to him a ring that would render him invisible, and advised him how to behave, and described the place where she would await him.

The people of the castle came to put him to death, and when they found nothing but the half of his horse, they were sorely grieved. He vanished from among them, went invisible to the maiden, placed his hand upon her shoulder as she had bid, and was conducted into a large and beautiful chamber. The maiden kindled a fire, gave Owain water with which to wash, and brought him food in vessels of gold and silver. And Owain ate and drank until late in the afternoon, when lo, they heard a mighty clamor in the castle, and Owain asked the maiden what that outcry was. "They are administering extreme unction," she said, "to the nobleman who owns the castle." And Owain went to sleep.

In the middle of the night they heard a woeful outcry. "The nobleman who owned the castle now is dead," said the maiden. And in the morning Owain watched from his window a vast number of women, both on horseback and on foot, and all the ecclesiastics of the city singing, and a boundless host that filled

103

the streets, so that the sky resounded with the vehemence of their cries. They were bearing the body of the Black Knight to the church. And, watching the procession, he beheld a lady stained with blood, and about her a dress which was torn. And it was a marvel that the ends of her fingers were not bruised from the violence with which she smote her hands together. And her cry was louder than the shout of the men or the clamor of the trumpets.

Then Owain inquired of the maiden who the lady was, for no sooner had he beheld her than he became inflamed with her love. "She is called the Countess of the Fountain," said the maiden, "the wife of him whom thou didst slay." "Verily," said Owain, "she is the woman that I love best." "Verily," said the maiden, "she shall also love thee not a little." And the maid arose, kindled a fire, filled a pot with water and set it to warm, brought a towel of white linen and washed Owain's head, shaved him, dried his head and his throat with the towel, brought him food to eat, and arranged his couch for him. "Come here," she said, "and sleep, and I will go and woo for thee." Owain lay down and the maid went out and shut the door.

For thus, apparently, was the law that prevailed at the Castle of the Fountain: whosoever slew the guardian became himself the guardian, the Black Knight, the lord and consort of the Lady of the Fountain. This is the same old law that Sir James G. Frazer discovered when he turned his attention to the custom of the ancient grove and sanctuary at Lake Nemi, just outside of Rome, and which he describes in his monumental study, *The Golden Bough*. [1] "In this mythological sacred grove there grew a certain tree round which at any time of the day, and probably far into the night, a grim figure might be seen to prowl. In his hand he

[1] Sir James G. Frazer, *The Golden Bough*, 1890, reissued in 12 volumes, 1907-15; one volume abridged edition, 1922. The passage quoted (one volume edition, p. 1) is reprinted by permission of The Macmillan Company, publishers.

carried a drawn sword, and he kept peering warily about him as if at every instant he expected to be set upon by an enemy. He was a priest and a murderer; and the man for whom he looked was sooner or later to murder him and hold the priesthood in his stead. Such was the rule of the sanctuary. A candidate for the priesthood could only succeed to office by slaying the priest, and having slain him, he retained office till he was himself slain by a stronger or a craftier." As Frazer demonstrates, the priest, who was called "The King of the Wood," was regarded as an incarnation of the god consort of Diana, the goddess of the lake and grove; and their marriage-union was the source of the fruitfulness of the earth, of all animals, and of mankind. [1]

Comparable is the case of the Black Knight and the Lady of the Fountain. She cannot be cast permanently into mourning by the death of the knight consort, for she symbolizes the perennial power of life, continuous and unbounded. She cannot be alienated by circumstance from her proper character, which is, precisely, persistence through all the vicissitudes of affliction and disaster. Therefore, the survivor, the stronger one, the knight triumphant in the contest, becomes her lord and carries on the custom of the castle.

The maiden who had assisted Owain into the castle's domain, acting in the service of the ageless powers of the miraculous sanctuary, carefully shut the door, leaving him to rest, and hastened to the chambers of her freshly widowed lady. When she came there, she found nothing but mourning and sorrow; and the countess in her chamber could not bear the sight of anyone for grief. The maiden entered and saluted her, but the countess answered her not. And the maiden bent down toward her and said, "What aileth thee, that thou answerest no one today?"

"Luned," said the countess, with a look of anger, "what change hath befallen thee that thou hast not come to visit me in my

[1] *Ibid.*, pp. 139-142.

grief? It was wrong in thee that thou didst not come to see me in my distress. That was wrong in thee."

"Truly," said Luned, the maiden, "I thought thy good sense was greater than I find it to be. Is it well for thee to mourn after that good man, or for anything else that thou canst not have?"

"I declare to heaven," said the countess, "that in the whole world there is not a man equal to him."

"Not so," said Luned, "for an ugly man would be as good as, or better than, he."

"I declare to heaven," said the countess, "that were it not repugnant to me to cause one whom I have brought up to be put to death, I would have thee executed for making such a comparison to me. As it is, I will banish thee."

"I am glad," said Luned, "that thou hast no other cause to do so, than that I would have been of service to thee where thou didst not know what was to thine advantage. And henceforth evil betide whichever of us shall make the first advance toward reconciliation to the other, whether I should seek an invitation from thee, or thou of thine own accord shouldst send to invite me."

With that the maiden went forth, and the countess arose and followed her to the door of the chamber and began coughing loudly. And when Luned looked back, the countess beckoned to her, and she returned to the countess.

"In truth," said the countess, "evil is thy disposition, but if thou knowest what is to my advantage, declare it to me."

"I will do so," quoth she.

And then the girl introduced the problem of keeping the fountain properly defended. "Unless thou canst defend the fountain, thou canst not maintain thy dominions; and no one can defend the fountain, except it be a knight of Arthur's household; and I will go to Arthur's court, and ill betide me, if I return thence without a warrior who can guard the fountain as well as, or even better than, he who defended it formerly."

"That will be hard to perform," said the countess. "Go, however, and make proof of that which thou hast promised."

When Owain was in due time introduced to her, the countess gazed upon him steadfastly and said: "Luned, this knight has not the look of a traveler."

"What harm is there in that, lady?" said Luned.

"I am certain," said the countess, "that no other man than this chased the soul from the body of my lord."

"So much the better for thee, lady," said Luned, "for had he not been stronger than thy lord he could not have deprived him of life. There is no remedy for that which is past, be it as it may."

"Go back to thine abode," said the countess, "and I will take counsel."

The next day the countess caused all her subjects to assemble, and she showed them that her earldom was left defenseless and that it could not be protected but with horse and arms and military skill.

"Therefore," said she, "this is what I offer for your choice: either let one of you take me, or give your consent for me to take a husband from elsewhere to defend my dominions."

So they came to the determination that it was better that she should have permission to marry someone from elsewhere; and, thereupon, she sent for the bishops and archbishops to celebrate her nuptials with Owain. And the men of the earldom did Owain homage. And Owain defended the fountain with lance and sword.

Had the countess, the Lady of the Fountain, been a human being, an ego, a personality responding to situations as an individual, it would have been fitting for her to yield to the sorrow of the personal loss brought upon her by the death of her consort. She might have resigned life and the joys of womanhood

107

and love. But, as the fairy mistress of the Fountain of Life, she is no less than the blind life force incarnate; she cannot resign. And in keeping with the custom of the Castle of Life, she and the deedsman who slew her former husband, his predecessor, belong to each other. The dead Black Knight is the bond between. She had been conquered by the Black Knight and the Black Knight by Owain. It must have been with a look very much like the one with which the nymph of the ancient sanctuary at Lake Nemi received the new priest, that the Lady of the Fountain bade welcome to her new consort. The blood of the slain old priest, dripping from the hands of his holy murderer, was the ointment of initiation that sacramentally installed him as successor to the holy office of the ritually slaughtered servant.

Thus Owain enters the world of faërie, the transcendental sphere of the higher cosmic powers. As the consort of the Lady of the Fountain and the guardian of the Everlasting Waters, the perfect knight exceeds the bounds of his humanity and becomes initiated in the source mysteries of the life force, bespelled by the task with which his superhuman conquest has invested him. As the master of the fountain, Owain is now a being apart, released and separated from the all-comprising stream of life that carries ordinary human existence in its flow. He is translated from the world he used to know—that of the normal knowledge of human beings, which is represented in the pictorial language of the romances of the Round Table as the fellowship of the knights and their common adventures, tournaments, and gallant festivals. The courageous adventurer is lost, lost to the world at large. He has been bewitched by the magic of the sphere of invisible forces that can be approached and entered by the elect alone.

And yet, he is a creature from the sphere of man. Owain is human. And the world will not resign the child it has brought forth, will not relax its claim. It will insist upon its portion, even in defiance of the transcendental sphere that has abstracted him and now holds him captive as its ensorcelled priest; for the two spheres—that of our common human knowledge and existence, and the higher one of the primal forces and their initiations—in mutual contrariety lay claim upon the human soul. And it is the central labor of the soul's development to make actual the proper balance between the two, to give to each its due. Wherefore, if the soul, rapt into enchantment by an initiation into the mysteries of the divine and higher sphere, so renounces the world of everyday that no longing ever stirs it to return, then that worldly sphere itself will send its summoner to rap at the door, shatter the supramundane spell, and rouse the enchanted one from his magic dream.

Thus it happened in the case of Owain. For King Arthur and his knights became uneasy about the continued absence of their departed comrade, and, after three years of gradually increasing anxiety, determined to set out on an expedition of search. Kynon, who had recounted to Owain the story of the Black Knight of the Fountain, suspected that he might have attempted the adventure, and so, when the company of great champions left the halls and courts of the kingly castle at Caerleon—King Arthur himself powerfully mounted and riding among them—it was he, Kynon, who took the part of guide.

They paused at the Castle of Abundance, and though the number of the retinue of King Arthur was great, their presence was scarcely observed in the castle, so vast was its extent. They came to the glade in the wilderness where the terrifying, one-eyed giant sat on his mound among the animals, and the stature of the man was even more surprising to Arthur than it had been represented to him. Finally they reached the fountain, and Kai, with the king's leave, threw a bowlful of water upon the slab. Immediately there came the thunder, and after the thunder the shower. Many of the attendants who were in Arthur's train were killed by the shower. After the shower had ceased the sky be-

109

came clear, and on looking at the tree they beheld it completely leafless. Then the birds descended upon the tree, and the song of the birds was far sweeter than any strain they had ever heard before. Then they beheld a knight on a coal-black horse, clothed in black satin, coming rapidly toward them. And Kai met him and encountered him, and it was not long before Kai was overthrown. And the knight withdrew, and Arthur and his host encamped for the night.

And when they arose in the morning, they perceived the signal of combat upon the lance of the knight. And Kai again went toward the knight. And on the spot he overthrew Kai and struck him with the head of his lance in the forehead, so that it broke his helmet and headpiece and pierced the skin and the flesh the breadth of the spearhead, even to the bone. And Kai returned to his companions.

After this, all the household of Arthur went forth, one after the other, to combat the knight, until there was not one that was not overthrown by him, except Arthur and Gawain. And Arthur armed himself to encounter the knight. "Oh, my lord," said Gawain, "permit me to fight with him first." And Arthur permitted him. And he went forth to meet the knight, having over himself and his horse a satin robe of honor. And they charged each other, and fought all that day until the evening, and neither of them was able to unhorse the other.

The next day they fought with strong lances, and neither of them could obtain the mastery.

And the third day they fought with exceeding strong lances. And they were incensed with rage, and fought furiously, even until noon. And they gave each other such a shock that the girths of their horses were broken, so that they fell over their horses' cruppers to the ground. And they rose up speedily, and drew their swords, and resumed the combat; and the multitude that witnessed their encounter felt assured that they had never before seen two men so valiant or so powerful. And had it been midnight, it would have been light from the fire that flashed from their weapons.

And the knight gave Gawain a blow that turned his helmet from off his face, so that the knight knew that it was Gawain.

Then Owain said: "My lord Gawain, I did not know thee for my cousin, owing to the robe of honor that enveloped thee; take my sword and my arms."

Said Gawain: "Thou, Owain, art the victor; take thou my sword."

And with that, Arthur saw that they were conversing and advanced toward them.

"My lord Arthur," said Gawain, "here is Owain, who has vanquished me, and will not take my arms."

"My lord," said Owain, "it is he that has vanquished me, and he will not take my sword."

"Give me your swords," said Arthur, "and then neither of you has vanquished the other."

Then Owain put his arms around Arthur's neck and they embraced. And all the host hurried forward to see Owain and to embrace him; and there was nigh being a loss of life, so great was the press.

Owain invited King Arthur and the knights and the great retinue to tarry with him and his lady in the Castle of the Fountain until all should have recovered from the fatigues of the extended journey. "For I have been absent from thee these three years," said Owain, "and during all that time, up to this very day, I have been preparing a banquet for thee, knowing that thou wouldst come to seek me." And they all proceeded to the castle of the Countess of the Fountain, and the banquet which had been three years preparing was consumed in three months.

When King Arthur was ready to depart, he sent an embassy to the countess to beseech her to permit Owain to go with him for three months. And the countess gave her consent, although it was very painful to her. So Owain took his leave of the magic sphere of the Fountain of Life and returned to his former life of chivalry among the nobles and fair dames of the island of Britain at King Arthur's court. And when he was once more amongst his kindred and friends, he stayed three years with them instead of three months. And thus the fountain remained without a guardian and the lady without her lord consort.

This second instance of forgetfulness is the counterpart of the first. Having been absorbed totally by the higher sphere, serving as initiated guardian of the Fountain of Life and the spellbound companion of the Lady of the Fountain in her domain of timelessness, the knight had neglected unduly the requirements of the world of ordinary human conduct, as represented by the social life of the knights of the Round Table. Inwardly absorbed—having penetrated to the ultimate source and fountain—Owain had forsaken the length and breadth of the stream of existence, turning his back completely on the sphere of his personal relations and the occupations of contemporary chivalry. Now that sphere, in revenge, rips him out of himself, gains complete possession of his being, and implicates him to such a degree in the vivid events of the normal sphere of externalization, that all memory of the mysteries of the utterly inward way is lost. And so the initiate loses recollection of his anointment; the higher mystic personality and rôle into which he had grown, as the Black Knight, falls away; and the elect is no longer the elect.

One may foresee that still another crisis lies before Owain—and a painful ordeal—before he discovers the secret of the balanced union of the two spheres of his soul's humanity. For the higher, like the lower sphere, when it has waited long in vain, knows how to summon again the delinquent. Its method, however, is somewhat less direct and manful.

Behold, one day a damsel made her appearance at King Ar-

thur's court, upon a bay horse with curling mane and covered
with foam, and the bridle and so much as was seen of the saddle were of gold. And the damsel was arrayed in a dress of yellow
satin. And she came up to Owain and took from off his hand the
ring that the Countess of the Fountain had bestowed on him as
a sign of their alliance. "Thus," said she, "shall be treated the
deceiver, the traitor, the faithless, and the disgraced; shame to
thy beard." And she turned her horse's head and departed.

Then his adventure came to Owain's remembrance and he
was sorrowful. The unconscious tie that had secretly united him
to the magic sphere having been thus rudely severed, he was
jolted to consciousness; the goddess had withdrawn even the
last token of her presence and existence. The waters of being that
he had discovered, that had absorbed him, that had sent him
forth reborn and then had supported him obscurely even in the
years of his forgetfulness, now had completely withdrawn, and
he was left stranded and alone. Owain departed from the court
for his own abode, and made preparations that night, and the
next day arose, but did not return again to the court. He wandered astray, out of Caerleon to the distant parts of the earth
and to uncultivated mountains.

Siegfried in the *Twilight of the Gods* undergoes an identical
trial. Like Owain, the young Siegfried is symbolical of the un-
spoiled heroic soul, entitled by its nature to communion with the
cosmic forces and eminently eligible for supreme fulfillment.
Like many figures of the world's mythological traditions, he was
not the offspring of human wedlock, but was of a somewhat
questionable and mysterious birth; like Zeus, like Krishna, he
was reared in secretness, and like Perseus he slew the dragon,
because—like Owain, like Gawain, like the Buddha—he knew no
fear. Siegfried possessed the golden ring that would yield, if his
youthful mind should ask for it, the boundlessness of cosmic
power. His sword was the sword of Wotan, Father of the Gods;

113

by forging it anew the hero proved his claim to it. Like Achilles, the son of a goddess, he was invulnerable. And like the hero sages of the East, he understood the language of the birds.

The great victory and sin of Siegfried were essentially the same as those of Owain. Having conquered his dragon, he made his way through a cosmic fire that encircled the summit of the divine mountain, and released Brünnhilde from her enchanted sleep. She was the favorite daughter of Wotan, and became the bride of the hero who released her. Thus he was joined to the transcendental forces precisely as Owain, by becoming the lord consort of a supernatural fairy mistress. And like Owain, when he descended the mountain again in quest of adventures in the inferior world of human affairs, Siegfried forgot completely the higher lady of his soul. Worse even than that, having drunk a potion of forgetfulness, he unwittingly exchanged her for an ordinary daughter of man. The vengeance taken was without mercy or bounds.

In the case of Siegfried, as in that of Owain, there was guilt without intent: innocence, but at the same time guilt.[1] For in the sphere of the superhuman the elect is not excused because of ignorance or good will. He is judged according to his adequacy and his acts. And since the powers of that sphere invisibly pervade everything in the visible world, everything the elect encounters is finally a test. Over and over again his decisions are his testing, and whenever he fails he dies, or he suffers what is equivalent to a death. The superhuman, sheer life force is as

[1] In the case of Perceval, the classic hero of the Grail Quest, we find again this dark theme of the unconscious guilt. Brought up by a widowed mother in the wilderness, aloof from King Arthur's court and in ignorance of the world of chivalry, he one day beheld a passing troop of knights, and following them, left his mother to die of a broken heart. That was the first great crime of his innocence. The second was incurred when at the height of his career he arrived at the Grail Castle and was privileged to attend the holy mystery. He failed to ask the secret meaning of what was being exhibited to his eyes, and thus brought upon himself the curse of the mystic realm.

114

revengeful as it is blind in its terrible onrush, the moment it feels itself disappointed and betrayed.

In keeping with this fearful law, the pretty maid Luned, who had conducted Owain into the presence of the Lady of the Fountain, was also hurled, at the same time as Owain, into the outer darkness; for she had assisted the wrong man to the estate of lord and master guardian of the fountain. Two vassals of the countess came one day and dragged her to a remote dungeon in the wilderness, into which they roughly hurled her, threatening her with death unless Owain himself should arrive to set her free before a certain day. And alas, she had no one to seek him for her. And the knight for whom she was condemned to wait was going mad.

Owain, after his loss of the ring and his recollection of his former state, had been unable to return to the society of the knights of the Round Table; for the spell had been broken which the shallow consciousness of the merely social existence in chivalry had temporarily cast upon him after his return with King Arthur to the court. As guardian-intimate of the cosmic powers, he had really outgrown that mode of life. The brief visit had been only temporary—a violent rocking to the forgotten side. But he now could not swing back to the other mode of existence either, for the goddess had rejected him; she had reclaimed her ring. Gone was the former lucidity of Owain's intuition, which once had guided him unconsciously and with unwavering stride into communion with the supernatural forces. Though the world of knighthood had dropped away, the earldom of the fountain could no longer be found or even sought. Owain was excluded from the human and from the superhuman. The romance describes how he sank below both to the only remaining extreme.

It is written that the hero in his misery dwelt and wandered in the wilderness "until all his apparel was worn out, and his body was wasted away, and his hair was grown long. And he went about with the wild beasts and fed with them, until they became familiar with him."

The powers had revenged themselves with a terrible ruthlessness. Having departed from their guidance, Owain had been left to sink to the lowest level of existence, that of the dim, instinctive unconsciousness and intuitive foraging of the animal world. We are reminded of the ordeal and metamorphosis of John Golden-Mouth, and of that strange notice, in the Book of Daniel, of King Nebuchadnezzar, who descended from his throne, and, on all fours, went to join the animals.[1] Both the saint and the king presently returned to the full possession of their reason. We may anticipate a similar development for the knight Owain.

He went about with the wild beasts and fed with them until they became familiar with him, but at length he became so weak that he could no longer bear them company. Thereupon he descended from the mountains to the valley, and he came to a park that was the estate of a certain widowed countess. And this countess, one day, together with her maidens, went forth to walk by a lake that was in the middle of the park. They saw the form of a man and were terrified. Nevertheless they approached, and touched him, and looked; and they saw that there was life in him, though he was exhausted by the heat of the sun. The countess returned to the castle, and took a flask full of precious ointment, and gave it to one of her maidens. "Go with this," she said, "and take with thee yonder horse and clothing and place them near the man we saw just now. And anoint him with this balsam near his heart, and if there is life in him he will arise through the efficacy of this balsam. Then watch what he will do."

And the maiden departed from her, and poured the whole of the balsam upon Owain, and left the horse and the garments hard by, and went a little way off and hid herself to watch him.

[1] Cf. pp. 52-66, *supra.*

116

In a short time she saw him begin to move his arms, and he rose up and looked at his person and became ashamed of the unseemliness of his appearance. Then he perceived the horse and the garments that were near him. And he crept forward till he was able to draw the garments to him from off the saddle. And he clothed himself, and with difficulty mounted the horse. Then the damsel discovered herself to him and saluted him. And he rejoiced when he saw her, and inquired of her what land and what territory that was.

"Truly," said the maiden, "a widowed countess owns yonder castle. At the death of her husband she received two earldoms, but at this day she has but this one dwelling that has not been wrested from her by a young earl, who is her neighbor, because she refused to become his wife."

"That is a pity," said Owain.

And he and the maiden proceeded to the castle, and he alighted there, and the maiden conducted him to a pleasant chamber and kindled a fire and left him. And the maiden came to the countess and gave the flask into her hand.

"Ha! maiden," said the countess, "where is all the balsam?"

"Have I not used it all?" said she.

"Oh, maiden," said the countess, "I cannot easily forgive thee this; it is sad for me to have wasted seven score pounds' worth of precious ointment upon a stranger whom I know not. However, maiden, wait thou upon him, until he is quite recovered."

And the maiden did so, and furnished him with meat and drink, and fire, and lodging, and medicaments, until he was well again. And in three months he was restored to his former guise and became even more comely than he had ever been before.

Owain rescued the countess from her undesired suitor. He rode up to the fellow when he arrived with a numerous army, reached out and drew him completely out of his saddle, and then returned with him disgraced to the portal of the castle, where he

117

presented him to the countess as a gift. "Behold a requital to thee for thy blessed balsam."

She was overjoyed. And the earl restored to the countess, as a ransom for his life, the two earldoms he had taken from her, and for his freedom he gave her the half of his own dominions, and all his gold, and his silver, and his jewels, besides hostages.

And Owain prepared to take his departure. The countess and all her subjects besought him to remain, but Owain chose rather to wander through distant lands and deserts. Having at one time been the guardian of the Fountain of Life and consort for three years of its fairy mistress, he could not be tempted now to dwell merely as a vastly rich country gentleman, with a magnificent feudal estate and a charming wife. On a beautiful black steed which the countess had given him, Owain rode away, a homeless wanderer, questing without any tangible aim between the two known but unapproachable spheres. This is the ageless way to the reintegration of the Self.

Then, of a day, as he journeyed, he chanced to hear a loud and terrible howl in a neighboring wood. And it was repeated a second and a third time. He quickly spurred to the spot, and beheld a huge craggy mound in the middle of the wood, on the side of which was a rock. There was a cleft in the rock and a serpent was within the cleft. And near the rock stood a black lion, and every time the lion sought to go thence, the serpent darted toward him to attack him.

Owain unsheathed his sword and drew near to the rock, and as the serpent sprang out, he struck him with his sword and cut him in two. And he dried his sword, and went on his way as before. But, behold, the lion followed him and played about him, as though it had been a greyhound that he had reared.

That evening Owain dismounted and turned his horse loose in a flat and wooded meadow. And he struck fire, and when the fire was kindled, the lion brought him fuel enough to last for three nights. And the lion disappeared. And presently the lion returned, bearing a fine large roebuck. And he threw it down before Owain.

Thus the knight had won a companion, a helpmate, a second ego, as it were. This lion was to rescue him, in the future, from a number of encounters against odds, which Owain would have lost had he been battling alone. The enemies were stronger than himself and dishonorable, and the knight always endeavored to engage them squarely, man to man, according to the code of chivalry. But the lion, unasked, even forbidden by Owain, would always eventually, and at precisely the fortunate moment, make his startling appearance on the field. A number of such timely rescues were necessary to convince the knight that he should acquiesce in his gallant decisions to the superior intuition of the kingly beast at his side. In the final stages of his quest he accepted the mute guidance of this animal alter ego as a kind of superior advice.

The slaying of the snake corresponds, symbolically, to the slaying of the dragon by Siegfried, Tristan, Perseus, Indra, and the other great dragon killers of the legends of the world. Owain, by that deed, gave expression to a decision in favor of the lion. The reward was the fellowship of the lion—a special variety and manifestation of the divine boon of superhuman power that always and everywhere issues from the deed of the killing of the dragon. For, unconsciously, Owain chose, of all beasts, the kingly one to be his companion and inseparable counterpart. Instinctively he recognized his own biological and spiritual kinship with the warm-blooded, noble mammal, when he elected to rescue it from the menace of the cold-blooded, venomous and cunning snake. The act endued him with animal power in its most elevated form—combining pride and strength with generosity and forbearance. Thus he discovered, so to speak, his totem animal, and integrated the power of that animal's instinct into his human personality as a salutary and obedient function, adding to the vigor of his reborn knighthood something of the force that overpowered him blindly when he became beastlike and lived among the creatures of the wood. The strength and wisdom of the kingly lion became his guide. Obedient, yet acting on its own as a sort of superior intuition, this externalization of the physical aspect of his being was to conduct him back to the mistress whom he forfeited when he became involved and absorbed in the merely worldly routines of social life, as represented by the company and vain formalities of the Round Table.

The first adventure that befell Sir Owain after his discovery and rescue of the lion boded well for the future. The grateful beast followed him like a dog for the remainder of the day, and that night brought him the roebuck for his evening meal. Owain took the kill and skinned it, and placed collops of its flesh upon skewers around the fire. The rest of the buck he gave to the lion to devour. And while he then was sitting watching his meat broil, he heard a deep sigh somewhere not far away, and a second, and a third. He called out to know whether the sound proceeded from a mortal, and he received the answer that it did.

"Who art thou?" said Owain.

"Truly," said the voice, "I am Luned, the handmaiden of the Countess of the Fountain."

"And what dost thou here?" said Owain.

"I am imprisoned," said she, "on account of the knight who came from King Arthur's court and married the countess. And he stayed a short time with her, but he afterwards departed for the court of Arthur, and has not returned since. And he was the friend I loved best in the world. And two of the pages in the countess' chamber traduced him and called him a deceiver. And I told them that they two were not a match for him alone. So they imprisoned me in the stone vault and said that I should be put to death unless he came himself to deliver me by a certain day and that is no further off than the day after tomorrow. And I have no one to send to seek him for me. And his name is Owain the son of Urien."

"And art thou certain that if that knight knew all this, he would come to thy rescue?"

"I am most certain of it," said she.

When the collops were cooked, Owain divided them into two parts between himself and the maiden. And never did sentinel keep stricter watch over his lord than the lion that night over Luned and Owain.

On the road then, with Luned up on the horse with him and the lion trotting like a dog beside, Owain paused at a castle very much like the earlier Castle of Abundance, only the present idyllic resort was cast under a pall of sorrow; for the two sons of the lord of the castle had been captured by a terrible giant—very much like the black, one-eyed giant, Woodward of the Wood—and were in danger of being devoured. Owain went to meet the monster, and the lion followed. And when the giant saw that Owain was armed, he rushed toward him and attacked. And the lion fought with the giant more fiercely than Owain did.

"Truly," protested the giant, "I should find no difficulty in fighting with thee, were it not for the animal that is with thee."

Upon that Owain took the lion back to the castle and shut the gate upon him, and then he returned to fight the giant as before. And the lion roared very loud, for he heard that it went hard with Owain. And he climbed up till he reached the top of the earl's hall, and thence he got to the top of the castle, and he sprang down from the walls and went and joined Owain. And the lion gave the giant a stroke with his paw which tore him from his shoulder to his hip, and his heart was laid bare, and the giant fell down dead. Then Owain restored the two rescued youths to their father.

Being a knight of the solemn circle of the Round Table, Owain, like Gawain and Lancelot, is the perfect man, according to the courtly conception of the Middle Ages; that is to say, as a social being and gentleman of the world, he is chivalry incarnate. On the other hand, the inarticulate lion, brute life force in its most majestic and generous aspect, represents, like the wonderful horse of the Conn-eda story, the intuitive guiding principle that conducts the hero to the sphere of supernatural power, which is at once above and beneath the social plane. The perfected human consciousness of the knight, joined to the sub- and super-human instinct of the king of beasts, proves stronger than even the titan of the wilderness, and prevails where human chivalry would have lacked both sagacity and strength.

When the knight with the lion had overcome the savage giant, he was besought to remain, but he refused, and taking leave of the grateful family, proceeded to the meadow where Luned was awaiting him. But when he came there, he saw a great fire kindled and two youths with beautiful auburn hair leading the maiden to cast her into the flame. They were the brutal pages from the castle of the Countess of the Fountain, who, the year before, had dragged Luned into the wilderness and were now come to execute their threat. Owain challenged, the two rode against him, the lion roared, and the battle was considerable. Owain was fatigued after his long struggle with the giant. Nevertheless, with the help of the lion, the maid was saved from being burned. And after that, Owain returned with Luned to the dominions of the Countess of the Fountain.

The details of the reunion and reconciliation of the knight with his supernatural mistress are not described by the Welsh text that we have been following, namely that of the *Red Book of Hergest*, but appear, with a new, French formality of decorum, in the version of the romance composed by Chrétien de Troyes. According to this courtly account, the lady herself had been present with her two pages when they came to strip and burn Luned (whose name

122

now, in the French, is Lunete), and she had witnessed the victory of the knight with the lion, but had not recognized him; for the armor that he was wearing was strange to her, and she did not know his name. Following the defeat of the two pages, they were both burned upon the pyre that they had kindled for the damsel, "for it is right and just that he who has misjudged another should suffer the same manner of death as that to which he had condemned the other." And Lunete was joyous at being reconciled with her mistress. Without recognizing the knight all present offered their service to him so long as life should last. and even the lady, who unknowingly possessed his heart, begged him to tarry until he and his lion should have regained their strength.

The knight replied: "Lady, I cannot tarry anywhere until my lady removes from me her displeasure and anger. Then the end of all my labors will come."

"Indeed," she said, "that grieves me. I think the lady cannot be very courteous who cherishes ill will against you. She ought not to close her door against so valorous a knight as you unless he had done some great wrong."

"Lady," he replied, "however great the hardship be, I am pleased by whatever may be her will. But speak to me no more of that, for I shall say nothing of the cause or crime, except to those who are informed of it."

"Does anyone know it, then, beside you two?"

"Yes, truly, lady."

"Well, tell us at least your name, fair sir; then you will be free to go."

"Quite free, my lady? No, I shall not be free. I owe more than I can pay. Yet, I ought not to conceal from you my name. You will never hear of 'The Knight with the Lion' without hearing of me, for I wish to be known by that name."

"For God's sake, sir, what does that name mean? For we never

123

saw you before, nor have we ever heard mentioned this name of yours."

"My lady, you may from that infer that my fame is not widespread."

Then the lady said: "Once more, if it did not oppose your will, I would pray you to tarry."

"Really, my lady, I should not dare, until I knew certainly that I had regained my lady's good will."

"Well then, go in God's name, fair sir, and, if it be His will, may He convert your grief and sorrow into joy."

"Lady," said he, "may God hear your prayer." Then he added softly under his breath: "Lady, it is you who hold the key, and though you know it not, you hold the casket in which my happiness is kept under lock." Then he went away in great distress, and no one had recognized him save Lunete, and she now rode with him and accompanied him a little distance.

Lunete alone kept him company, and he begged her insistently never to reveal the name of her champion. "Sire," said she, "I will never do so." Then he further requested her that she should not forget him, and that she should keep a place for him in his mistress's heart whenever the chance arose. She told him to be at ease on that score, for she would never be forgetful, nor unfaithful, nor idle. Then he thanked her a thousand times, and he departed pensive and oppressed because of his lion that he must needs carry, being wounded and unable to follow him on foot. He made for him a litter of moss and ferns in his shield. When he had made a bed for him there, he laid him in it as gently as he could, and carried him before his saddle thus stretched out full length on the inner side.[1]

[1] Chrétien de Troyes, *Le Chevalier au Lion* (Yvain), vv. 4533 ff., edited by Foerster, Max Niemeyer Verlag, Halle, 1887; translated by W. Wistar Comfort, *Arthurian Romances by Chrétien de Troyes*, Everyman's Library No. 698, pp. 239-241.

The romance of Chrétien de Troyes describes a number of further adventures, illustrating the mutual loyalty of the lion and his master, and then brings the errant knight to the point of his ultimate task—that of the difficult reunion with the Goddess of Life. Still accompanied by his animal companion, he arrived one day at the miraculous fountain beneath its wonderful tree, and, repeating the mysterious and well-known ritual, dipped up the water and poured it on the stone. The thunderclap shook the countryside, toppling walls within the domain of the castle. The great tree was stripped of its leafage, and after the storm the numerous birds arrived and beautifully sang. Owain sat and waited. But there was no Black Knight to defend the fountain. The inhabitants of the castle and its town were so stricken with terror that they did not know what to do. "Confounded be the man," said they, "who first constructed a house in this neighborhood, and all those who built this town. In the wide world they could not have found so detestable a spot, for a single man is able here to invade and worry and harry us." And the lady herself was in great fear.

The maid Lunete, who had for weeks been preparing her lady for the return of the knight, made quick and brilliant use of the opportunity. "Surely," she urged, "you are in a bad predicament, my lady, if you do not devise some plan."

The countess replied: "Do thou, who art so wise, tell me what plan I can devise, and I will follow thy advice."

"Indeed, my lady," said Lunete, "if I had any plan, I should gladly propose it to you, but you have great need of a wiser counselor. So I shall certainly not dare to intrude, and in common with the others I shall endure the rain and wind until, if it please God, I shall see some worthy man appear here in your court, who will assume the responsibility and burden of the battle."

But the countess insisted on hearing some suggestion, and

125

Lunete then stated that she thought the Knight with the Lion
would be a competent defender. The countess agreed; she had as
yet no suspicion that he was her husband. Lunete rode and met
the knight, who was still waiting at the fountain. And she gave
him safe conduct to the castle. And although the countess was
indignant when the visor was lifted and she discovered that the
knight to whom she had pledged herself was her delinquent and
rejected spouse, she nevertheless abandoned her hauteur and
acquiesced when he abased himself. [1] The couple were reconciled, and after a season of great happiness, Owain found the
Lady of the Fountain willing to return with him to the gallant
world of the Round Table. "When he went thence," we read, "he
took the countess with him to Arthur's court." [2] And so he reached
his goal and integrated the two contrary spheres—which all the
while had been the obscure objective of his seeking.

For the two spheres are one, in spite of the apparent duality
of their phenomenal manifestations. And, in a preliminary way,
Owain had already reunited them when he achieved and established his silent and mysterious companionship with the lion.
That had been the secret of his power to return. The new name
that he gave himself, *Le Chevalier au Lion,* which was the
mask, the new personality, by means of which the countess was
appeased, was the symbol of a spiritual rebirth. The goddess
would never have accepted the knight in his former character.
But he now had been augmented by a mute, profound relationship with the instinctive principle in himself and in the realm of
nature. He had become the irresistible Lion-Man—the master,
the consummate champion, of the two worlds.

Mythology at large knows several instances of the Lion-Man—
not to speak of a multitude of other impressive figures combining
animal traits with human. Vishnu in India, for example, assumed

[1] Chrétien de Troyes, *op. cit.*, vv. 6527-6813.
[2] *Red Book of Hergest, op. cit.*, pp. 174-175.

the monstrous shape known as the "Half-Man, Half-Lion" (Nara-simha—a human body, but with a lion head and lion claws) in order to annihilate a certain stupendous demon, Golden Garment by name, who had upset the order of the world. And in the myths of Greece, we are told of another great Lion-Man—closer to our own imagination and therefore more easily deciphered—namely Herakles, who, by his heroic deeds, became the model for antiquity, just as Owain for the peoples of the basically Celtic world of the medieval North. Herakles, however, linked himself with the "lion" principle in the Greek fashion—a manner precisely the reverse of the Celtic. He was not followed by his beast as by a faithful dog, but conquered, slew, and flayed it, in the form of the invincible lion monster of Nemea; then he donned the skin, which he wore thenceforward as his characteristic costume, both to boast of the victory and to frighten friend and foe. With the terrible claws crossed over his heroic chest, the fierce mouth with its gaping jaws towering over his head, and the tail dangling behind, he stalked about the land as a two-legged super-lion, the man conqueror of lionhood, i.e., the man conqueror of the whole animal kingdom by virtue of his conquest of its king.

But Herakles killed also the Hydra, the titanic snake. In the pictorial script of the old mythologies, that is as much as to say that the elect among men, on his ascent to perfection, overpowered *both* of the mutually antagonistic spheres of the animal realm. The ideal hero of the Greek civilization—paving the way to Christianity and the age of modern man—rid the mind of its archaic reverence for those animal features and forms that had been so conspicuous in the earlier mythologies and religions of Mesopotamia and Egypt. Moses and the Prophets, in their establishment of the Jewish faith of the Old Testament, effected a comparable transformation when they resolutely battled, time and time again, against the relapses of their people into the

127

worship of the local bull-shaped divinities of the Mediterranean: the "golden calf" of the Bible, and the other beast gods of the surrounding pagan world. The Greeks and the Hebrews brought to pass a humanization of the sphere of the divine, which represented the dawn of a new age and was to lead to modern man, a decisive break with the thenceforth archaic tradition that had been inherited by the ancient world from primitive man, who felt and reverenced in himself an intrinsic kinship with the animal domain.

Archaic man regarded himself as a part of the animal world of nature and identified himself with the traits and powers of the more impressive among his surrounding animal neighbors. The Celtic tradition (as we may judge from the story of Conn-eda as well as from that of Owain) was in this sense archaic. And throughout the Middle Ages this very ancient monitor of feeling and belief, speaking through numberless fairy tales, romantic lais, and courtly epics of adventure, repeated its old lesson to medieval man, who was then undergoing a process of humanization under the dual influence of the Christian faith and the chivalric ideal, pointing out the opposite, the "other" way to perfection; the way, namely, not of killing the animal soul inside and setting ourselves apart from it, but of converting the beast to the human cause—winning it over, so that it should serve as a helpmate in the great and very difficult task of forging a union between the human and the extrahuman powers that inhabit not the cosmos only but also ourselves. The Arthurian romance of the Knight with the Lion stands for an accord between Christian chivalric humanity, as symbolized in the knightship of the Round Table, and the sheer powers of life, as represented by the holy, secret fountain (the source out of which all the life powers perennially well), the Lady of the Fountain, and the guiding kingly lion who assisted the hero to the goal.

If the animal within is killed by an overresolute morality, or even only chilled into hibernation by a perfect social routine, the conscious personality will never be vivified by the hidden forces that underlie and obscurely sustain it. The interior animal asks to be accepted, permitted to live with us, as the somewhat queer, often puzzling companion. Though mute and obstinate, nevertheless it knows better than our conscious personalities, and would be known to know better if we could only learn to listen to its dimly audible voice. The voice is the voice and urge of instinct, and that voice is the only thing that can effect our rescue from the impasses into which our conscious personalities will be continually conducting us as long as we remain wrapped in the self-pride of being completely human, disdainful, and destitute of all intuitive contact with the occult fountain of the life of the world.

Owain, thus, is a Lion-Man diametrically opposed to the ideals of the Greek and modern tradition. As a symbol of human perfection, he was shaped by the mind and spirit of the Celt, in consonance with an attitude toward the demonic-superhuman that distinctly suggests the archaic Orient more than the later Occident. The motif of the black lion in conjunction with the gigantic snake also suggests the East, specifically Syria and Mesopotamia. And the symbol of a well yielding the precious water of life is one long familiar to the sunstricken countries of the Near East, which are forever haunted by the fear of drought and the danger of death by thirst; it is not an image inspired, in the first instance, by the rain-drenched climate of the British Isles.

Long before the Roman Conquest, old Mother Asia bestowed a portion of her bountiful mythological heritage on the remote peoples of the western isles. The Phoenicians, sailing from the coast of Palestine, voyaged through the Gates of Hercules and came to port in Cornwall to exploit the tin mines there, so valuable to the great bronze civilizations of their time. The symbols and tales of the preclassic Egypto-Babylonian civilizations were thus carried directly to the pre-Celtic and Celtic populations of Britain, Wales, and Ireland. And though those remote domains were overwhelmed, subsequently, by the Christian, then the Germanic-English, and the Chivalric-Norman invasions, wave upon wave, the earlier wisdom, nevertheless, survived. To this day the genius of the Celtic race remains second to none in its power to weave the magic tapestries of the everlasting mythical romance of the human heart. Continental Europe was enchanted by its wizardry for centuries, up to the very dawn of the Renaissance. And today it touches us anew, charming the soul of modern man (a very old soul, by the way) through such poetry as that of William Butler Yeats, Fiona Macleod (William Sharp), John Synge, and the others of the Celtic Revival, as well as through the Arthurian Parsifal and Tristan of Richard Wagner.

It is difficult to estimate the degree of understanding with which the medieval redactions of the archaic symbolic tales were composed and received, but there is a cogency about them that would seem to suggest the persistence of an effective conscious tradition. Not all the poets knew what they were doing, by any means, but on the other hand there were certainly a number who did. The distinctly courtly romances betray many signs of a not altogether remote derivation from the pre-Christian, and one can even say pre-European, past.

The knight, Sir Owain, in his adventure, overcomes as a merely preliminary test the two trials that constituted the whole of the adventure of Sir Gawain. At the Castle of Abundance he survives the temptation of sensual self-indulgence, which was the sense of Gawain's affair inside the curtains of the bed, and before the one-eyed black Ward of the Wood he outfaces the terror of death, which Gawain knew when he stretched out his neck to the ax. Owain's long adventure, after that, is concerned with a further and higher meaning. By a process of laborious reintegration he gradually wins back what he originally possessed, when, moving as it were in a dream, he first made his way to the Fountain of Life. He achieves a harmonious fusion of the conscious and the unconscious personalities, the former aware of the problems and controls of the visible phenomenal world, the latter intuitive of those deeper springs of being from which both the phenomenal world and its conscious witness perennially proceed. Such a harmoniously integrated style of life is the boon which nature bestows upon every infant, in a preliminary, undecisive way, and which the growing child then loses with the development of its self-conscious individuality. The romance of Owain teaches, through its pictorial script, how to win back that boon on the level of maturity, the bliss of the kingdom of heaven: innocence reborn and strength re-established according to the pattern of that primitive state of enlightened childhood which Christ points to as the model for the perfect.

III. LANCELOT

1

When you buy a pack of ordinary French playing cards, in Paris or anywhere else in France, you discover, perhaps with some surprise, that the face cards all bear names. The kings are called after four celebrated monarchs of the past: David, Alexander, Caesar, and Charlemagne. The queens are Rachel and Judith of the Old Testament (motherhood and feminine heroship respectively), and two Greek goddesses. The knights, or knaves, are led off by Lancelot, the jack of clubs. He is followed by one of the paladins of Charlemagne, Roger the Dane, as the knave, or jack, of spades, then by Hector of Troy, jack of diamonds,[1] and La Hire, the jack, or knight, of hearts.[2] In a number of the games of the sixteenth to eighteenth centuries (bezique, for example), these four gallant knight-bachelors serve to upset the harmony of the married life of the kings and queens. Thus Sir Lancelot maintains his celebrated illicit role to this day in the popular French imagination.

Lancelot du Lac is, without question, the most attractive and splendid of the knights of the Arthurian Round Table, even though he betrays his allegiance to his king, disgraces the ideal of stainless knighthood, and renders himself, through his life-long sin of adultery, incapable of the culminating Christian-chivalric quest of the Holy Grail. A mysterious warning voice cried out to him when he attempted to approach the sanctuary: "Sir Lancelot, more harder than is the stone, and more bitter than is the wood, and more naked and barer than is the leaf of the fig tree; therefore go thou from hence, and withdraw thee from this holy place." And when he heard this he knew not what to do, and so departed weeping, and cursed the time that he was born: "My sin and my wickedness have brought me unto great dishonor; for when I sought worldly adventures for worldly desires, I ever achieved them and had the better in every place, and never was I discomfit in no quarrel, were it right or wrong. And now I take upon me the adventures of holy things, and now I see and understand that mine old sin hindereth me and shameth me." [3] Lancelot reforms temporarily under the inspira-

---

[1] Hector's son, Astyanax, or Francillon, is supposed to have escaped from the ruins of Troy to become the mythical ancestor of the royal lineage of the kings of France. In the same way, Aeneas is supposed to have escaped to Italy and founded Rome.

[2] La Hire, or Etienne de Vignolles (*ca.* 1390-1443), was one of the chief officers at the court of King Charles VII of France. King Charles, aided by Joan of Arc, brought the Hundred Years' War to an end; and it was King Charles who assigned these names to the face cards of the French pack.

[3] Malory, *Morte d'Arthur* xiii, 19.

tion of the quest, and so comes as close to success as a sinner may; but after the Grail has been achieved by his illegitimate son, Sir Galahad, and he himself has returned to Arthur's court, he relapses helplessly into his old love again, which presently brings disaster upon the fellowship of the Round Table. Through it the queen is disgraced, many knights are slain, Sir Gawain is killed by Sir Lancelot, and Lancelot himself is banished. A catastrophic series is set in motion that results, at last, in the death of the king and the expiration of the cycle.

The legend of this brilliant warrior and lover, spellbound his whole lifetime by the secret yet all too well-known passion for Queen Guinevere, retained a greater interest for later generations than the deeds and sufferings of the other knights of Arthur's entourage. This most popular, most dashing figure was charged with a special magic. He represented something very different from the heroic medieval ideals of his companions, something much less timely, more profoundly human and enduring.[1] Sir Lancelot is an incarnation of the ideal for manhood that exists, not in the world of masculine social action, but in the hopes and fancies of the feminine imagination. He is an example, that is to say, of what the modern analytical psychologist terms the "animus archetype," the dream image of manliness that inhabits the woman's psyche. Gawain and Owain, on the other hand, and the majority of the other knights of the Round Table. stand for the medieval masculine psyche itself, in the throes of its characteristic male adventures and decisions.[2]

[1] Sir Gawain is the *real* hero of early English chivalry (as often emphasized by J. L. Weston).

[2] In contrast to the paucity of animus-figures in the Arthurian romances, representations of the opposite, the anima-archetype, abound. Apparitions of the "dream woman" of the male—that elusive, attractive and dangerous, mischievous and benevolent, ambiguous 'mistress of his unconscious longing are ubiquitous in those fairies of the lake that act as helpmates of the hero, wicked queens who bewitch and harass him, glamorous ladies and beautiful damosels continually and everywhere imploring his assistance: Nimue, the Lady of the Lake, who be-

133

The name of Lancelot has become proverbial for the gallant and reckless lover, in which respect it ranks with the name of Tristan, the lover of the Irish princess, Queen Isolt. The two were heroes of the same mettle, cursed and blessed by the destiny of the same forbidden passion, each spellbound by the wife of his liege. They encountered each other once in a great tournament, with opposing armies, and though Tristan was momentarily unhorsed by Lancelot, he resumed the combat with such vigor and endurance that in the end the two yielded their swords to each other, and embraced.[1] An eternal friendship was concluded,

---

stows on King Arthur the unfailing sword, Excalibur, and its sheath which renders the possessor invulnerable; Morgan le Fay, whose spell is cast over the king and many of his knights; Niniane, who conjures the wizard Merlin, the most inspired and inspiring figure of the whole cycle, into a living grave.

Merlin is a perfect example, by the way, of the archetype of the Wise Old Man, the personification of the intuitive wisdom of the unconscious. By his inspiration and secret advice he guides the conscious personality, which is represented by the knights and the king. The figure of Merlin is descended, through the Celtic druids, from the ancient tribal priest and medicine man, supernaturally endowed with cosmic wisdom and the power of witchcraft, the poet and divine who can conjure invisible presences with the magic of his songs. Like Orpheus, the singer and master of the mysteries and initiations of ancient Greece, whose harmonies tamed the wild animals and moved the mute stones to arrange themselves into walls and buildings, Merlin can command the stones. By magic he transported the great stone circle of Stonehenge, "the dance of the giants," all the way from Ireland to the Salisbury plain. Merlin is the Master of the Enchanted Forest, that is to say, of the realm of the unconscious with all its powers and enigmas; his castle of innumerable windows opens to a view of them all. Omniscient, he knows the past and the future. His gaze penetrates to the hidden depths of the earth, and he can behold there hidden dragons rocking the foundations of a tower. Time and again, in the guise of an old man "of four score years," he accosts unexpectedly the knights and King Arthur, his special pupil, forecasting events to come and imparting warning and advice. He can also appear as a child of fourteen, pouring forth wisdom beyond all age and time. Thus he resembles the Chinese Old Man, Lao-tse, "The Old One," whose name at the same time means "The Old Child." In his role as supervisor and guide of King Arthur's career and court, Merlin strongly resembles the Hindu type of the guru, or house priest, the magician and spiritual teacher of the Hindu householders and kings. By creating the Round Table itself and guiding Arthur from infancy to paramount kingship, he was the moving principle of the entire legend.

[1] Morte d'Arthur x, 67-86.

for the two were attracted by the identity of their natures; they were ruled by the one demonic spell. Dante celebrates both in the fifth Canto of his *Inferno,* in the Second Circle (that of the carnal sinners), where Tristan, side by side with Paris of Troy, appears for a moment in the smoke, carried along in the fiery whirlwind of unquenchable desire. A few lines later, Francesca da Rimini, locked with the brother of her husband under the doom of an insatiable embrace, woefully confesses how she had been led to sin and disaster by reading with her lover of the first kiss of Guinevere and Lancelot: "We were alone, and without suspicion. Many times that reading brought our eyes together, and changed the color of our faces, but at one point only were we overcome. When we read of the desired smile being kissed by such a lover, he who never shall be divided from me kissed my mouth, all trembling. And in the book we read no more that day."[1]

The spiritual initiation of Sir Lancelot is not the way of the high quest in sanctity. His halo is that of inextinguishable guilt, the sign of the wayward, ambiguous initiation of the reckless forces of insatiable passion. There is something inhuman, demonic, elfish, about his blind addiction to the forbidden food of his soul, his effrontery and miraculous skill in eluding public opinion and disgrace. And this is the very occasion of his fame, the very secret of his hold on us. For he is not a mere human gallant, but a supernatural, a kind of changeling, who has aligned on his side the secret potencies of the fairy realm and is blessed by the interdicted powers of the soul.

Sir Lancelot was of human parentage, being the son of King Ban of Benwick, and he was baptized not Lancelot but Galahad, the name that was handed on, at last, to his son. But Lancelot, this first Galahad, while still an infant, was carried away and reared by the Lady of the Lake—the same who bestowed on

[1] *Inferno* v, 129-238.

135

King Arthur Excalibur, the magic sword. And he was reared in a miraculous, inhuman land under waves, the mythical kingdom of the elemental sheer life force; fostered there by the fairies and elves, not human beings; and he remained there until he was eighteen. The Lady of the Lake, his patroness, bestowed on him a magic ring that had the power of dispelling witchcraft and would make him a match for dragons and all other such superhuman things. And it was she who named him Lancelot du Lac, Lancelot of the Lake. The name bespeaks his second character, his humanity augmented by the elemental powers that saturated his personality during the boyhood spent in the Land under Waves.

2

The legend of the sword of Sir Lancelot is another sign of his double character. According to the conventions of the universal picture language of myth and legend, the weapon by which a hero accomplishes his deeds is a counterpart of himself, symbolical of the force that he wields. The sword of Sir Lancelot—that invincible weapon with which he dealt the deathblow to his former companion-in-arms, Sir Gawain—came, as might be expected, from the mysterious domain of faërie. Its first human possessor was the tragic, strange, and fatal Northumbrian hero, Sir Balin, noble in purpose yet ever doing the wrong thing, who not only dealt the terrible Dolorous Stroke, "whereof shall fall great vengeance," but fought and killed his beloved brother, Sir Balan, in "the marvellest battle that ever was heard of, and they were buried both in one tomb." Sir Balin was called "The Knight with the Two Swords," a title suggestive of his split personality; and his brother with whom he battled, who bears almost the same name as himself and is "the best friend," "the man he most loves in the world," is practically himself again in another form. Both are continually longing to see each other and be united, but by a fairy trick inherent in the character and fatal destiny of the sword, which was later to be passed along to Lancelot (together with its perverse and dangerous power), they encountered not in love but in battle, and discovered their mistake too late.

The story of Sir Balin is worth reviewing in full length, not only because of its own doom-heavy beauty, but because it discloses something of the fatality of the entire cycle. Malory places it close to the opening of his great compilation, where it stands as a prefigurement and foreboding of the melancholy catastrophe which the sin of the inheritor of Balin's sword is to actuate. Noteworthy also is the role that Merlin plays in the wonderful tale. We begin to know and feel the force of his permanent, sustaining presence. Merlin's occasional, timely apparitions are like the condensations of an enwrapping atmosphere into a human figure; he is the enchantment, the Providence, that inhabits, moves, foreknows, and designates; he is the Weird of all these initiations, tests, catastrophes, and illusions of joy.

There had come a damsel to King Arthur's court, and she had been girt with this selfsame sword; and that was the first the world had ever seen of it. She had been "sent on message from the great lady Lile of Avelion." And the king had had great marvel, and he said: "Damosel, for what cause are ye girt with that sword? It beseemeth you not."

"Now I shall tell you," said the damosel. "This sword that I am girt withal doth me great sorrow and cumbrance; for I may not be delivered of this sword but by a knight. But he must be a passing good man of his hands and of his deeds, and without villainy or treachery, and without treason. And if I may find such a knight that hath all these virtues, he may draw out this sword out of the sheath."

"This is a great marvel," said Arthur, "if this be sooth. I will

137

myself assay to draw out the sword; not presuming upon myself that I am the best knight, but that I will begin to draw at your sword in giving example to all the barons that they shall assay every each one after other when I have assayed it."

Then Arthur took the sword by the sheath and by the girdle and pulled at it eagerly, but the sword would not out.

"Sir," said the damosel, "you need not to pull half so hard; for he that shall pull it out shall do it with little might."

"Ye say well," said Arthur. "Now assay ye all my barons; but beware ye be not defiled with shame, treachery, nor guile."

Most of all the barons of the Round Table that were there at that time assayed; but without success.

"Alas!" said the damosel, "I weened in this court had been the best knights, without treachery or treason."

"By my faith," said Arthur, "here are good knights, as I deem, as any be in the world, but their grace is not to help you; wherefore I am displeased."

Then fell it so that at that time there was a poor knight with King Arthur, that had been prisoner with him half a year and more for slaying of a knight, the which was cousin unto King Arthur. The name of this knight was called Balin, and by good means of the barons he was delivered out of prison; and so he went privily into the court, and saw this adventure. And as the damosel took her leave of Arthur and of all the barons, so departing, this knight Balin called unto her; and said: "Damosel, I pray you of your courtesy, suffer me as well to assay as these lords."

The damosel beheld the poor knight, and saw he was a likely man; but for his poor arrayment she thought he should be of no worship without villainy or treachery. And then she said unto the knight: "Sir, it needeth not to put me to more pain or labor, for it seemeth not you to speed there as others have failed."

"Ah! fair damosel," said Balin, "worthiness, and good tatches, and good deeds, are not only in arrayment, but manhood and worship is hid within man's person, and many a worshipful knight is not known unto all people, and therefore worship and hardiness is not in arrayment."

"By God," said the damosel, "ye say sooth. Therefore ye shall assay to do what ye may."

Balin took the sword by the girdle and sheath, and drew it out easily; and when he looked on the sword it pleased him much. Then had the king and all the barons great marvel.

"Certes," said the damosel, "this is a passing good knight, and the best that ever I found, and most of worship without treason, treachery, or villainy, and many marvels shall he do. Now, gentle and courteous knight, give me the sword again."

"Nay," said Balin, "for this sword will I keep, but it be taken from me with force."

"Well," said the damosel, "ye are not wise to keep the sword from me; for ye shall slay with the sword the best friend that ye have, and the man that ye most love in the world, and the sword shall be your destruction."

"I shall take the adventure," said Balin, "that God will ordain me."

The damosel departed, making great sorrow; and Balin sent for his horse and armor, and made him ready to depart from King Arthur. The meanwhile there came into the court a lady that hight the Lady of the Lake; and she came on horseback, richly bysene, and saluted King Arthur. She asked him a gift that she declared he promised her when she gave him the sword Excalibur.

"That is sooth," said Arthur, "a gift I promised you. Ask what ye will and ye shall have it, an it lie in my power to give it."

"Well," said the lady, "I ask the head of the knight that hath won the sword, or else the damosel's head that brought it; for he slew my brother, and that gentlewoman was causer of my father's death."

"Truly," said King Arthur, "I may not grant neither of their heads with my worship. Therefore ask what ye will else, and I shall fulfill your desire."

"I will ask none other thing," said the lady.

When Balin was ready to depart, he saw the Lady of the Lake. By her means she had slain Balin's mother, and he had sought her three years. And when it was told him that she asked his head of King Arthur, he went to her straight and said: "Evil be you found. Ye would have my head, and therefore ye shall lose yours." And with his sword lightly he smote off her head before King Arthur.

"Alas, for shame!" said Arthur; "why have ye done so? Ye have shamed me and all my court; for this was a lady that I was beholden to, and hither she came after my safe-conduct. I shall never forgive you that trespass."

"Sir," said Balin, "me forthynketh of your displeasure; for this same lady was the untruest lady living, and by enchantment and sorcery she hath been the destroyer of many good knights, and she was causer that my mother was burnt, through her falsehood and treachery."

"What cause soever ye had," said Arthur, "ye should have forborne her in my presence. Therefore, think not the contrary, ye shall repent it; for such another despite had I never in my court. Therefore withdraw you out of my court in all haste ye may."

Then Balin took up the head of the lady, and rode forth out of the town.

Sir Balin, thus ignominiously banished, but possessed of the fairy sword, rode away on adventure. And whatever enemy he met, he dealt him a deadly blow, but at the same time, unawares, and by the same blow, he caused some disaster. He overthrew the son of the King of Ireland who came against him to avenge

140

the murder of the Lady of the Lake; and a damosel that had loved the prince slew herself on the prince's sword when she saw him slain. Merlin appeared then and prophesied that on the spot where the two young lovers were buried Tristan and Lancelot du Lac should fight "the greatest battle betwixt two knights that was or ever shall be." And Merlin turned to Balin. "Thou hast done thyself great hurt," he said. "Because of the death of this lady thou shalt strike a stroke most dolorous that ever man struck, except the stroke of our Lord; for thou shalt hurt the truest knight and the man of most worship that now liveth, and through that stroke three kingdoms shall be in great poverty, misery, and wretchedness twelve years, and the knight shall not be whole of that wound for many years."

And Balin said: "If I wist it were sooth that ye say I should do such a perilous deed as that, I would slay myself to make thee a liar." And therewith Merlin suddenly vanished away.

The terrible Dolorous Stroke that had been thus foretold by the Wise Old Man was brought about by a peculiar adventure. Balin was giving safe-conduct to a young lover one day, when there passed someone who rode invisible and smote the young knight that went with Balin through the body with a spear. "Alas," said the young knight, "I am slain under your conduct, and by a knight called Garlon. Therefore take my horse that is better than yours, and ride to the damosel; and follow my quest as she will lead you, and revenge my death when ye may."

"That shall I do," said Balin, "and that I make a vow to knighthood." And so he departed from this knight with great sorrow.

Balin found the damosel, and he rode together with her into a forest. And there they met with a knight that had been a-hunting; and when he had joined them, and as they came by a hermitage even by a churchyard, there passed the knight Garlon, invisible again, and smote this second knight, Perin de Mountbeliard, through the body with a spear.

"Alas," said Balin, "it is not the first despite he hath done me."

And there the hermit and Balin buried the knight. And Balin and the damosel rode on. And they came after many days to a castle where King Pellam, "the man of most worship that now liveth," was holding feast. Garlon was there, among many knights of worship, and he was the brother of the good King Pellam, and his face was black. He was pointed out to Balin, and when Garlon espied that this Balin was watching him, he came and smote Balin on the face with the back of his hand, and said: "Knight, why beholdest me so? For shame therefor. Eat thy meat, and do what thou came for."

"Thou sayest sooth," said Balin. "This is not the first despite that thou hast done me, and therefore, I will do what I came for." And he rose up fiercely and clave his head to the shoulders.

All the knights arose from the table to set on Balin, and King Pellam himself stood up fiercely, and said: "Knight, hast thou slain my brother? Thou shalt die therefor or thou depart."

"Well," said Balin, "do it yourself."

"Yes," said King Pellam, "there shall no man have ado with thee but myself, for the love of my brother."

Then King Pellam caught in his hand a grim weapon and smote eagerly at Balin; but Balin put the sword betwixt his head and the stroke, and therewith his sword burst in sunder. And when Balin was weaponless he ran into a chamber for to seek some weapon, and so from chamber to chamber, and no weapon could he find, and always King Pellam after him.

And, at the last, he entered into a chamber that was marvelously well dight and richly, and a bed arrayed with cloth of gold the richest that might be thought, and one lying therein, and thereby stood a table of clene gold with four pillars of silver that bare up the table, and upon the table stood a marvelous spear strangely wrought. And when Balin saw that spear, he gat it in his hand and turned him to King Pellam, and smote him pass·

ingly sore with that spear, so that King Pellam fell down in a swoon, and therewith the castle roof and walls brake and fell to the earth, and Balin fell down so that he might not stir foot nor hand. And so the most part of the castle, that was fallen through that dolorous stroke, lay upon Pellam and Balin three days.

Then Merlin came thither and took up Balin, and gat him a good horse, for his was dead, and bad him ride out of that country.

"I would have my damosel," said Balin.

"Lo," said Merlin, "where she lieth dead."

And King Pellam lay so, many years sore wounded, and might never be whole till Galahad, the haughty prince, healed him in the quest of the Sangreal.

Then Balin departed from Merlin, and said, "In this world we meet never no more." So he rode forth through the fair countries and cities, and found the people dead, slain on every side. And all that were alive cried, "O Balin, thou hast caused great damage in these countries; for the dolorous stroke thou gavest unto King Pellam, three countries are destroyed, and doubt not but the vengeance will fall on thee at the last."

A most remarkable adventure! This is the dark prelude to the legend of the quest of the Holy Grail. Sir Galahad, the son of Sir Lancelot, was to make good this damage wrought upon the Grail King, the castle, and the realm, by the original wielder of Sir Lancelot's magic power as embodied and symbolized in the fairy sword. For the fairy powers that have been joined to the human are equivocal in their modes of manifestation. Whereas in Galahad they will show their redemptive power and King Pellam will be healed, in Balin they are destructive. Sir Balin is to Sir Galahad as death to rebirth, twilight to dawn, November to May; and between their two adventures stretches the long night, the winter sleep of the soul, which is our life in sin. This

143

interim is the period of Sir Lancelot and of the mission of the fellowship of the Round Table for the salvation of the world.

Through the demon power that Balin acquired with the sword, he succeeded where another would have failed; he rid the world of the mischievous, invisible rider, Garlon. But in conquering, he wrought havoc; for the superhuman power that he had hoarded to himself when he refused to give back the weapon was beyond his personal control. It lifted him above the level of normal human heroship, but strewed the path of his exploits with disaster, and would continue to do so as long as he proceeded along his now terrible way. The curt parting from the Wise Old Man, Merlin, the wizard of prophecy who had forewarned him, amounted to a final severance of submission to the advice of the unconscious. It was a reiteration of the same willfulness that had cut him off from the fairy maiden when she had appeared at the court with the now devilish sword. Such a bluff self-confidence was something very different from the courteous acquiescence of Sir Gawain in the requirements of the mysterious presences from the transcendental realm, something that could never lead to the bliss and glory of the hero-elect, but only to world destruction, self-destruction, and the destruction of the man that was most loved in the world.

Sir Balin rode from the three countries he had destroyed, and when he was past them he rode eight days before he met with adventure. Then he came upon a fair knight who sat on the ground and made great mourning. And this knight complained of his lady who had promised to meet him here and had failed. He was about to slay himself with the sword that she had given to him, but Balin restrained his hand, promising to help him seek her. And they rode until they arrived before her castle. "I will go into the castle," said Balin, "and look if she be there." So he went in. He searched from chamber to chamber. Then he looked into a fair little garden, and under a laurel tree he saw her lying with a knight in her arms, the foulest knight that ever he saw. And the two were fast asleep.

Balin returned to the betrayed lover, told how he had discovered her, and conducted him to the garden. And when the knight beheld her so lying, for pure sorrow his mouth and nose burst out bleeding, and with his sword he smote off both their heads, and then he made sorrow out of measure. "O Balin," he said, "much sorrow hast thou brought unto me, for haddest thou not shewed me that sight I should have passed my sorrow." And therewith suddenly he rove himself on his sword unto the hilts.

Thus again, and innocently, Balin has wrought disaster. Wherever he appears and intervenes with his good intentions, wherever he makes a friend or lends his hand to human affairs, inadvertently he gives only ruin to the world. He shatters the new friendship and isolates himself from mankind again in the isolation of the lonely errant knight. And so, wherever he goes he is known now as Balin le Savage, for the boon retained from the fairy realm has made him one apart. He is a man possessed. It was long ago that he parted from his brother Balan, his counterpart wearing but one sword, who has vanished from his sight; and he could now no more drop his fateful weapon than Abu Kasem his bewitched and bewitching slippers.

When Sir Balin saw the lady and the two knights dead, he rapidly spurred away, lest folk should say that he had slain them. And so he rode forth; and within three days he came by a cross, and thereon were letters of gold that said, "It is not for no knight alone to ride toward this castle." But that was precisely Balin's doom: to be the knight alone, and so it was a moment of terrible foreboding as he stood before that boundary cross. Then he saw an old hoary man coming toward him—a double, or counterpart, as it were, of the wizard Merlin. "Balin le Savage," this personage cautioned, "thou passest thy bounds to come this way. Therefore turn again and it will avail thee." And he vanished.

145

And with that, Balin heard a horn blow, as if it had been the death of a beast. "That blast," said Balin, "is blown for me; for I am the prize, and yet I am not dead."

He was very brave. The same valor that had made it possible for him to draw the sword of extrahuman power now would hold him to the way of self-destruction that he knew to lie before him. He would not turn back. And so he pressed on beyond the forbidding cross, and came very soon to a fair castle that was on an island, and it was guarded by a knight. And the towers of the castle stood full of ladies—like the *Château Merveil* of Sir Gawain. It was the Realm of the Mothers to which he had come, the Land of No Return.

"Sir," said a certain knight, that was before the ferry, "methinketh your shield is not good; I will lend you a bigger."

The shield and arms, during the Middle Ages, served to identify the knight who rode and gave battle with his visor closed. The devices were the signs and symbols of his personality, derived from some major and celebrated deed of his, or they heralded his lineage and so announced the ideals for which he fought. They represented the rationale of his conscious action, the manner of his conscious ego, the tangible, visible aspect of his being, as met by friend or foe. Balin, by the resignation of his shield, would be made anonymous at the very moment of stepping into the sphere of the fairy powers. He would relinquish there his personal character and conscious being.

And so Balin took the shield that was unknown and left his own; and put himself and his horse into a great boat, and so rode to the island.

And when he came on the other side he met with a damosel, and she said: "O knight Balin, why have ye left your own shield? Alas, ye have put yourself in great danger; for by your shield ye should have been known."

"Me repenteth," said Balin, "that ever I came within the

146

country, but I may not turn now again for shame; and what adventure shall fall to me, be it life or death, I will take the adventure that shall come to me." And then he looked on his armor, and understood he was well armed, and therewith made the sign of the cross and mounted upon his horse.

Then before him he saw come riding out of the castle a knight, his horse trapped all red, and himself in the same color. This was Balan, Balin's brother; but he did not know him—"the man he most loves in the world," whose destruction the fairy maiden had prophesied when Balin had refused to return the sword. Like Owain at the castle of the Lady of the Fountain, Balan was serving here in the priestly role of the lord and captive of the Sanctuary of Life. And like the black armor of the Black Knight, his red was the vestment of his office.

Balan, the priest and guardian of the Women's Isle, failed to recognize his brother even though Balin carried his two swords, "because he knew not his shield." "And so they aventryd their spears and came marvellously fast together, and they smote each other in the shields. . . ." And they were of exactly the same strength, two aspects of one and the same single being: Balan the self that Balin had been before he took and retained the fairy sword. And so they fought there together till their breaths failed. And all the place there as they fought was blood red.

Balan, the younger brother, withdrew him a little and laid him down. Then said Balin le Savage: "What knight art thou? For or now I found never no knight that matched me."

"My name is," said he, "Balan, brother unto the good knight Balin."

"Alas," said Balin, "that ever I should see this day." And therewith he fell backward in a swoon.

Then Balan moved on hands and knees to him and put off the helm, but could not know him, his visage was so battered and full of blood.

147

When Balin awoke, he said: "O Balan, my brother, thou hast slain me and I thee."

"Alas," said·Balan, "that ever I saw this day."

"We came both out of one tomb, that is to say one mother's belly, and so shall we lie both in one pit."

And the lady of the tower buried them both in that same place where the battle was done. And so all the ladies and gentlewomen wept for pity. And the lady let make a mention of Balan, how he was there slain by his brother's hands; but she knew not Balin's name.

The two sides of the sundered personality, the demonic and the innocent human, having proceeded through life along separate lines, ever longing for, yet unrecognizable to, each other, had embraced only by ceasing to exist, reconciled through mutual destruction and united in a common grave.

Balin, because of his boylike fearlessness, his valor without blemish, was endowed with superhuman powers and privileged to draw the fairy sword. He was representative of the perfect man. But he became caught and dominated by the forces that might have served him, after his willful refusal of the fairy messenger's request. The extrapersonal, infrahuman element, which every human being carries within, then surged against and overbore his conscious human personality, carrying him, as on a wave, to destruction. When the shield of his chivalric personality was taken away, he lost his human face, and then, carried anonymously on the tide of the powers, crashed against the likewise anonymous, reciprocally enchanted presence of his brother, and in the act of killing each other, each killed himself: Balin-Balan, the two aspects of the one being, the demonic and the human, undid each other and sank to their mutual doom.

Merlin came in the morning, and he let write Balin's name on the tomb with letters of gold: that here lieth Balin le Savage that was the knight with the two swords, and he that smote the dolorous stroke. And Merlin took Balin's sword, and took off the pommel and set on another pommel. So Merlin bade a knight that stood afore him handle that sword, and he assayed, and he might not handle it. Then Merlin laughed.

"Why laugh ye?" said the knight.

"This is the cause," said Merlin; "there shall never man handle this sword but the best knight of the world, and that shall be Sir Lancelot or else Galahad his son. And Lancelot with his sword shall slay the man that in the world he loved best; that shall be Sir Gawain." And Merlin let write all this in the pommel of the sword.[1]

3

Every blow that Balin dealt with the sword proved, inadvertently, to be a Dolorous Stroke; for when the personality is invaded by extrapersonal forces, the freedom of judgment and power to measure action, which distinguish the rational consciousness, are overthrown. The individual becomes enthralled to an irresistible fatality, victim and agent at once of the pressures that have mastered him. And so Balin le Savage, though he foreknew the end, had to continue to his doom.

Similarly Lancelot. Like the Knight of the Two Swords, whose fairy weapon he inherited, Lancelot was split in his nature, on the one hand human, but on the other a prodigy of the magic of the "Lake." His entire being was pervaded by the witchery of his fairy patroness and, himself bewitched, he bewitched everyone who beheld him—Queen Guinevere, King Arthur, even Dante's poor Paolo and Francesca. But this power is also an isolating factor. Like Balin, Lancelot was cut off from normal human life and the fulfillments of a real man's existence. He was

[1] Malory, *Morte d'Arthur*, II.

never to become a husband or the father of a family, but was doomed to remain the bachelor gallant. In this fixed role of the perfect though unvirtuous lover, he was both something more and something less than human. He dominated the society of the Round Table and to this day can captivate the imagination. Even in his great defeat, Sir Lancelot was more interesting, more human, than the knights whose hearts were pure.

Only once, and then through sorcery, was Lancelot ever seduced from his faithfulness to the lady of his life. And it was a mortifying episode, though great glory redounded from it to the fellowship of the Round Table of the king. Lancelot had been out riding on adventure, shortly following his tournament with the great lover of Queen Isolt, Sir Tristan, and after rescuing a grateful lady who had been five years boiling in a chamber "that was as hot as any stew," he went against a dragon inhabiting a nearby tomb. On the tomb a prophecy was written in letters of gold: "Here shall come a leopard of king's blood, and he shall slay this serpent; and this leopard shall engender a lion in this foreign country, the which lion shall pass all other knights." Not pausing to consider the implications, Queen Guinevere's knight lifted up the cover, and there came out a dragon, spitting fire. He drew his sword, and fought with the dragon long. When he had slain it, the king of that country arrived, a good and noble knight, and desired to know his name.

"Sir," said Sir Lancelot, "wit you well my name is Sir Lancelot."

"And my name is," said the king, "Pelles, king of the foreign country, and cousin nigh unto Joseph of Arimathæa." [1]

---

[1] Malory's source for this adventure is the French *Prose Lancelot*, whereas his source for the Balin story was the *Prose Merlin*. These two great thirteenth-century productions drew their legends independently from the vast and not altogether self-consistent fund of the medieval Arthurian tradition. In the Balin story we saw the castle of the Grail King destroyed; here it will be found still intact, but under a curse; it is in some kind of "danger." The name of the king in the Balin

Then either of them made much of the other, and so they went into the castle to take their repast. And fain would King Pelles have found the means to have had Sir Lancelot to lie by his daughter, fair Elaine; for the king knew well that Sir Lancelot should get a child upon his daughter, the which should be named Sir Galahad the good knight, by whom all that foreign country should be brought out of danger, and by him the Holy Grail should be achieved.

Then came forth a lady that hight Dame Brisen, and she said unto the king: "Sir, wit ye well Sir Lancelot loveth no lady in the world but only Queen Guinevere; and therefore work ye by my counsel, and I shall make him to lie with your daughter, and he shall not wit but that he lieth with Queen Guinevere."

"O fair lady, Dame Brisen," said the king, "hope ye to bring this about?"

"Sir," said she, "upon pain of my life let me deal"; for this Dame Brisen was one of the greatest enchantresses that was at that time in the world living.

Then anon, by Dame Brisen's wit, Sir Lancelot was told that Queen Guinevere was visiting in a certain castle of Case but five miles thence. And when Sir Lancelot heard that, wit ye well he was never so fain; and he thought to be there that same night. And then this Dame Brisen let send Elaine to the castle of Case, and Sir Lancelot against night rode unto that castle, and there anon he was received worshipfully.

story was Pellam ("Pellean" in Malory's French source), here it is Pelles. Both texts, however, describe the kingly figure as a close relative of Joseph of Arimathæa, who, according to the thirteenth-century legend, brought the cup of the Last Supper (the cup that received Christ's blood at the Crucifixion) and the lance that pierced Christ's side to this reliquary chapel of the Grail. The holy treasures were here preserved and guarded by the Grail King, Pellam-Pelles, for the well-being of Christendom.

The Grail Castle is a Christianization of the pagan-Celtic motif of the castle of the Fountain of Life, the source of the well-being and bounty of the created world. For a discussion of the Celtic backgrounds of the Grail legend, *cf.* Roger S. Loomis, *op. cit.*, pp. 139-270.

When Sir Lancelot was alit, he asked where the queen was. So Dame Brisen said she was in her bed; and then the people were avoided, and Sir Lancelot was led unto the chamber. And then Dame Brisen brought Sir Lancelot a cupful of wine; and anon as he had drunken that wine he was so assotted and mad that he might make no delay, but withouten any let he went to bed. And he weened that maiden Elaine had been Queen Guinevere. Wit you well that Sir Lancelot was glad, and so was that lady Elaine that she had gotten Sir Lancelot in her arms. For well she knew that same night should be gotten upon her Galahad that should prove the best knight of the world. And so they lay together until undern of the morn; and all the windows and holes of that chamber were stopped, that no manner of day might be seen. And then Sir Lancelot remembered him, and he arose up and went to the window, and anon as he had unshut the window the enchantment was gone; then he knew himself that he had done amiss.

"Alas," he said, "that I have lived so long. Now I am shamed."

So then he gat his sword in his hand and said: "Thou traitoress! What art thou that I have lain by all this night? Thou shalt die right here of my hands."

Then this fair lady Elaine skipped out of her bed all naked, and kneeled down afore Sir Lancelot, and said: "Fair, courteous knight, come of king's blood, I require you have mercy upon me; and as thou art renowned the most noble knight of the world, slay me not. For I have in my womb him by thee that shall be the most noblest knight of the world."

"Ah, false traitoress," said Sir Lancelot, "why hast thou betrayed me? Anon tell me what thou art."

"Sir," she said, "I am Elaine, the daughter of King Pelles."

"Well," said Sir Lancelot, "I will forgive you this deed." And therewith he took her up in his arms, and kissed her; for she was

152

as fair a lady, and thereto lusty and young, and as wise, as any that was that time living.

And so Sir Lancelot arrayed him and armed him. Then she said: "My lord Sir Lancelot, I beseech you see me as soon as ye may; for I have obeyed me unto the prophecy that my father told me. And by his commandment to fulfill this prophecy I have given the greatest riches and the fairest flower that ever I had, and that is my maidenhood that I shall never have again. And therefore, gentle knight, owe me your good will."

And so Sir Lancelot arrayed him and was armed, and took his leave mildly of that young lady Elaine. And so he departed.[1]

After Galahad was born and the news was abroad, Lancelot had to assuage the jealousy and suspicion of his lady. The great crisis came when Elaine, with twenty knights and ten ladies and gentlewomen to the number of a hundred horses, made her appearance at Camelot, King Arthur's court. When Sir Lancelot beheld her he was so ashamed that he would not salute her nor speak to her, and yet he thought she was the fairest woman that ever he saw.

Elaine saw that Sir Lancelot would not speak to her, and she was so heavy that she weened her heart would have burst; for wit you well, out of measure she loved him. And then Elaine said to her woman, Dame Brisen: "The unkindness of Sir Lancelot slayeth me near."

"Ah, peace, madam," said Dame Brisen. "I will undertake that this night shall he lie with you, and ye would hold you still."

"That were me liefer," said Dame Elaine, "than all the gold that is above the earth."

"Let me deal," said Dame Brisen.

So when Elaine was brought unto Queen Guinevere, either made other good cheer, by countenance, but nothing with

[1] Malory, *Morte d'Arthur*, xi. 1-3.

hearts. But all men and women spake of the beauty of Dame Elaine, and of her great riches.

Then at night the queen commanded that Dame Elaine should sleep in a chamber nigh her chamber, and all under one roof. And so it was done as the queen commanded. Then the queen sent for Sir Lancelot and bad him come to her chamber that night: "Or else I am sure," said the queen, "that ye will go to your lady's bed, Dame Elaine, by whom ye gat Galahad."

"Ah, madam," said Sir Lancelot, "never say ye so; for that I did was against my will."

"Then," said the queen, "look that ye come to me when I send for you."

"Madam," said Lancelot, "I shall not fail you, but I shall be ready at your commandment."

This bargain was soon done and made between them, but Dame Brisen knew it by her crafts. So when time came that all folks were abed, Dame Brisen came to Sir Lancelot's bedside and said: "Sir Lancelot du Lake, sleep you? My lady, Queen Guinevere, lieth and awaiteth upon you."

"O my fair lady," said Sir Lancelot, "I am ready to go with you where ye will have me."

So Sir Lancelot threw upon him a long gown, and took his sword in his hand; and then Dame Brisen took him by the finger and led him to her lady's bed, Dame Elaine; and then she departed and left them in bed together. Wit you well the lady was glad, and so was Sir Lancelot; for he weened that he had another in his arms.

Now leave we them kissing and clipping, as was a kindly thing; and now speak we of Queen Guinevere that sent one of her women unto Sir Lancelot's bed. And when she came there she found the bed cold, and he was away. So she came to the queen and told her all.

"Alas," said the queen, "where is that false knight become?"

Then the queen was nigh out of her wit, and then she writhed and weltered as a mad woman, and might not sleep a four or five hours.

But now Sir Lancelot had a condition that he used of custom: he would clatter in his sleep, and speak oft of his lady. So as Sir Lancelot had waked as long as it pleased him, then by course of kind he slept, and Dame Elaine, both. And in his sleep he talked and clattered as a jay of the love that had been betwixt Queen Guinevere and him. And so as he talked so loud, the queen heard him there as she lay in her chamber. And when she heard him so clatter, she was nigh witless and out of her mind, and for anger and pain wist not what to do.

And then she coughed so loud that Sir Lancelot awaked, and he knew her hemming. And then he knew well that he lay not by the queen. And therewith he leapt out of his bed as he had been a mad man, in his shirt, and the queen met him on the floor; and thus she said: "False traitor knight that thou art, look thou never abide in my court, and avoid my chamber; and be not so hardy, thou false traitor knight that thou art, that ever thou come in my sight."

"Alas," said Sir Lancelot; and therewith he took such an hearty sorrow at her words that he fell down to the floor in a swoon. And therewith Queen Guinevere departed. And when Sir Lancelot awoke of his swoon, he leapt out at a bay window into a garden, and there with thorns he was all scratched in his visage and his body. And so he ran forth he wist not whither, and was wild mad as ever was man. And so he ran two years, and never man might have grace to know him.

When Dame Elaine heard the queen so to rebuke Sir Lancelot, and also she saw how he swooned, and how he leaped out at a bay window, then she said unto Queen Guinevere: "Madam, ye are greatly to blame for Sir Lancelot, for now have ye lost him; for I saw and heard by his countenance that he is mad forever.

Alas, madam, ye do great sin, and to yourself great dishonor; for ye have a lord of your own, and therefore it is your part to love him; for there is no queen in this world hath such another king as ye have. And if ye were not, I might have the love of my lord Sir Lancelot. And cause I have to love him; for he had my maidenhood, and by him I have borne a fair son, and his name is Galahad, and he shall be in his time the best knight of the world."

"Dame Elaine," said the queen, "when it is daylight I charge you and command you to avoid my court. And for the love ye owe unto Sir Lancelot discover not his counsel, for an ye do, it will be his death."

"As for that," said Dame Elaine, "I dare undertake he is marred forever. And that have ye made; for ye nor I are like to rejoice him; for he made the most piteous groans when he leapt out at yonder bay window that ever I heard man make. Alas," said fair Elaine, and "Alas," said the Queen Guinevere; "for now I wot well we have lost him for ever." So on the morn Dame Elaine took her leave to depart, and she would no longer abide.[1]

Sir Lancelot ran two years mad, suffered and endured many sharp showers, and lived by fruit and such as he might get. And then upon a day he came by adventure into the town and the castle garden of the King Pelles, and there, as he slept beside a well, Dame Elaine's maidens espied where he lay, and they showed him to Elaine. And when she beheld him, she knew him for Sir Lancelot; and therewithal she fell on weeping so heartily that she sank to the earth. And when she had thus wept a great while, then she arose and called her maidens and said she was sick. And so she went out of the garden, and she went straight to her father.

"Sir," said Dame Brisen, "we must be wise how we deal with him; for this knight is out of his mind, and if we awaken him

[1] *Ibid.*, xi, 7-9.

rudely, what he will do we all know not. But ye shall abide, and I shall throw such an enchantment upon him that he shall not awake within the space of an hour"; and so she did.

Then within a little while after, the king commanded that all people should avoid that none should be in that way there, as the king would come. And so when this was done, four men as the king most trusted, and Dame Elaine, and Dame Brisen, laid hand on Sir Lancelot; and so they bare him into a tower, and so into a chamber where was the holy vessel of the Sangreal. And by force Sir Lancelot was laid by that holy vessel. And there came an holy man and uncovered that vessel. And so by miracle and by virtue of that holy vessel, Sir Lancelot was healed and recovered. And when that he was awaked he groaned and sighed, and complained greatly that he was passing sore.

Sir Lancelot lay more than a fortnight or ever that he might stir for soreness. And then upon a day he said unto Dame Elaine these words: "Lady Elaine, for your sake I have had much travail, care and anguish. I need not rehearse it; ye know how. Notwithstanding I know well I have done foul to you when that I drew my sword to you, to have slain you, upon the morn when I had lain with you. And all was the cause, that ye and Dame Brisen made me for to lie by you maugre mine head; and as ye say, that night Galahad your son was begotten."

"That is truth," said Dame Elaine.

"Now will ye for my love," said Sir Lancelot, "go unto your father and get me a place of him wherein I may dwell? For in the court of King Arthur may I never come."

"Sir," said Dame Elaine, "I will live and die with you, and only for your sake. And I will go to my father, and I am sure there is nothing that I can desire of him but I shall have it. And where ye be, my lord Sir Lancelot, doubt ye not but I will be with you with all the service that I may do."

"Well, daughter," said the king, "sith it is his desire to abide in these marches he shall be in the Castle of Bliant, and there shall ye be with him, and twenty of the fairest ladies that be in the country, and they shall all be of the great blood; and ye shall have ten knights with you. For, daughter, I will that ye wit we all be honored by the blood of Sir Lancelot."

And so it came to pass that Sir Lancelot du Lac, that model bachelor, the knight of the fairy powers, cursed and blessed by the necessity to love sinfully and forever the one forbidden woman, passed for a time into what for a normal man might have been the moment and opportunity of release. With Elaine, who, as she herself had declared, was the proper wife for him and the mother of his child, he dwelt for fifteen years in the castle of his proud father-in-law, King Pelles; the Castle of Bliant, that stood on an island, surrounded by the fairest waters. And when they were there, Sir Lancelot let call it the Joyous Isle. But his thoughts were never removed from the queen that had banished him. Once every day, in spite of all that the ladies and his wife could do to make him mirth, he would gaze toward the realm of Logres, where King Arthur was with Queen Guinevere, and he would weep as though his heart would break. And he dropped his name, calling himself by a new one which should secretly attest to his guilt in having betrayed involuntarily the love that was the dominant of his existence. "Le Chevaler Mal Fet," he now chose to term himself; that is to say, "the knight that hath trespassed." And through this designation, upon which he strictly insisted, he struck out, silently, the marriage bond that was uniting him with Elaine. The idyll in the Joyous Isle, thus, for all its gentleness, had no validity. The moment two comrades of the Round Table arrived, dispatched for him by Queen Guinevere, who could no more sustain the longing, he mounted his horse and briefly took his leave.[1]

[1] *Ibid.*, XII, 1-9.

"One thing you lack," a damsel once told him. "You are a knight wifeless, that you will not love some maiden or gentle-woman, and that is great pity. But it is noised that you love Queen Guinevere and that she has ordained by enchantment that you shall never love none other but her." So it was, and so it remained even into their late middle age, when the quarrels between them were becoming petty and the magic of youth had long departed from their limbs.

The unhappy lot recounted in the well-known story of the innocent, love-ready but desperate lily maid of Astolat—the second Elaine in the life of this now cut and dried old warrior of innumerable tournaments—bears witness to the persistence, long past the time of nature, of his miraculous animus-brilliance and charm: For ever she was about Sir Lancelot all the while she might be suffered; and ever she beheld Sir Lancelot wonderfully. "I would have you to my husband," she finally pleaded with him; "for but if ye will wed me, or else be my paramour at the least, my good days are done." And she cast such a love unto Sir Lancelot that she could never withdraw her love; wherefore she died.[1]

His dedication to Guinevere, the long life with and without her, had so filled his being with the magnetisms of love that he was like a demon presence that set the mind astray. But he himself was likewise astray, under the spell of the singular passion that possessed him. One might say that the personalities of Lancelot and Guinevere had become, both, entirely invaded and enchanted by the powers of the "lake" of the unconscious, possessed and beset by a trans-personal, compulsive, unrationalized and rationally ungovernable animus-anima interlinkage. Their conscious individualities had been overwhelmed at first

[1] *Ibid.*, xviii, 9-20. The story of the second Elaine is retold in Tennyson's *Lancelot and Elaine.*

sight by an archetypal, rather than personal, experience. Each had discovered in the other, not a devoted human companion, but the perfect counter-actor on an ideal, superhuman stage of abstract yet fatal passion. Each was related to the other, not as to a human being, but as to a discovery of a lost, required, separated portion of the soul. They were not two, but one: each a projection of the unconscious of the other. And if their normal human biographies became annihilated in this demonic spell, that was because the timelessness of their relationship left little within them of time. Their charm held the world about them spellbound. And though it strewed the stage with disaster and disgrace, nevertheless, not even their closest intimates could presume to reproach them. In the presence of their representation of the timelessness of the two sexes in their experienced identity, all the proprieties, conventions, ideals, and virtues of the court fell into insignificance. The symbol of the Round Table lost power. The court of the Christian king became the temple of a divine connubium that knew nothing of the historical mission of Christianity: the holy joy of an un-Christian god and goddess in their mystery of eternal union—something similar to the union of the Hindu Shiva and Satī, which we shall ponder in our later chapters of The Romance of the Goddess.[1]

4

The poets and chroniclers of the Middle Ages seem to have had some dim sense of the pre-Christian, un-Christian sanctity of the great sin of Lancelot and the queen. They might not have recognized or credited the psychological interpretation that we have suggested for the enchantment cast upon the world by their guilty love, but the supernatural explanation they knew.

[1] *Infra,* pp. 239 ff.

They rendered it in terms of faërie and enchantment. Through this device they redeemed the guilt of the spellbound reckless lovers, retaining their haloes of divinity and letting the traces of their divine radiance of yore remain, even in the context of the chivalric, Christian, medieval love dilemmas and trials. Not as animus and anima, but as god and goddess in mutual worship, the two stood justified in their Olympian fault.

We can descry something of the ancient mythical outlines in the most celebrated and important of the adventures of Lancelot and the queen, that remarkable tale recounted in the earliest written record of the knight: Chrétien's epical verse romance of "The Knight of the Cart."

Now Chrétien de Troyes was a court poet, a very sophisticated man of his day, and not at all interested in the mythical backgrounds of his narrations; but he knew how to utilize mythical materials for the entertainment and edification of his contemporary courtly audience. He had opened his career with a translation of the Latin poet Ovid into twelfth-century French; and he was inspired by the worldly-wise psychology of love and passion represented in Ovid's renditions of such traditional heroes and heroines as Pyramus and Thisbe. Chrétien's success in the court of Marie de Champagne, and in the general field of medieval letters, seems to have been chiefly founded on his ability to convey to a chivalric audience something of the complexity and sentimentalism of the Hellenistic manner of interpreting the passion and the gallantries of love. But the retention and utilization of the earlier supernatural elements was one of the delicacies of this sophisticated art. That is how it happens that in Chrétien's romances, just as in the tales of Ovid (though certainly more obscurely), beneath the surface of contemporary costume, contemporary psychologizing, and ethical problemizing, the old stream of mythical tradition flows on, silently, stealthily, carrying into the new age the ageless symbols of the trials and victories of the soul.[1]

Chrétien's romance of "The Knight of the Cart," *Le chevalier de la charrette* (Lancelot), opens with an apparition and challenge as sinister as that of the opening of Gawain and the Green Knight. A man unknown and in full armor, well-equipped, came into the court at Camelot, when King Arthur and Queen Guinevere were sitting at table, holding feast, upon a certain Ascension Day. And the knight gave no greeting, but spoke directly to the king.

"King Arthur, I hold in captivity knights, ladies, and damsels who belong to thy dominion and household; but it is not because of any intention to restore them to thee that I make reference to them here; rather do I wish to proclaim and serve thee notice that thou hast not the strength or the resources to enable thee to secure them again. And be assured that thou shalt die before thou canst ever succour them."

The king replied that he must needs endure what he had not the power to change; nevertheless he was filled with grief.

Then the knight made as if to go, but after reaching the door of the hall, stopped and turned, and spoke again: "King, if in thy court there is a single knight in whom thou hast such confidence that thou wouldst dare to entrust to him the queen that he might escort her after me out into the woods whither I am going, I will promise to await him there, and will surrender to thee all the prisoners whom I hold in exile in my country if he is able to defend the queen and if he succeeds in bringing her back again."

Now the queen was the life and soul of King Arthur's court

[1] Four of the epics of Chrétien de Troyes are readily available in Everyman's Library, No. 698: *Arthurian Romances by Chrétien de Troyes*, translated by W. Wistar Comfort. Our quotations in the following paragraphs will be taken from this volume, pp. 270-359. The Old French text of the romance may be read in the edition of Foerster, 1899.

The king had won her, together with the Round Table, by dint of great exploits at the opening of his chivalric career, after he had proved his right to the throne of paramount kingship. To lose her would be to suffer a major calamity, symbolical as well as personal. But to refuse the challenge would also amount to a calamity; for to protect womanhood and innocence against ruthless aggression was the supreme sense and mission of the noble association of the Round Table. Thus the high fellowship was at this moment in imminent danger of collapse. Many who were in the palace at the time had heard the challenge, and the whole court was in an uproar.

Unfortunately, the knight who first arose to the occasion was the seneschal Sir Kai. He was the senior among the knights, and he compensated for an all too well warranted feeling of inferiority before the more dashing deeds of the vigorous youths, by harboring and demonstrating on every possible occasion a ridiculous self-conceit. Sir Kai, by a clever ruse, forced the king to consent that he should be the one to meet the challenge. He first pretended that he wished to resign from the dishonored fellowship. Both the king and the queen begged him to remain. Then he stipulated as his condition that the king should grant him a boon, and when Arthur was sworn, stated his demand for permission to champion the court. And so, with the queen very reluctantly committed to his protection, he started away, the whole company making such a general lament as if she already lay dead upon a bier.

On Sir Gawain's advice, King Arthur and all the knights, after a little interval, followed at a distance, to rescue Guinevere if Sir Kai should be overthrown. But as they approached the forest they saw Kai's horse running out, and when they rode in all haste to the place of the combat, not only the queen and the strange challenger had disappeared, but their overbold champion as well. Sir Gawain pressed on in advance of the rest of the party, with two horses that he had brought along for the queen and Kai, and on his way through the wilderness presently saw coming a knight whom he did not recognize, riding a horse that was sore, painfully tired, and covered with sweat. The unknown knight saluted and then begged graciously for the loan of one of the mounts. The moment the request was granted he leapt upon the horse that was the nearer to him and rode off. Then the one he had left fell dead from sheer exhaustion.

Gawain spurred in pursuit, and when he had gone some distance, found the horse dead that he had just given to the knight, and he observed that the ground had been trampled and that broken shields and lances lay strewn about, as though a fierce battle had taken place. Sir Gawain rapidly passed on, until he saw again the unknown knight all alone on foot, completely armed, with helmet laced, sword girt on, and his shield hanging from his neck. He had just overtaken a cart.

"Now in those days," explains the poet Chrétien, "such a cart served the same purpose as does a pillory now; and in each good town where there are more than three thousand such carts nowadays, in those times there was only one, and this, like our pillories, had to do service for all those who commit murder or treason, and those who are guilty of any delinquency, and for thieves who have stolen others' property or have forcibly seized it on the roads. Whoever was convicted of any crime was placed upon a cart and dragged through all the streets, and he lost henceforth all his legal rights, and was never afterward heard, honored, or welcomed in any court. The carts were so dreadful in those days that the saying was then first used: 'When thou dost see and meet a cart, cross thyself and call upon God, that no evil may befall thee.' "

The knight on foot, and without a lance, was walking behind the cart. The driver, a dwarf, was sitting on the shafts, with a long goad in his hand.

164

PLATES

1. Head of the Dancing Shiva

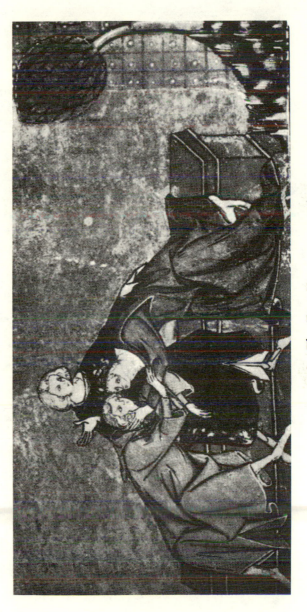

2. The First Kiss

3. The Knight of the Cart

4. The Sword Bridge

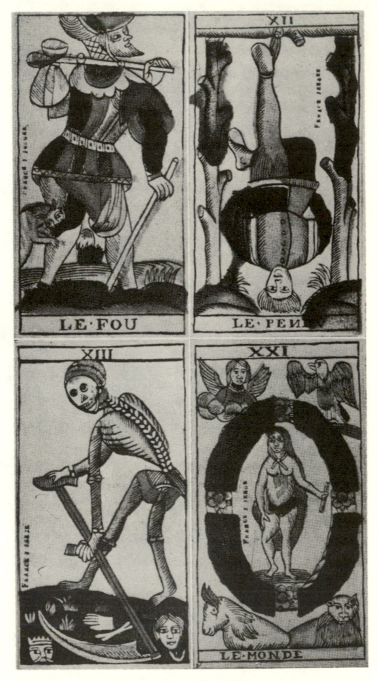

5. Four Cards of the Tarot

6. Pārvatī

"Dwarf," cried out the walking knight, "for God's sake, tell me now if thou hast seen my lady, the queen, pass by here."

The miserable, lowborn dwarf would not give him any news of her, but replied: "If thou wilt get up into the cart I am driving, thou shalt hear tomorrow what has happened to the queen." Then he kept on his way, without giving further heed.

The knight hesitated for only a couple of steps before getting in. "Yet, it was unlucky for him," Chrétien remarks, "that he shrank from the disgrace and did not jump in at once; for he will later rue his delay." Apparently, he has here met with the first of a series of trials to test his fitness for rescuing the queen from the country that holds captive so many of the former subjects of King Arthur's rule. Of that country we are told that it is "the kingdom whence no stranger returns":

> Et si l'a el reaume mise
> Don nus éstranges ne retorne,
> Més par force el pais sejorne
> An servitude et an essil:[1]

"but perforce the voyager must remain in that country, in servitude and banishment"—which is as much as to say that Queen Guinevere, the life and soul of the domain of King Arthur, has been abducted into the kingdom of death. Like the goddess Persephone in the well-known classical myth, this Queen of Life, the muse and inspiration of all romance and chivalry, has been ravished into the netherworld of no return.

On the way to rescue her, Sir Gawain and the anonymous knight (who in a later dramatic meeting with the queen was to be revealed as none other than Sir Lancelot) would meet with a succession of such adventures as befit, and in all mythologies characterize, the transit into the world beyond. "There are many

[1] Chrétien de Troyes, Le chevalier de la charrette, Foerster's ed., p. 25, vv. 644-647.

obstacles and difficult passages," said a damsel whom they later encountered on the way. "However, it is possible to enter by two very perilous paths and by two very difficult passageways. One is called 'the water-bridge,' because the bridge is under water, and there is the same amount of water beneath it as above it, so that the bridge is exactly in the middle, and it is only a foot and a half in width and in thickness. This choice is certainly to be avoided, and yet it is the less dangerous of the two. The other bridge is still more impracticable and much more perilous, never having been crossed by man. It is just like a sharp sword, and therefore all the people call it 'the sword-bridge.' Now I have told you all the truth I know."

The test of the cart, then, was the first of an increasing series. Lancelot hesitated only for a couple of steps and jumped in, feeling no concern about the shame; for "love was enclosed within his heart." Sir Gawain, on the other hand, when he rode up to the cart and was briefly told by the dwarf to get in if he wished to know anything of the queen, considered the command great foolishness, and said that he would not; for it would be dishonorable to exchange a horse for a cart.[1] And so he followed the cart with Lancelot and the dwarf in it, preserving for himself the dignity of knighthood, while the people of the next town, greatly amazed to see the other in the cart, took no pains to conceal their feelings, but great and small, old and young, shouted their taunts in the streets.

The dwarf conducted the knight to a lodging place, a tower which stood on the same level over against the town, and Gawain, following the horse and cart, dismounted and entered the tower

[1] [The exchange is a great degradation, representing, metaphysically, the exchange of the solar vehicle for the human body, the latter being a "cart" in the sense of the Platonic, and Indian, "chariot symbolism." This is the point at which Gawain, as every solar hero does *once*, "hesitates" ("May this cup be taken from me"; the Buddha's hesitation to preach; etc.). Hence the importance of what to a casual reader seems a minor point.—AKC.]

also. Here Lancelot and Gawain spent the night together and were put to their second trial. A bed was dressed for each, and besides these two beds there was a third, particularly sumptuous, which "possessed all the excellence that one could think of in a bed"; and the knights were warned that they should not attempt to lie on that bed of state. "In that one yonder," the instructing damsel of the tower told them, "no one ever lay who did not merit it." Lancelot, however, was not deterred. He at once disrobed in the bed and lay down to sleep. But at midnight mischance nearly overtook him. For at that hour a lance suddenly descended from the rafters, as with the intention of pinning him through the flanks to the white sheets. The pennon attached to it was all ablaze, and the whole bed immediately caught fire. But Lancelot escaped the lance with a mere scratch; "it cut the skin a little, without seriously wounding him." Remaining in the bed, he put out the fire, and taking the lance, swung it into the middle of the hall; then he lay back and returned to sleep.

This bed evidently is another of the set of the "marvel beds," *lits merveils,* such as the one that Sir Gawain wooed and mastered on his adventure into the "isle of women"—the Realm of the Mothers—that other manifestation of the world of the departed. The adventure of this night, then, had been Lancelot's test of courage. The other necessary test—the test in the castle of lust —would be the next to come.

But Sir Gawain, meanwhile, only reposed in peace.

In the morning the two knights were apprised of the two bridges by the directing damsel, and Lancelot gave the choice to his companion. Sir Gawain elected what had been described as the lesser difficulty, and so started along the road that would lead to the water-bridge; while Sir Lancelot, now mounted, took the other path pointed out to them, and so arrived presently at a ford, where he overcame the guardian knight and continued on his way. But the road was long. And in the late afternoon a

167

certain damsel, well attired and richly dressed, very fair and winsome, greeted him prudently and courteously. "Sire, my house is prepared for you," she said, "if you will accept my hospitality; but you shall find shelter there only on condition that you will lie with me. Upon these terms I propose and make my offer."

"Not a few there are who would have thanked her five hundred times for such a gift," remarks the poet; but Lancelot was much displeased and made a very different answer: "Damsel, I thank you for the offer of your house, and esteem it highly, but, if you please, I should be very sorry to lie with you."

"By my eyes," the damsel said, "then I retract my offer."

Whereupon, since it was unavoidable, he let her have her way, though his heart grieved to give consent; and the damsel conducted him to her abode.

It was a majestic fortified castle with a quantity of handsome rooms and a large and roomy hall. A table was laid; they washed their hands and sat to eat. Just before bedtime Sir Lancelot discovered that he had to rescue his hostess from the assault of an undesirable, violent lover; and when he had passed this test she led him to the bed in which they were to sleep together, and which had been set up for them in the midst of the main hall. The damsel lay down first and Sir Lancelot, in accordance with his contract, followed. But he took great care not to touch her; and when he was in bed, he turned away from her as far as possible, and spoke not a word to her, "like a monk to whom speech is forbidden."

So she said to him, after a little while of this quietness: "My lord, if you will not feel hurt, I will leave and return to bed in my own room, and you will be more comfortable. I do not believe that you are pleased with my company and society. Do not esteem me less if I tell you what I think. Now take your rest all night; for you have so well kept your promise that I have no right to make further request of you. So I commend you to God, and shall go away." For as she understood the case, he had on hand a more perilous and grave affair than any ever undertaken by a knight. "And may God grant," she prayed when she had got to her bed, "that he succeed in it."

These, however, had been only minor troubles, preliminary initiations, the first of the testings through which the elect must pass to the realization, manifestation, and enactment of his inborn perfection. The following day, after two or three comparatively slight exchanges, the hero arrived at a curious sort of church with many tombs, and a very old monk led him around. He read the inscriptions: "Here Gawain is to lie, here Louis, and here Yvain." Inadvertently Lancelot had ridden into the Land of Death, where there is a place in store for everybody among the living. Turning to the monk, the knight inquired: "Of what use are these tombs here?" And the monk replied: "You have already read the inscriptions; if you have understood, you must know what they say and what is the meaning of the tombs." Walking on, as if in a dream, Lancelot reached "a very large sarcophagus, larger than any that ever was made; one so rich and well-carved was never seen." He demanded: "Now tell me, what is this large one for?" And the hermit answered: "You need not be concerned with that, for it can never do you any good; you will never see inside of it. There is an inscription on it which says that anyone who can lift this stone of his own unaided strength will set free all the men and women who are captives in the land, whence no slave or noble can issue forth, unless he is a native of that land. No one has ever come back from there, but they are detained in foreign prisons." At once Lancelot went to grasp the stone and raised it without the slightest trouble, more easily than ten men would do who exerted all their strength. And the monk was amazed, and nearly fell down at the sight. Apparently this tomb was meant for Lancelot himself. Lancelot

169

questioned the old guardian: "Now tell me, who is to lie in this tomb?" "Sir," the monk replied, "he who shall deliver all those who are held captive in the kingdom whence none escapes."

Shortly following this exploit, which foretold his ultimate triumph, Lancelot encountered, in the borderland of the kingdom of King Death, the first of the captive inhabitants. These greeted him as their savior and advised him how to proceed. They guided him toward the terrible sword-bridge defending the central stronghold of the king, which was to be his supreme trial. And they meanwhile praised him with many and joyous voices:

"This is he," they cried, "who is to deliver us all from the durance and misery in which we have so long been confined. We ought to do him great honor when, to set us free, he has passed through so many perils and is ready to face many more." Their praise had a ring very like that of the psalm with which Adam and Eve and the other ancestors of mankind greeted Christ at the mouth of the netherworld, between the hour of His Crucifixion and the day of Resurrection, when He descended into Hell.[1]

For fundamentally, in spite of the chivalric gear, Sir Lancelot, this harrower of the kingdom of death, is a mythical savior. Instead of the "Two Worlds" of Life and Death we have, in his romance, feudal kingdoms and their quarrels; in the place of the dead we have abducted hostages; and as the supreme representative of the soul we have the queen. And so, by releasing Guinevere, the feminine life-giving principle, the highest symbol of the chivalrous love and life of the Round Table, life force in its visible human incarnation, the knight, Sir Lancelot, would break the hold of death upon the soul, that is, would be the restorer of our immortality. That was the hidden meaning of the pledge given by the sinister knight when he challenged the king and carried off the queen: if he should be overcome and Queen

[1] *The Gospel of Nicodemus II:* "The Harrowing of Hell," xxi.

Guinevere restored, then he would yield up all the prisoners from King Arthur's realm that he was holding captive. And so now, in the person of Sir Lancelot, the restoring hero was actually making his triumphant way past all the barriers.

"Hades said, Who is this King of Glory? And the angels of the Lord said, The Lord strong and mighty, the Lord mighty in battle. And immediately, at this word, the brazen gates were broken, and the iron bars were crushed, and all the dead that were bound were loosed from their bonds. And the King of Glory entered as a man, and all the dark places of Hades were lighted up." [1]

After battles and trials, out of all of which he came victorious, Sir Lancelot arrived eventually at the sword-bridge. "And if anyone asks of me the truth," writes Chrétien, "there never was such a bad bridge, nor one whose flooring was so bad. The bridge across the cold stream consisted of a polished, gleaming sword, but the sword was stout and stiff and was as long as two lances. At each end there was a tree trunk in which the sword was firmly fixed." The water cascading beneath was a "wicked-looking stream, as swift and raging, as black and turgid, as fierce and terrible as if it were the devil's stream; and it is so dangerous and bottomless that anything falling into it would be as completely lost as if it fell into the salt sea." Two lions or two leopards were tied to a great rock at the other end of the bridge. And the water and the bridge and the lions were so terrible to behold that anyone standing before them all would tremble with fear.

This bridge suggests an origin in the mythical traditions of the East.[2] Just such a long keen knife blade, crossing the abyss of damnation, constitutes one of the main testing devices in the ancient Persian mythology of the Last Judgment. The souls are

[1] *The Gospel of Nicodemus II:* "The Harrowing of Hell," xxi.
[2] Cf. D. L. Coomaraswamy, "The Perilous Bridge of Welfare," *Harvard Journal of Asiatic Studies* 8, Aug. 1944, pp. 196-213.

compelled to cross, and the sinful will fall into the abyss, but for the pious the edge broadens out into a smooth and pleasant way, leading to Paradise. The "lions or two leopards" also suggest the Orient.

Sir Lancelot, before this barrier, prepared himself as best he might, and in a manner that may occasion some surprise: "He removes the armor from his feet and hands. He will be in a sorry state when he reaches the other side. He is going to support himself with his bare hands and feet upon the sword, which was sharper than a scythe. But he preferred to maim himself rather than to fall from the bridge and be plunged into the water from which he could never escape. He passes over with great pain and agony.[1] Creeping on his hands, feet, and knees, he proceeds until he reaches the other side. Then he recollects the two lions which he thought he had seen from the other side; but, on looking about, he does not see so much as a lizard or anything else to do him harm . . . there was not a living creature there." But the blood from his wounds was dripping on his shirt and on all sides.

He saw before him a castle which was so strong that never had he seen such a strong one before. This was the Castle of Death. The king and his son were looking out of a window, having watched his exploit. Exactly as in the story of Gawain and the Green Knight, Death is here never properly unveiled and named. Death there, in lifting his visor, simply called himself a certain "Bernlak de Hautdesert," a nobleman, a human being. So here again, the mythical sphere is overlaid with a chivalric reinterpretation. King Death is described as King Bademagu, "very scrupulous and precise about matters of honor and what was right, and careful to observe and practice loyalty above all else." That designates the sovereign impartiality and fairness of Death, before whom all are equal, Death's utter justice and de-

[1] "A sharpened edge of a razor, hard to traverse,
A difficult path is this" (*Katha Upanishad* 3:14).

mocracy. But, on the other hand, Death's son, his alter ego, Prince Meleagant, is declared to be exactly the reverse: "for he found his pleasure in disloyalty, and never wearied of villainy, treason, and felony." So, too, is Death—when it deals its sudden blow, slaying the innocent, ravishing the bloom of youth, and meanwhile sparing the scoundrel to a mean old age.[1] This Meleagant is the one who carried Queen Guinevere away and with whom Lancelot will have to engage in his final battle of redemption. Meleagant is to be outpointed in a great and solemn tournament, the queen therewith redeemed, and all the other captive inhabitants of the realm set free.

I do not wish to dwell on the details of the knightly battle, on the numerous lesser engagements that followed it, or on Meleagant's various nasty devices to hinder the final departure of Lancelot, the queen, and the other subjects, to the kingdom of the living. Suffice to say that by a ruse Sir Lancelot was imprisoned for a time in a dungeon, so that the queen had to be conducted back to Arthur's court by his earlier companion of the adventure, Sir Gawain. The latter, in spite of the fact that he had elected the lesser of the two dangerous bridges, had suffered a very bad mischance. Overtoppled in his crossing, he had been swept away by the torrent: "One moment he rises, and the next he sinks; one moment they see him, and the next they lose him from sight." But his rescuers made such efforts that they succeeded in raising him with branches, poles, and hooks. He had nothing but his hauberk on his back, and on his head was fixed his helmet, and he wore his iron greaves, which were all rusty with his sweat, for he had endured great trials and had passed victoriously through many perils, and assaults. His body was full of water, and until

---

[1] Compare the brothers King Pellam and Garlon in the Balin story. Compare, also, in the Gawain story the two aspects of the Green Knight, and in the tale of Owain the benign host of the Castle of Abundance and the monstrous Ward of the Wood.

he got rid of it, they did not hear him speak a word. But when his speech and voice and the passageway to his heart were free, and as soon as what he said could be heard and understood, he inquired for the queen.

The imprisoned Sir Lancelot presently was released from his lonely tower by a grateful young lady whom he once had served, and he returned to Camelot, where he met the prince of death again. This time, in a final combat before the whole magnificent court of Camelot, Meleagant was slain. And thus was completed the epochal restoration of the queen to the world of life.

There is one detail of the romance that I should like to recall, namely that curious one of the cart which has given its name to the whole adventure and to Lancelot himself as "The Knight of the Cart." Chrétien's audience must have shuddered between horror and admiration as they read of the faithful knight, "feeling no concern about the shame," jumping into a vehicle that should disgrace him forever in the eyes of his world. According to the point of view of the lords and ladies of the age of chivalry, that was an exploit second to none. And its sequel was even more of a delight to read. The poet saved it for the great moment in the Castle of Death, when Sir Lancelot, having won the release of the queen, was about to receive her greeting and stood in expectation of her smile.

King Bademagu, the benign father of Prince Meleagant, led Sir Lancelot into the castle by the hand. But when the queen saw them enter, she rose before the king, and looked displeased and spoke not a word.

"Lady, here is Lancelot come to see you," the king said, "you ought to be pleased and satisfied."

"I, sir? He cannot please me. I care nothing about seeing him."

"Come now, lady," said the king, who was very frank and

174

courteous, "what induces you to act like this? You are too scornful toward a man who has served you so faithfully."

"Sir, truly he has made poor use of his time. I shall never deny
that I feel no gratitude toward him." And she did not utter
another word, but returned to her room.

Lancelot was dumbfounded. He tried, soon after, to kill
himself, and the queen, when she heard that he was dead, nearly
died of grief. Many complications followed, but then, at last,
the two lifelong lovers were together again, and the queen explained.

"Did you not hesitate for shame to mount the cart? You showed
you were loath to get in when you hesitated for two whole steps.
That is the reason why I would neither address nor look at you."

"May God save me from such a crime again," Lancelot replied, "and may God show me no mercy, if you were not quite
right!"

Chrétien and his audience must have greatly relished this
episode. It made a nice point in illustration of the extreme punc-
tiliousness that governed the courtly game of love. But how,
we may ask, could the queen in her captivity have known that her
knight had failed her in this minute circumstance, which no one
but Lancelot himself could have been quite aware of, and which
no one but Sir Gawain and the dwarf could have seen?

Evidently she is omniscient, so that what has taken place far
away is present to her mind. She has the omniscience of a goddess, for a goddess she is. And, like a true goddess, she takes
umbrage at the slightest lack of due reverence and subservience.
She is incensed at the most trifling affront. The moment she becomes aware that her devotee has fallen short of absolute, perfect
devotion, she waxes in ire and resentment. This is the manner of
archaic and primitive divinities everywhere—and of that still
more primitive being that we all carry within. The goddess of

life is—of course—jealous and demanding, and from the pious servant on whom she has bestowed her supreme favors she will brook nothing less than wholehearted and total surrender. For her he should sacrifice, without even feeling that he is making a sacrifice, such trifles as his social values and reputation. Is he not to devote to her his very life? Chrétien and the courtly audience insisted on this identical point in their exquisite code and cult of the divinity of love. The fulfillment of perfect love might entail every sort of social disgrace; it was itself the end that rendered noble all the means.

But the detail of the cart holds still another and even more significant charge of meaning. As we have said, in coming up with the cart the two knights confront the first of the tests that they are to endure in their quest for the queen. Lancelot has already demonstrated his greater eagerness and devotion: he has ridden a horse to death and fought an advance battle, while Gawain has been coming at a fast but not unreasonable pace. Gawain overtakes him only when he is reduced to plodding along afoot. Both knights inquire after the queen from the mocking dwarf of the cart, and they receive identical answers: if they wish to learn of her, they are enjoined to discard their knightliness, to sacrifice the cherished social standard of their conscious personality. That is the social ideal for which they have fought innumerable battles and tournaments and which constitutes the measure of their life, their honor among men, and their everlasting fame. They are asked to exchange this supreme value of their conscious lives for the vague hope of somehow tracing the queen and the unknown enemy who has spirited her away. Gawain declines to take this foolish step; that is why he fails in the later, supreme adventure. He remains but the perfect all-round knight, a cavalier of the world, not intended for the higher task of confronting and outmatching the demonic superhuman powers of the realm of death, which have taken into their clutches the goddess of life. Gawain, in this adventure, is not the superhero of the stature for the descent into Hell.[1]

Sir Lancelot is an example of the archetypal figure of the "Savior" which appears not only in the Christian but in numerous pre-Christian traditions of belief. Jesus was branded and mocked as a criminal before being committed to the gallows and pillory of the Cross; He was regarded as worse than Barabbas, the murderer, who was released from execution in his stead. And Jesus was crucified between two thieves. Comparably Lancelot, this "Savior" in disguise: he has to surrender his social character of unsullied knighthood and incur the ignominy of the pillory, before he can proceed on his quest into the kingdom of death and rescue there the soul of life. Sir Lancelot has to submit, symbolically, to civil death; following that, and again symbolically, to physical death—when he passes through the graveyard chapel, where he finds the empty tombs that await his friends, and is confronted with his own sarcophagus. These two steps, the social death and the physical, would seem to represent two stages in some esoteric ritual of initiation, requiring of the candidate a gradual surrender of the whole earthly personality in exchange for the boon of a higher spiritual nature and the *summum bonum* of the experience of immortality.

The same symbolism, curiously enough, seems to underlie and to have inspired the somewhat puzzling pictures of medieval French playing cards: the so-called Tarot. (The *Tarot de Marseilles* goes back at least to the fourteenth century.) Besides the

[1] That supreme and cosmic adventure is precisely the typical one of the Divine Lovers of Antiquity. The goddess Ishtar of the Babylonian mythology descended into the netherworld, passing through the seven successive gates, to rescue Tammuz (Adonis), her deceased lover, from the bondage of the hell-queen Ereshkigal. And now it is Lancelot, the disgraced rider in the cart, not Gawain, the unsullied horseman, who is to accomplish the terrible journey again. Like Christ, the divine adventurer who descended into Hell and released from eternal death Adam and Eve and all the patriarchs and prophets, Sir Lancelot is to harrow and redeem the abyss.

four suits—"swords," "clubs," "cups," and "coins"—this pack contained a superior series of twenty-two picture cards. One of these, "The Fool," bore no number; it was, apparently, the forerunner of the present-day Joker. The other twenty-one were numbered to denote an increasing series. Now it is my belief that the pictorial script of these face cards represented the degrees of an esoteric order of initiation, employing largely Christian signs, but masking the formulae of the heretical Gnostic teaching that was so widespread in Southern France up to the fifteenth century.[1] The initiate, passing through twenty degrees of gradually amplifying enlightenment and beset by as many characteristic temptations, at last arrived at the stage of a mystical union with the Holy Trinity, and this is what was symbolized in the culminating image of the series, "The Dancing Hermaphrodite." The Soul was the bride of the Lord; in the figure of the Hermaphrodite the two were one. The figure is immediately suggestive of the Dancing Shiva; Shiva unites in himself the female and the male.[2] Such a bisexual symbol represents the embodiment in a single form of all the pairs of opposites, a transcendence of the contraries of phenomenality; and this incarnate Form of forms is then conceived of as the One whose dance is the created world. The candidate is to realize and impersonate this attitude as the effective symbol of his supreme metaphysical realization.

Something similar would seem to be indicated by the divine bed of Sir Lancelot and the queen: the two lovers are one, and each is both. In their realization of this identity they embody and make manifest the singular Form of forms which is beyond all space and time; their love play is the dance of that Cosmic

[1] There have been proposed a number of interpretations of the Tarot symbolism. The above seems not to have been hit upon before.

[2] For an elucidation of the symbolism of the Dance of Shiva, *cf.* Zimmer, *Myths and Symbols in Indian Art and Civilization*, Bollingen Series No. 6, 1946, pp. 151-175.

178

Hermaphrodite;[1] and their reunion in the Castle of Death is symbolic of the renewing moment that restores the life of the world.

Midway along the perilous path to this realization as represented in the honor series of the Tarot pack, that is, at the sinister station of Card XIII, we are shown the unmistakable symbol of Death: the skeleton with the scythe mowing down the flowers on the meadow of life. And this is preceded by the figure of "The Hanged One," *Le Pendu* (Card XII), where the initiate is hanging by the left ankle, head down, condemned to the other death of social disgrace on the social gallows. Card XII is the counterpart of Sir Lancelot's initiation of the cart; Card XIII corresponds to his passage of the tomb.

5

In terminating this all too sketchy portrayal of the most interesting and inspiring animus-figure of the Western tradition, I should like to suggest that it is out of his archaic pagan origins that Lancelot's bewitched and bewitching attitude of spellbound recklessness proceeds. He is bound indissolubly, blindly, and forever, to the goddess of sheer life force, in the role of her rescuing devotee. And out of those origins must have proceeded also the traits that rendered him unfit to achieve the Christian adventure of the Grail. "Sir Lancelot," the warning voice commanded, "more harder than is the stone, and more bitter than is the wood, and more naked and barer than is the leaf of the fig tree; therefore go thou from hence, and withdraw thee from this holy place." He was not the one to enact the leading part in such a purely spiritual quest. He might watch the mystery from afar,

[1] Compare the Oriental images of god and goddess, Zimmer, *op. cit.*, Figs. 34, 35.

but was never to approach. And when he realized that, then he understood, at last, the limits of one devoted not to the Queen of the Spirit but to the Queen of the Life of the World. And we have already heard his lament: "When I sought worldly adventures for worldly desires, I ever achieved them, and never was I discomfit in no quarrel, were it right or wrong. And now I take upon me the adventures of holy things, and now I see and understand that mine old sin hinders me so that I had no power to stir nor to speak when the holy blood appeared before me."

Nevertheless he was not long disconsolate. For the voice of the life force, the dynamism of the cosmos, that had saturated his personality when he dwelt, in his youth, with the fairy goddess in the waters of the "Lake," very soon consoled him. "Thus he sorrowed till it was day," we read, "and heard the fowls sing, then somewhat he was comforted."

Lancelot's alter ego, the son who bears the name that Lancelot himself received in baptism from his human father (before the Lady of the Lake abstracted, initiated, and renamed him "Lancelot of the Lake"), will achieve the holy adventure of the Grail; for, as in the symbolism of dreams, the child, the son, here connotes a higher transformation of the personality. The child is the self reborn in pristine perfection, the perfect being that we ought to be, that we are striving to become, and that we hoped to become, so to say, when we entered our present body. It is the symbol of the entelechy, or secret model, of our destination.

Thus Sir Galahad, the immaculate, is the redemption of the ambiguous, brilliant father whose "Christian" name he reaffirms and bears. He is the redemption because he is the re-embodiment of the father. The virtues of this triumphant saintly son are those of the essence of the father himself. And so, that father— Sir Lancelot of the Lake, but Sir Galahad of the Baptismal Font —is revealed to have combined in himself the energies of the two

180

spheres, the worldly sphere of desires, and the higher one of the purely spiritual adventure. This is the final secret of his charm.

IV. MERLIN

The growth of the heathen religions of northern Europe was nipped in the bud when the peoples who had practiced them came within the sphere of Christian influence. The Church did more than Roman culture to deprive the mythology of the Celts, the Teutons, and the pre-Celtic primitive population of the British Isles of the old creed in which it lived, moved, and had its being. Nevertheless it survived, without foundation or foothold, no longer a cult, and shorn of its ancient ritual. As elsewhere under similar circumstances, mythology became transformed into poetry and saga, became secularized, and lost its binding power; and since in this form there was nothing about it that the Church could attack, it continued to develop through the Middle Ages, supplying a rich nourishment for the soul, when the Church with its theology of salvation had nothing comparable to offer. Medieval man dreamed out his broken youth in the images and figures of Celtic and pre-Celtic myths and sagas; and it was these, in the form of the Grail and other romances of the Arthurian cycle, that became the popular novels of the knightly and courtly circles of the whole of Europe.

At the core of this saga cycle is the figure of Merlin. He represents for the West something which in other cultures is a frequent and compelling personage: the magician as teacher and guide of souls. He is comparable, for example, to the *guru* as the house priest and master of initiation ceremonies in India, or to the medicine man as the oracle and spiritual leader of the primitive tribe. Merlin dwells in the "enchanted forest," the "Valley of No Return," which is the Land of Death, the dark aspect of the

181

world. The magic forest is always full of adventures. No one can enter it without losing his way. But the chosen one, the elect, who survives its deadly perils, is reborn and leaves it a changed man. The forest has always been a place of initiation; for there the demonic presences, the ancestral spirits, and the forces of nature reveal themselves. There man meets his greater self, his totem animal. And thither the medicine man conducts the youths of the tribe in order that they may be born again through gruesome initiation rites, as warriors and men. The forest is the antithesis of house and hearth, village and field boundary, where the household gods hold sway and where human laws and customs prevail. It holds the dark forbidden things—secrets, terrors, which threaten the protected life of the ordered world of common day. In its terrifying abyss, full of strange forms and whispering voices, it contains the secret of the soul's adventure. Somewhere in this monstrous region, this seat of darkness, the castle of Merlin stands. Its countless windows look out upon the secrets that lurk around it, the doors are open to travelers from every quarter of the globe, and paths lead from the castle into the farthest reaches of the world. The castle is the heart of darkness; its countless eyes see and know all, and it offers to each of the elect a different approach to the mystery.[1]

But Merlin is not only the master of the forest who entices the chosen one into the field of the perilous tests, he is also the founder and guide of the knightly Round Table and the teacher of King Arthur, its lord. In the normal daylight world, that is to say, he calls together the numbers of the elect and then sends them out, one by one, into the darkness, to confront the tests by which they are to become transformed. Merlin is the master of

[1] For descriptions of the forest of Merlin, see Geoffrey of Monmouth, *Vita Merlini*, ed., John Jay Parry, University of Illinois Studies in Language and Literature, vol. x, No. 3, August 1925, especially lines 74 ff., 347 ff., 533 ff. The house with seventy doors and windows is described in lines 555 ff.

the entire cycle—the shapeshifter, the mysterious, benign, yet frightening pedagogue, the summoner, the tester, and the bestower of the ultimate boon; he is Meleagant and King Bademagu, Bernlak de Hautdesert, the host of the Castle of Abundance, and the Ward of the Wood.[1]

---

[1] An account of Merlin's transformation into the Ward of the Wood appears in the Old French *Livre d'Artus*, where the young hero Calogrenant is in the role that was assigned to Kynon and Owain in the version which we quoted (pp. 99 ff. *supra*) from the Welsh *Red Book of Hergest*.

" 'It came to his (Merlin's) mind to go and divert himself in the forest of Broceliande and to do something for which he should be spoken of forever. So on the day when the three messengers departed from Calogrenant, he transformed himself into such a shape as no man ever saw or heard of before. He became a herdsman, a great club in his hand, clad in a great hide, the fur of which was longer than the breadth of the largest hand known, and it was neither black nor white but smoked and browned and seemed to be a wolf skin. He took his place in a great clearing on the border of a ditch, right over the bank, leaning on an old mossy oak, and held his club down to the bottom of the ditch and bent over it. He was large, bent, black, lean, hairy, old with a great age, shod without in marvelous leggings that reached to his girdle. He was transformed so that his ears hung down to his waist, wide as a winnowing fan. He had eyes in his head, large and black, and a head as big as a buffalo's, and hair so long that it brushed his girdle, all bristly, stiff, and black as ink. His mouth was as large and wide as a dragon's, and gaped up to the ears; his teeth were white; and his thick lips were always open so that the teeth showed all around. He had a hump behind on his spine, as big as a mortar. His two feet were where the heels ought to be in an earthly man, and the palms of the hands where the backs should be. He was so hideous and ugly to see that no man living would not be seized with great dread, unless he were brave and valiant. He was so tall when he stood up that a rod of eighteen feet would not reach him and, in proportion to his height, he had the breadth of a thin man. His voice was so loud when he spoke that it seemed like a trumpet when he spoke a little loud. When Merlin had turned himself into this shape and placed himself on the road by which Calogrenant was traveling, he caused by his art stags, hinds, bucks, and all manner of wild beasts to come and graze around him; and there were such a multitude that no one could tell the number. He ruled them so that when he scolded one roughly, it did not dare to eat or drink till he commanded.'

"When Calogrenant saw the 'hom sauvage' he set himself in a posture for defense, but turned toward him to ask the way. To his question, what man he was, the herdsman replied: 'Vassal, what would you do? I am such as you see, for I am never anyone else, and I watch over the beasts of these woods and the forest, of which I am wholly lord. For there is no beast so bold that when I have chidden or rebuked it will dare to eat or drink until I bid. They go to drink in a fountain

In the Arthurian tradition of the twelfth century, Merlin was represented as the son of a demon-incubus and a virgin. This, of course, was the Christian version and rationalization. The old gods of the Britons, shrunk to demons, were declared to have begotten an antichrist in their effort to buttress their dying power against the growing might of the Savior, and a propagandistic turn was thus given to the universal mythological motif of the Virgin Birth. For the hero destined to perform miracles, slay the dragon, and create a new world order can have no earthly father. It is impossible that he should spring from an ordinary marriage within the snug circle of ordinary human beings; his seed has to be planted by heavenly powers. His mother, however, is earthly, and so he is born both god and man. Always the chosen one unites within himself in this way the two spheres. Perseus, for example, was the fruit of the golden seed that Zeus poured into the womb of the princess Danaë. Conquering the Medusa and rescuing Andromeda from the sea dragon, he freed the world of men from the might of monsters. And Indra, also a dragon slayer and the son of a virgin, by virtue of his cosmic deeds rose

---

of mine near by, which a friend of mine guards.' Then follows a description of the storm-making fountain and its defender, Brun sans Pitié. 'Now tell me,' said Calogrenant, 'on what you live. Have you a manor in the neighborhood where you sleep or retreat where you take your meat and whatsoever you need to live?' He answered that he ate nothing but herbs and roots of the wood just like the other beasts, 'for I do not care for other food, and these are all my arts, and I have no desire to have an abode but only a rough oak where I may rest at night, and when it is cold and stormy, to be clad as you see. If it is cold and I need to warm myself, I have a fire as long as I like; and if I wish to eat meat I always have as much as I want.' 'Truly,' said Calogrenant, 'you are a lord when you thus have your desires.' The 'hom sauvage' then directs Calogrenant to a hermitage, where he is well entertained before going on to the fountain." (*Livre d'Artus*, ed., H. O. Sommer, *Vulgate Version of the Arthurian Romances* VII, pp. 124-126, as cited and translated by Roger S. Loomis, *op. cit.*, pp. 131-132. Passage reprinted by permission of Columbia University Press.)

Another account of Merlin as the terrifying keeper of the beasts will be found in the *Roman de Merlin*, 26-28, Sommer's ed., pp. 38-40. There are numerous examples of Merlin's transformations in the *Vita Merlini*.

to the rank of a god. Merlin, however, though akin through his supernatural origin to such figures as these, is not, like them, a warrior hero but a magician; his weapons are magic and knowl-edge rather than deeds. He does not himself create the new world order as Indra did, but brings Arthur, its destined king, to life, and then presides over the founding of the Round Table. This formula is an expression of the pre-Christian culture of the British Isles, a culture in which the druids, the priests and seers, by virtue of their magic power and knowledge, overshadowed, instructed, and ruled the kings, as do the Buddhist priests today in Lamaistic Tibet.

Merlin's mother was a princess. In all innocence she suc-cumbed to the demon, and, having conceived her fairy child, gave birth to it in a dark dungeon, outcast and alone. But the infant comforted his poor mother in her sorrow; he knew whence he had come and why. And he was not afraid of the road he was to travel. He proved his supernatural descent in many ways. This "gospel of childhood," with its miracles and prophetical sayings betraying the child's high destiny, belongs to the tradi-tional mythical career of the chosen one. In Merlin's case, the story is told of King Vortigern, who, after a bloody conquest of the throne, built himself a tower as a refuge and a hiding place. But his tower tottered and his two magicians were unable to save it. And so the king, having learned of the existence of the boy versed in magic, sent for him. Merlin revealed the secret of the tower: two dragons were struggling with each other in the depths of the earth just under it, and their activities were con-tinually shaking the foundations. That put the two official court magicians to shame. And then the wonderful boy went on to prophesy that when the white dragon should overcome the red, Vortigern's reign would end. That was the foreknowledge of the coming order of King Arthur; this child himself had been born to bring that order into being. And so he triumphed not only over

185

the magicians but also over the king. These self-confident forces, which had reared their heads in boastful self-assertion, were doomed to pass and die. Merlin himself was to initiate the new order. The Round Table in all its splendor would be the work of his hands.[1]

Merlin's first problem was to bring together the royal couple who were to become Arthur's parents, King Uther Pendragon and Igerne, or Igraine, who at the time was the wife of the Duke of Cornwall. He accomplished this by magic arts.[2] And then he himself watched over Arthur's youth, preparing him in secret for his hour of destiny. Merlin created the Round Table (a copy of which may still be seen in Winchester) and became the guide and inspiration of the knightly fellowship, a seer in the pre-Christian druidical sense, the king's counselor and magician, like a Brahminical *guru* at the court of an Indian prince.

After the passing of the Middle Ages, Merlin, from his retreat in Wales, remained as the prophetic figure of the Celtic world. It was a common custom of the peoples of the Middle Ages to formulate their thoughts about their own time and their dreams of the future in a style suggesting mysterious prehistoric prophecies—a type of revelation influenced by the Greek prophecies of the sibyl, and the Hebrew prophets of the Old Testament and Apocalypse. In Wales, Merlin's songs and his conversations with his sister formed a chain of folk utterances that stretched on for hundreds of years, and which, even in the sixteenth century, exerted so much power that they were included in the *Index* by the Council of Trent.[3] And so, through the mask of the wizard

[1] Geoffrey of Monmouth, *Historia Britonum* vi-vii, Everyman's Library, vol. 577; also *Roman de Merlin* 1-23, Sommer's ed., pp. 1-34.

[2] *Historia Britonum* viii, 19-20, *Roman de Merlin*. 50-72, Sommer's ed., pp. 57-71; also Malory, *Morte d'Arthur* i, 1-2.

[3] Rabelais parodies and ridicules the prophecies of Merlin in *Gargantua*, and in *Pantagruéline prognostication certaine, véritable et infaillible*, composed about 1533.

without age, the genius of the Celtic people raised its voice against contemporary political forces and conditions. He was a representation of the prophetic spirit of the race, like those seers and magicians, druids and primitive workers of weather magic, who dream the dreams of their tribe and interpret them, and he remains for his people a significant figure whose comforting and healing powers long outlast the mythical years of his life on earth.

Merlin and Arthur, Vortigern, and Arthur's parents, were all actual figures of British history in the bloody time when the Romans relinquished the island, when the Scots from the north and the Irish from the west broke into Britain, and the Angles and Saxons invaded from the Continent. Vortigern was the British king who summoned the Saxons into his country to help defend him from his neighbors, and then found himself cheated and his people permanently subdued by the invited allies. An old Welsh chronicle, *Brut Tysilio*, one of the sources of Geoffrey of Monmouth's *Historia Britonum*, tells how Vortigern tried unsuccessfully to erect a castle against his enemies, and of his meeting with the wise child Merlin.[1] Arthur, the son of Uther, the chronicle goes on to say, was one of the great leaders of the Britons against their foreign foes. In a successful overseas campaign he beat back a Viking invasion, reached over into Gaul, threatened there the late Roman rule, and even planned an expedition against Rome itself, aiming, like Charlemagne three centuries later, at the imperial crown. But Arthur was halted by news of treachery at home.

At home in Britain—so the story goes—Modred, King Arthur's nephew, had risen against him and stolen his queen. Arthur returned, slew Modred and shattered his army, but was himself

[1] O. Jones *et al.*, editors, *The Myvyrian Archaiology of Wales*, Denbigh, 1870, pp. 476-554.

fatally wounded in the battle. Seeking a miraculous cure, he visited the fabulous island sanctuary of Avalon; but, like the visit of Sir Gawain to the *Château Merveil,* that was his journey to the Land of No Return. The last journey to the magic island was the return home of the mythical hero, not the voyage of a historical king. Arthur was transported to the Blessed Isles. The "Passing of Arthur" was the home-coming of an old god, who, at the close of his mission, retires from the world and vanishes into the beyond out of which he came.[1]

Like the figures in the tales of E. T. A. Hoffmann, Merlin and Arthur move on two planes—that of history as recorded in the chronicles, and that of the timeless mythological world. To the historical traits are added superhuman deeds and characteristics from the great world treasure chest of folklore and myth, so that the hero becomes even in this world immortal, as the transfigured body of an idea. The characteristics of old vanished gods overgrow the historical memory, and figures which in the baldness of the chronicles appear as little more than mute names begin to speak with the timeless language of dream.

One of the most vivid of the mythical episodes added to the history of the Celtic captain, Arthur, is that of the deed by which he was disclosed to be the predestined king. His father, Uther Pendragon, had died, and the powerful lords of the kingdom were all grasping for the crown. By Merlin's advice and counsel it was finally decided that the supernatural powers should be left to determine the troubled issue. Before the greatest church in London a stone had appeared in which a sword was buried; and letters of gold were to be seen on the stone around the sword, to the effect that the one who could draw the blade should be recognized as king. Many tried in vain. Then, at last, this unknown youth, Arthur, who had been reared secretly under the

[1] *Morte d'Arthur,* xxi.

guardianship of Merlin, rode up to the church and, ignorant of the magic of his deed, pulled out the sword.[1]

This striking symbol of the hero's election and sacred power is derived from the prehistoric period at the close of the Age of Stone. Swords were not made until after the discovery of bronze and iron; before that time there were only spears and arrows and axes. And so, who is the one who frees the metal from the stone? The culture-hero, the magic smith, who released the world from the Stone Age and taught mankind the art of smelting bronze and iron from the ore. The hero who can draw the iron sword from the stone is not necessarily a great warrior, but always a powerful magician, lord over spiritual and material things; a seer comparable, in terms of the Iron Age, to the modern inventor, chemist or engineer, who creates new weapons for his people. And just as today we live in awe—and some fear—of the man of science, so is it only natural that the folk of that faraway other day should have thought of the one who freed for them metal from stone as the chosen master of the secrets of existence.

The hero in those days was the maker of his own weapons, literally the "forger of his own fortune," and so his power and prestige were in large measure bound up with his ability to forge a weapon that would not break in his hand. The warrior depended for victory as much upon the magic of his sword as upon his courage and strength: the magic and the capacity were thus mythical equivalents, and in essence identical with the secret of the new-found superior technical equipment of mankind. The supreme miracle and sign would be the sword imperishable, the marvelous weapon absolutely endowed. And it was the great dream of the youthful metal age to possess this imperishable blade, just as it had been the dream of the Age of Stone to possess a magic missile which should return to the hand that

[1] *Roman de Merlin*, 88-99, Sommer's ed., pp. 84-92; *Morte d'Arthur*, I, 5-7.

189

threw it, like the hammer of Thor, or the thunderbolts of Zeus and Indra.

The virtue of the weapon forged by the hero, or bestowed on him by the gods, is a part of himself and the sign of his magic strength. The weapon goes with him into the grave, or can be received from him only by one fitted to wield it, because it is a counterpart in some way of the hero himself. So it was with the bow of Ulysses, which none of the wooers could draw. So it is with Arthur's sword in the stone. The weapon has preserved itself for the chosen heir; and he arises, young and unknown, from the midst of older and more celebrated names; and then, after his performance of the deed that proves his calling, he turns out to be the son of the old king.

Another sword was won by Arthur in combat with a giant, King Rion.[1] The weapon wrested from a defeated foe is the power of the vanquished in tangible form, which then is transferred to the victor; the human being who conquers such a giant and appropriates his sword is, therefore, a "giant man." a super-giant, and, employing the weapon in combat, is endowed with the giant's might. A third sword was yielded to Arthur by a supernatural fairy hand that held it out to him from the water of the "Lake" when his first sword shattered in a battle. This was the great Excalibur. But because the first had failed him he had been unable to conquer King Pellinor, and as a consequence his dominion was doomed to remain, for a time, incomplete.[2]

The Round Table had been originally entrusted by Merlin to Arthur's father, and at his death came into the hands of a certain King Leodogran of Camelot, who was the father of the beautiful princess Guinevere. Arthur rescued Leodogran from a host of enemies, was rewarded with the hand of his daughter, and on the day of the marriage came into possession of the Round

---

[1] *Roman de Merlin*, 308-314, Sommer's ed., pp. 245-251.
[2] *Morte d'Arthur*, I, 23-25.

Table. The original members of the fellowship were knights who had been in the service of King Leodogran. Others were chosen by Arthur at Merlin's behest. Then the last empty seat (except for the "seat perilous" which was to remain free awaiting secret future happenings) was assumed by the undefeated King Pellinor, who bowed willingly now to Arthur's majesty. And so the dominion of the paramount king of Celtic Christendom was made perfect.[1]

A new day had dawned. Arthur had been married to Guinevere, the fellowship of the Round Table was completed, and the members were all prepared for wondrous deeds. Life seemed full of promise and meaning. The assembled knights lifted up their swords and swore by the circling cup to change wrong into right, to feed the hungry and help the weak, to abide by the laws, and never to refuse help to a woman in distress. But no sooner had the oath crossed their lips than the strangest events began to come to pass.

With a great barking of dogs and the mysterious sound of horns, a wild hunt broke full into the hall, a white stag in the lead, and on his heels a small swift bloodhound, followed by a pack of dogs. The hunt swept around the Table, and suddenly the stag, in desperation, leapt over Gawain, tipping him backwards. The little bloodhound followed, but Gawain caught him, and, as though immediately bewitched, was dragged into the chase, which rushed from the hall on the heels of the stag.

The knights of the Round Table sat as though in a dream. Whereupon a girl mounted on a white palfrey appeared in the doorway, mourning for her little dog. "They must not take him from me," she lamented. "Think on your oath, King Arthur. I am in need, and you have sworn never to refuse help to a woman in distress."

[1] *Roman de Merlin*, 48-54, 177-206, 289, 410-414, Sommer's ed., pp. 54-60, 150-169, 232-233, 320-324; *Morte d'Arthur*, III, 1-4.

The king remained silent, his hand on the pommel of his sword. When he had taken the oath he had been dreaming of quite other deeds than the restoring of a little dog to a sorrowing girl. Before he could collect himself, a shadowy black knight rode into the hall, seized the bridle of the white palfrey, and before the knights could move, led the weeping girl away. The mysterious horns could still be heard in the distant hills.

Everyone sat thunderstruck, and Arthur turned in his bewilderment to Merlin: "What is the meaning of all these things, O great magician? Did they emanate from your enchanted forest? Are they spirits?"

Merlin threw back the hood that concealed his lined face, and the moment his features became visible they were transformed. The familiar countenance, with its long white beard and crowned with druidic mistletoe, had become the radiant visage of an ageless boy, with leaves of the laurel in his golden hair. When he spoke he smiled, and his voice had the ring of the distant hunting horns. "Was this not a magic hunt and a fairy maid?" he said. "Are you not man enough to seek adventure with the spirits, and to ride in pursuit of fairy beings? Why are you gathered here together, if not to follow the example of Gawain?" Whereupon he covered his face again and disappeared.[1]

It had not been granted to Arthur and his knights long to rejoice in the completion of the Round Table, or in the mystic marriage of the king and queen, which was also a symbol of the attainment of a certain degree of perfection. A wind summoned by Merlin blew through the castle and everything was transformed; the knights lost heart; and yet it was only a white hunted stag that had passed, and a helpless weeping girl. This ironical answer to their lofty oath tormented their minds and oppressed

[1] *Suite du Merlin*, Huth MS., fol. 157-158, ed., Gaston Paris and Jacob Ulrich, Paris, 1886, vol. II, pp. 76-79.

their hearts, for it was a sign to them of the emptiness of their splendor.

Every moment of achievement in the life of the chosen one is a step that bears within itself the seed of death; for the moment he believes that what he has attained is the end, the result is a withering away into staleness, monotony, and repetition. The tangible world in so far as it is conquered is laid waste, in so far as it is safe and well ordered, without real perils and adventures, is inert. And then dangers arise from the unknown, from the magic forest, the Castle Perilous, the Valley of No Return. The knights now understood this. The maintenance of chivalrous perfection can become a game, a complacent routine, as can any phase of spiritual progress for the chosen one, if he pauses in it along his path—even though, at the level of the ordinary mortal, that mode of activity may be the very breath of life, ordained by nature. Where there are no further adventures in store, the civil world has nothing to offer the chosen one but the position of a dignitary. The real field of endeavor must then become the adventure of the soul. The Round Table companion must array himself for the lonely quest of the supernatural.

The forest shimmers in a lovely twofold light; there are new dangers, new initiations. The Celtic forest is not an opposing world, like the hell of the Christian theology, but a realm of the soul itself, which the soul may choose to know, to seek therein its most intimate adventure. This was the quick choice of Gawain when he followed the little dog and the white stag. There is a pure strength that preserves the hero, but he cannot forgo the call of the abyss. All that is dark and tempting in the world is to be found again in the enchanted forest, where it springs from our deepest wishes and the soul's most ancient dreams.

The real task of the knights now lies before them. Merlin, their guide, has revealed the meaning of the hunt. They are face to face with the adventure to which everything else has been but a prelude, intended to cement the circle of the fellowship of the chosen. As members, all, of the Round Table, they are united in a common bond, and their paths, though predestined for each one of them alone, will meet, cross, and intertwine. They will be led through similar dangers to similar ends. And like the deeds of Herakles, the voyage of the Argonauts, like Theseus' heroic life, and Ulysses' journeys, their romances will represent and interpret differing ways of initiation, transformation, and the realization of perfection.

The romances of the Arthurian cycle are the Celtic counterparts of the great myths of the Classic civilization. They were one of the principal correctives of medieval Christianity (another was the encounter with Islam and its ancient tradition), towering out of the most remote antiquity, and pointing the way through suffering and initiation to a higher humanity. Their magic, the magic of the druidical Merlin, inspired and ensorcelled the heart of European man until well into the Renaissance, when the deep dream symbolism of the knightly journeys and quests, worn thin in the popular romances, was made ridiculous by the wit of Rabelais and received its death stroke in the figure of Don Quixote. Merlin himself, however, had long since withdrawn from the world in which he had worked with his initiates, first uniting them in the circle of the Round Table, and then scattering them forth again on the paths of their several transformations.

Merlin's end is well known. In the forest, one day, he met the beautiful Niniane, said to have been the daughter, by a rich nobleman named Dyonas, of Diana, the Sicilian siren. Her mother had endowed her with many wondrous gifts, and, thanks to these, it had been preordained that she should enrapture Merlin. He entertained her with a magic game. He broke a twig and drew a circle; immediately a company of knights and ladies appeared, holding hands and singing more beautifully than anyone

194

could imagine. Minstrels played on many kinds of instruments, so that it seemed one was listening to the music of the angels. Then when the sun climbed high, a cool shady hedge sprang up round about, and flowers and herbs appeared in the long grass. Niniane could not have enough of the music, although she understood only one verse of it: "Bitter suffering ends the sweet joys of newborn love."

Niniane made Merlin promise to teach her his art, and they swore to love one another eternally. They took one another, and in the joys of love-making Merlin taught her many singular things. They could hardly bear to part; and every time they met, the wizard found himself more closely bound to her. And so he taught her more and more. He knew very well that the day would come when she would completely enchant him with his own magic. Nevertheless he continued. And he took his leave of Arthur and the world of his fame.

When Merlin returned from his last visit to Camelot and rejoined Niniane in the magic forest, she received him more winningly and passionately than ever. "Teach me," she besought him, "how, without fetters or prison walls, I can enchain a man, purely by magic, and in such a way that he shall never escape me unless I choose to set him free."

Merlin sighed and bowed his head. Then, keeping nothing back, he taught her all the arts and elements of so powerful a spell. Niniane was beside herself with joy, and gave him so freely of her love that he would never know happiness again except with her.

And so they meandered hand in hand through the forest of Broceliande, and when they were tired, sat down under a whitethorn tree, heavy with sweet-smelling blossoms. There they delighted each other with tender words and kisses, until at last Merlin laid his head in her lap, and she stroked his face and entwined her fingers in his hair until he slept. As soon as she was

195

sure that he was sound asleep, she softly rose, took her long veil, and wound it around the whitethorn bush. Then, using the spells that Merlin had taught her, she stepped nine times around the bush within a circle that she had drawn, whispered nine times the proper magic words, and knew that after that the spell was unbreakable. Whereupon she sat down, and again took Merlin's head in her lap.

The wizard awoke and looked around him; he seemed to be lying on a bed inside an incredibly high tower. "If you do not stay with me forever," he said, "you have betrayed me; for no one but you can release me from this tower."

"My dear love," answered Niniane, "I shall often rest in your arms."

And she kept her word. Very few days or nights ever passed that she did not spend with him. And he could not stir from the spot, but she herself could come and go as she pleased. After a little time, however, she would have given him his freedom gladly, for she was sorry to see him always a prisoner; but the spell had been made too strong, and it was not in her power. So she remained with him, a perpetual sadness in her heart. [1]

It is a shimmering romance, full of the sweet nostalgia of Tristan and shadowed with a gentle melancholy—a tale of the age-old enchantment of the love spell, colored and retouched with the amorous rococo of medieval France. The courtly element appears only in the stylization; the mythical material itself is immensely old.

But there is a special nuance to this tale. The wizard gives up his magic lore. But he does not give it to his prodigies, the knights of the Round Table, or even into the hands of their lord, his special charge, King Arthur. For the world ultimately is not to be guided by a circle of wise men, a group of mahatmas from

[1] *Roman de Merlin*, 277-280, 526, 554-557, Sommer's ed., pp. 223-226, 451-452, 482-484.

196

beyond the Himalayas, Sarastros and Cagliostros from their temple halls, or any other group of perfected initiates. Merlin is too
wise to share with such as these any dream of disentangling the
world-skein, to weave from it a carpet of perfection according to
some ideal design. His prophetic eyes can watch the images of
the future unroll, as well as those of the present, and he knows
what is to come to pass. And so he bequeaths the power of his
magic wisdom into the bewitching fingers of lovely folly, his
fairy mistress. She is the personification of the spellbinding energy of life itself, and she receives in her thoughtlessness his gift,
which is powerful beyond all thought. And all that she can think
of to do with it is to bewitch the master of magic himself. Thus
the lord of the enchanted forest is made spellbound, wittingly
and willingly, in his own domain, and by an enchanting fairy
child who is the incarnation of the magic depths of the forest
itself.

Merlin withdraws, that is to say, into the power that is himself. It only looks as though he had succumbed to it. He returns
home into its perfumed, silently blossoming existence voluntarily, having been for so long the power that worked in the world
outside it. Merlin was the face and the voice of the forest; but
the face is hidden now, and the voice has died away into the
silence that gave it birth, the silence whence the message came
which it transmitted into the world of space. So the unconscious,
when it has clothed itself for a while with words and gestures,
when it has ruled for a while as the conscious, returns in silence
to its own slumber. Niniane's trickery is an illusion; Merlin's
abandonment to it is knowledge. In the girl's bright eyes he can
recognize the quintessence of his own being.

The abyss, in its wisdom and supreme indifference, is what
lured Merlin to submit to the spell that withdrew him from the
work and triumphs of the world. Merlin had gone forth into the
world; he came home to the forest. What is the world to the

forest? What is consciousness to the unconscious? That is a question which only Merlin can ask, which only he can answer. What is history, in space and time, to the abyss? But he has given us his answer. The answer is that he allows the forest, the abyss, to swallow him back, and he becomes again the magic wood and all its trees. For he is the lord of the forest and its essence, whereas the knights of the Round Table are children of men, lords of castles, and heroes of the world. The unconscious, through Merlin, has manifested itself to the world in revealing symbols, and sinks again into its own primeval stillness.

In abandoning himself to Niniane's magic arts, which are also most peculiarly his own, knowing at every step of the way what he is losing and what the end must be, Merlin rises to the calm heights of an Indian god who withdraws, after a period of manifestation, back into his own silence, knowing that he has no further part to play in saving or judging the world. Such was the gesture of Shiva, when in silent devotion he abandoned himself to the loving turbulence, the tender insatiability, of his goddess, and, motionless before her, committed the world drama of birth, fulfillment, and decay into her creating hands.

Arthur and his knights were distressed beyond measure at the departure of Merlin. They waited in vain, and for many years wandered seeking him through the world. Once when Gawain was thus riding sadly through the forest of Broceliande, he thought he heard a voice, but it was only a faint rustle and he could not discover whence it came. Again he heard it. "Be not sad, Gawain, everything that must happen, happens."

"Who are you that calls me by name?" cried Gawain.

"Do you not know me, Sir Gawain?" called the soft, teasing voice. "Once you knew me well. The old saying must be true— leave the court, and the court leaves you. When I served King Arthur I was known and loved by everyone. Now I am a stranger, and this could not be, were there any faith or faithfulness on earth."

Then cried Gawain: "O Master Merlin, now I know your voice. Come forth, that I may look upon your face."

"You will never see my face," answered Merlin, "and you are the last to hear my voice; after you I shall speak to no man again. No one will ever again reach this spot, even you are here for the last time. I can never find my way out to you, no matter how it grieves me that I must stay here forever. Only she who holds me here has the power to come and go as she pleases, she is the only one who may see me and speak to me."

"What, dear friend," cried Gawain, "are you so bound that you will never be free? How can this have come upon you, the wisest of men?"

"I am also the greatest fool," answered Merlin. "I love another more than I love myself, and I taught my beloved how to bind me to herself, and now no one can set me free."

Sadly Gawain turned and left him, to carry the news back to court. And great was the mourning when he told the knights that no one would ever see Merlin again or hear his voice, and when he told whose power it was that held him captive. They wept as they heard how he had blessed them all, the king and the queen, the nobles, and the kingdom.[1]

What we find enshrined and celebrated in this story of the end of Merlin is the overwhelming power of the fairy world—a primeval motif in the myths and sagas of the Celts. The magic of love and the senses, the power of nature and the unconscious, are a more imperious force than will and renunciation, consciousness and reason. There is here a nostalgic worship of dissolution, a loving sense for the mysterious descent into the womb of the generating powers: that return to the "Mothers," which we have already noted in the earlier romances, and which Richard Wag-

[1] *Roman de Merlin*, 558, 565-569, Sommer's ed., pp. 484-485, 492-496.

ner celebrated in the song of the Love-death, the *Liebestod*, of Tristan and Isolde's indissoluble merging. A theme of wonderful fascination, but on the other hand of fearful dangers too; for this sympathy with death can be aroused to a demonic evil, which pursues and entwines anyone who tries to escape from its toils. In the romance of the end of Merlin, as in that of Tristan and Isolde, it is the morality of elves and fairies, of the powers of water and forest, the old nature religion and the essential mysticism of the Celtic tribes, that celebrates its victory.

The course of world history has decided against the morality of the Celts, against Merlin's divine squandering of himself, his abandoning himself to the beguiling being to whom he entrusted the golden ropes of his own captivity. Englishmen, not Irishmen, or Welshmen, have founded the greatest empire since Rome, and the world is all in favor of Round Table government, voyages of discovery, and the adventure of good-willed intervention. But the whitethorn hedge blossoms imperishably, and in it Merlin is living still. Can that wizard who is at home in timelessness— the seer that sees the future as a changing flow of pictures in a crystal ball, while he floats beyond the flood—can he struggle against the waves of time?

There is food for thought in Merlin's end. There are worse fates for the body and for the soul. To be driven everlastingly around the world on adventures that never end, no matter how varied they may be, is finally a monotony as narrow and confining as the magic circle under the flowering thorn. Ulysses wearies at last of all the monsters he has conquered, the difficulties mastered, the Circes and Calypsos at whose sides he has slept his soul away; wearies of the islands with their cliffs and harbors that have arisen, hostile or friendly, before him, fading into twilight behind; wearies of the wine-dark sea and the starry silence; and he longs for the less eventful repetition of the well-known things of everyday, longs for his little island, his house, and his aging wife. For the heart of man is committed to two worlds. On the one hand, there is the wild forest of experience, which is without as well as within, pathless, full of monsters and adventures, fairies and enchantresses, and of spellbound lovely beings who require to be rescued and who then bewitch their rescuers. And, on the other hand, there is the dense sweet-smelling whitethorn hedge; and all longing for far spaces comes home to rest under its cloud of flowers, painfully yet blissfully stilled. The serpent coils into its last sleep. And this is the eve of the day of creation, the dark night before the myriad forms and events of the visible world have burst from the sanctuary whose veil no hand has ever raised.

Merlin and Niniane seem, in the end, to have exchanged sexes. He is content to be vanquished and to rest peacefully, while she, with the knowledge he has given her, is free to come and go. Her presence enthralls and delights him. And the Round Table, meanwhile, which by its high deeds and noble purpose has given rise to a new world order, sinks into oblivion; for Merlin, the master and guide, has cast away his wand. The inner principle that conceived and sustained the idea of the fellowship of the Round Table, chose and guided and foreknew the destiny of its members, has withdrawn into itself, dissolved in the twilight of its own timeless being.

THE KING AND THE CORPSE

1

It was remarkable, the way the king became involved in the adventure. For ten years, every day, there had been appearing in his audience chamber, where he sat in state hearing petitions and dispensing justice, a holy man in the robe of a beggar ascetic, who, without a word, would offer him a fruit. And the royal personage would accept the trifling present, passing it along without an afterthought to his treasurer standing behind the throne. Without making any request, the mendicant would then withdraw and vanish into the crowd of petitioners, having betrayed no sign either of disappointment or of impatience.

Then it happened one day, some ten years after the first appearance of the holy man, that a tame monkey, having escaped from the women's apartments in the inner palace, came bounding into the hall and leaped upon the arm of the throne. The mendicant had just presented his gift, and the king playfully handed it over to the monkey. When the animal bit into it, a valuable jewel dropped out and rolled across the floor.

The king's eyes grew wide. He turned with dignity to the treasurer at his shoulder. "What has become of all the others?" he asked. But the treasurer was unable to say. He had been tossing the unimpressive gifts through an upper, trellised window into the treasure house, not even bothering to unlock the door. And so he excused himself and hurried to the vault. Opening it, he made his way to the part beneath the little window. There, on the floor, lay a mass of rotten fruit in various stages

202

of decay and, amidst this debris of many years, a heap of price-less gems.

The king was pleased, and he bestowed the entire heap upon the treasurer. Of a generous spirit, he was not avid for riches, yet his curiosity was aroused. Therefore when the ascetic next morning presented himself, tendering in silence his apparently modest offering, the king refused to accept it unless he would pause awhile and speak. The holy man stated that he wished an interview in private. The king granted the desire, and the mendicant at last presented his request.

What he required, he told the king, was the help of a hero, a truly intrepid man, to assist in an enterprise of magic.

The king was interested in hearing more.

The weapons of true heroes, the magician explained, are renowned in the annals of magic for their peculiar exorcising powers.

The king permitted his petitioner to continue.

The stranger thereupon invited him to come, on the night of the next new moon, to the great funeral ground, where the dead of the city were cremated and the criminals hanged.

The king, undaunted, gave assent; and the ascetic—who bore the appropriate name of "Rich in Patience"—took his leave.

The appointed night arrived: the night of the next new moon The king, alone, girded on his sword, wrapped himself in a dark mantle, and with muffled countenance set forth on the questionable adventure. As he approached the dreadful burial ground, he became increasingly aware of the tumult of the specters and demons hovering about the uncanny place, feasting upon the dead, and celebrating their horrible carousals. Fearlessly he continued. When he crossed into the burning-area, by the light of the still smoldering funeral pyres his alert eyes half discerned, half guessed, the charred scattering of the blackened skeletons and skulls. His ears throbbed to the hideous uproar of the ghouls.

He proceeded to the rendezvous, and there was his sorcerer, intently drawing a magic circle on the ground.

"Here I am," the king said. "What can I do for you?"

The other hardly lifted his eyes. "Go to the other end of the burning ground," he said, "and you will find the corpse of a hanged man dangling from a tree. Cut it down and bring it here."

The king turned, and crossing again the extensive area, came to a giant tree. The moonless night was illuminated only by the dim flickering of the exhausted pyres; the goblins made an inhuman din. Yet he was unafraid, and perceiving the hanged man dangling there, he ascended the tree and cut the rope with his sword. When the corpse fell, it gave a moan, as though it had been hurt. The king, thinking there must still be life in it, began to grope over the rigid form. A shrill laugh broke from its throat, and the king realized that the body was inhabited by a ghost.

"What are you laughing at?" he demanded.

The instant he spoke, the corpse flew back to the limb of the tree.

The king ascended and again cut the body down. He lifted it without a word this time, placed it on his shoulder, and began to walk. But he had not taken many steps when the voice in the corpse began to speak. "O King, let me shorten the way for you with a tale," it said. The king did not reply, and so the spirit told its story.

There was, once upon a time, a certain prince who went on a hunting party with a young friend; the friend was the son of the chancellor of the prince's father. And losing touch with their companions, they strolled aimlessly through the forest, until they arrived at a pleasant lake where they paused to rest. The prince saw a beautiful maiden bathing on the farther bank, who, unobserved by her companions, was already making signals to him across the water. He was unable to understand the signs, but the chancellor's son was catching their meaning very well. She had communicated her name, that of her family, and that of the kingdom in which she lived, and was announcing her love. When she turned and vanished into the foliage, the two youths at last got up and ambled home.

Another day, under the pretext of another hunting party, the two friends set off again into the jungle, detached themselves, and went to the town in which the girl lived. They found lodging in the house of an old woman, whom they bribed to serve as messenger. The girl was so cunning that she was able to formulate a reply which the old woman did not recognize as the arrangement of a rendezvous. The signals were deciphered by the clever son of the chancellor. Then, for lunar reasons, the rendezvous had to be postponed, and the girl described, again by signals, how the prince might climb into her father's garden and ascend to her lofty chamber. He entered, as arranged, through her window, and the two young lovers found delight in each other's arms.

The girl was both passionate and cunning. When she learned that her signals had been deciphered not by the prince but by his friend, she was immediately afraid that her affair would be betrayed, and so she determined to poison the interpreter. He, however, was her match, and had even foreseen that this would come to pass. He had devised a plan that would teach her, once and for all, that he knew how to take care both of himself and of his prince.

The young man disguised himself as a beggar ascetic, persuaded the prince to play the role of the ascetic's pupil, and then, by a clever stratagem, brought the girl into suspicion as a witch. He convinced the king of the country that she had been the cause of the recent sudden death of his infant son, and he produced such proof that she was condemned to a disgraceful death. Exposed naked outside of the town, she was left prey to the beasts of the surrounding jungle. But the moment she was abandoned, the two young men, having procured swift horses for themselves, snatched her up and fled with her to the prince's realm, where she became his bride and future queen. Grief over the disgrace and loss overcame the aged parents of the maid; their hearts broke and they died.

"Now who was guilty of the death of those two?" suddenly demanded the specter in the corpse. "If you know the answer and do not reply, your head will burst into a hundred pieces."

The king believed that he knew the answer, but suspected that if he uttered a word the corpse would go flying back to the tree. Nevertheless, he did not wish his head to explode.

"Neither the maid nor the prince was guilty," he said, "because they were inflamed by the arrows of love. Nor was the son of the chancellor guilty, for he was not acting upon his own responsibility but in the service of his master. The only one guilty was the king of that country, who let such things come to pass within his realm. He did not see through the subtle trick played on the natural grief that he felt for his infant son. He failed to note that the mien of the beggar ascetic was no more than a disguise. He had never taken cognizance of the activities of the two strangers in his capital; he was not even aware that they were there. Therefore, he is to be judged guilty of failure in his kingly duty, which was to be the all-seeing eye of his kingdom, the all-knowing protector and governor of his folk."

When the last word of the judgment had left the speaker's tongue, the burden, groaning in mock agony, vanished from his back, and he knew that it was hanging again from the arm of the tree. He returned, cut the corpse down, shouldered the load, and tried again.

"My dear sir," said the voice, addressing him anew, "you have encumbered yourself with a difficult and curious charge. Permit me to while the time away for you with a pleasant tale.

"Now, once upon a time there were three young Brahmins who had lived a number of years in the home of their spiritual teacher. All three had fallen in love with their teacher's daughter, and he did not dare to bestow her on any one of them for fear of breaking the others' hearts. But then the maid was stricken with a serious illness and died, and the three young men, equally desperate, committed her body to a funerary pyre. When it had been cremated, the first decided to give vent to his grief by wandering through the world as a beggar ascetic, the second gathered the beloved bones from among the ashes and proceeded with them to a celebrated sanctuary beside the life-giving waters of the holy Ganges, while the third, remaining on the spot, constructed a hermit's hut over the place of the fire, and slept on the ashes of the body of his love.

"Now the one who had decided to roam through the world was one day the witness of an extraordinary event. He saw a man read from a book a magic charm that restored a child to life whose body had already been consumed to ashes. Stealing the book, the young lover hurried back to the cremation scene, and arrived just when the one who had gone to the Ganges also returned, the latter having dipped the bones into the life-giving stream. The skeleton was reassembled among the ashes, the charm was read from the book, and the miracle came to pass. The thrice-beloved arose again, more beautiful than ever. So at once the rivalry was resumed, but more hotly now; for each claimed to have earned the right to her: one having guarded her ashes, one having dipped her bones in the Ganges, and the third having pronounced the spell.

"And so to whom does she belong?" said the voice in the corpse. "If you know the answer but do not reply, your head will explode."

The king believed he knew, and so was forced to reply. "The one who recalled her to life with the magic spell and had little trouble in doing so is her father," he said, "and the one who rendered the pious service to her bones fulfilled the duty of a son. But the one who slept on the ashes, did not depart from her, and devoted his life to her, may be termed her spouse."

A wise enough judgment—yet the moment it was given, the corpse was gone. Doggedly, the king returned, cut it down, and started again the unrewarding walk. The voice resumed. The king was given another riddle to solve, and again compelled to retrace his path. And so it went, time after time, the unrelenting specter in the corpse spinning tale upon tale of twisted destinies and tangled lives, while the king was driven to and fro. All of life with its joys and horrors was described. And the threads of the fantasies always twisted into knots of right and wrong, tangles of conflicting claims.

There was a story, for example, of the posthumous son of a thief, who was faced by a delicate problem when he went to make an offering to his dead father at a sacred well. His grand-mother had been left a widow while still very young; and since her relatives had defrauded her of the inheritance, she had been compelled to go out into the world with only her little daughter. The night of her departure from the village, she came upon a thief who had been impaled and was on the verge of death. In terrible agony, hardly able to breathe, he expressed a desire to marry the little daughter, then and there—with the thought that the marriage would give him spiritual rights over her future son, even though the latter should be engendered by an-other, and this son then would be eligible to make the offerings due to the soul of a deceased father. In compensation, he would tell where he had concealed a certain stolen treasure.

The marriage was concluded in an informal though binding

208

manner, the thief died, and the mother and daughter had a considerable fortune. The girl fell in love, in due time, with a handsome young Brahmin, and he consented to become her lover, but insisted on a payment, because there was a certain courtesan whose fee he wished to be able to pay. The young woman conceived a son, and following the instructions of a dream, deposited the babe, together with a thousand gold pieces, at the threshold of the palace of a certain king. Now this king, who was without offspring and desirous of an heir to the throne, had happened that very night to dream that a child was about to be deposited at his door. He accepted the sign, and brought up the foundling as his son and heir.

Many years later, when the benevolent king had died, the young prince, incumbent to the throne, went to make an offering to his departed father. He proceeded to a holy well, where the dead were accustomed to stretch forth their hands to receive the proffered gifts. But instead of a single hand, three hands appeared to take his oblation: that of the impaled thief, that of the Brahmin, and that of the king. The prince did not know what to do. Even the priests attending the offering were at a loss. "Well," challenged the specter in the corpse, "into which hand should the prince consign his oblation?"

Again threatened with the explosion of his skull, the king pronounced judgment: "The oblation should be placed in the hand of the thief, for neither the Brahmin who begot the child nor the king who reared him has any valid claim. The Brahmin sold himself. The king received his compensation in the gold pieces. The man who made it possible for the prince to be born was the thief; his treasure paid for both the begetting and the fosterage. Furthermore, the thief had title to the child by marriage." Immediately, the corpse was off, and still another walk brought the king back to the tree.

209

Then there is that curious tale of the transposed heads, the tale of two lifelong friends and a girl.[1] The maid married one of the two, but the marriage was not particularly happy. Shortly following the wedding, the couple, together with their bachelor friend, set forth on a visit to the parents of the bride. On the way, they came to a sanctuary of the bloodthirsty goddess Kālī, and the husband excused himself, for a moment, to go into the temple alone. There, in a sudden excess of emotion, he decided to offer himself to the image as a sacrifice, and, with a keen-edged sacrificial sword that was there, lopped his head from his shoulders and collapsed in a pool of blood. The friend, having waited with the bride, went into the temple to see what had happened, and when he beheld the sight was inspired to follow suit. At last the bride came in, only to take flight again, intent on hanging herself from the limb of a tree. The voice of the goddess commanded her to halt, however, and sent her back to restore the lives of the two young men by replacing the heads. But because of her distraction, the young woman made the interesting mistake of putting the friend's head on the husband's body, and the husband's on the friend's. "To which now does she belong?" demanded the specter in the corpse, "the one with the husband's body, or the one with the husband's head?"

The king thinks he knows, and, to keep his own head from bursting, gives his answer: "The one with the husband's head; for the head ranks supreme among the members, just as woman among life's delights."

Again the corpse has vanished and again the king is trudging back to the fateful tree.

[1] Cf. Thomas Mann, *The Transposed Heads*, 1940. The inspiration for this short novel was an earlier version of the present essay, "Die Geschichte vom indischen König mit dem Leichnam," which appeared in the Festival Volume in honor of Dr. C. G. Jung's sixtieth birthday, *Die kulturelle Bedeutung der komplexen Psychologie*, Verlag Julius Springer, Berlin, 1935.

2

When will the ordeal end? Is it some kind of serious test or a joke? In all, twenty-four riddles are propounded; and the king can announce a solution to all but the last.

This last concerns the case of a father and son. They were members of a hill tribe of huntsmen, the father a chief. And the two had gone out on a hunting party, when they happened on the footprints of two women. Now the father was a widower and the son as yet unmarried, but the father in his sorrow for his deceased wife had rejected every suggestion that he should rewed. Still, the footmarks were particularly charming: the practiced eyes of the hunters judged that they had been left by a noble mother and daughter, fugitives of some aristocratic house—perhaps even a queen and a princess. The larger prints suggested the beauty of the queen and the smaller ones the fascination of the princess. The son was very much excited. But the father had to be persuaded. What the son proposed was that the father should marry the woman of the larger footprints and himself the smaller, as befitted their rank and age. He had to argue the point for some time, but at last the chieftain acquiesced, and the two took a solemn oath that that was the way it should be.

Then they made haste along the trail. And they came, at length, upon the two unhappy creatures, a queen and princess indeed—just as the tribesmen had suspected—in anxious flight from a situation that had developed at home when the king had unexpectedly died. But there was this disillusioning complication: the daughter was the one who had the larger feet. According to their oath, therefore, the son would be forced to marry the queen.

Father and son conducted their quarry into their mountain

village, and there made wives of them; the daughter became the wife of the chief, and the mother of the son. Then the two women conceived.

"Now just how were the two male children that were born related to each other?" asked the voice of the specter in the corpse. "Precisely what was each to the other, and precisely what were they not?"

The king, carrying his burden, was unable to find any unequivocal term for this complicated relationship. The enigma had at last been found that could strike him dumb. And so he walked along with a remarkably buoyant stride, bemusing the problem in silence. The children would be living paradoxes of interrelationship, both this and that: uncle and nephew, nephew and uncle, at once on the father's side and on the mother's.

But is it not always so—with all things—in some secret respect? Is not everything, in some deep way, its own opposite? Even though the discriminating intellect, the categorizing logic of human language and thought, may refuse to accept the paradoxical fact, nevertheless every feature, every moment of life, includes, somehow, qualities diametrically opposed to those apparently implied. In the kingly person there can lie concealed a secret unkingliness, a streak of inadvertence, for example, which may lead, on occasion, to the inadequate supervision of possibly dangerous strangers, or perhaps a tendency to underestimate gifts that arrive in humble wrappings. Similarly, unholiness can reside beneath the robe of a religious mendicant. Having seemingly renounced the world of power and ambition, the beggar monk can be addicted, nevertheless, to black magic, and devote his nights to the sinister practices of necromancy.

Have we here hit upon the hidden lesson of this wild symposium of the twenty-four tales of the specter in the corpse?

Is this the meaning of the bizarre initiation? Was the king wiser in his silence than in the perspicacity of his replies?

Driven back into the problem of his own character and present predicament, he walked in silence, but with an admirable nimbleness of step that seemed heedless of the night's long ordeal. And apparently the specter was impressed, for when the voice spoke again, it was altered to a tone of respect.

"Sir," it said, "you seem cheerful in spite of all this weird tramping back and forth across the funeral ground; you are unafraid. I am pleased by the spectacle of your determination. You may have this corpse, therefore. Take it with you. I am about to quit it."

But this was not the end. If it were, the adventure would have been of little avail—a test of valor, perhaps, but more like a practical joke; or the whole affair of the burning-ground and the specter in the corpse would have amounted to little better than a macabre literary device for the framing of a number of unrelated tales. The collection is witty and entertaining, but at the same time portentous and profound; this king and his specter are linked by a deeply hidden enigma of the soul.

Before taking its departure, the voice warned that the projects of the magician ascetic were of terrible danger to them both; beneath the holy garment of renunciation throbbed a boundless lust for power and blood. The necromancer was about to use the king in a great enterprise of black magic, first as accomplice and then as a living human sacrifice.

"Listen, O King," the specter warned, "listen to what I have to tell you, and, if you value your own good, do exactly as I say. That beggar monk is a very dangerous imposter. With his powerful spells he is going to force me to re-enter this corpse, which he will then use as an idol. What he plans to do is to place it in the center of his magic circle, worship me there as a divinity, and, in the course of the worship, offer you up as the victim. You

213

will be ordered to fall down and do me reverence, first on your knees, then prostrate, in the most slavish attitude of devotion, with your head, hands, and shoulders touching the ground. He will attempt then to decapitate you with a single stroke of your own sword.

"There is only one way to escape. When you are ordered to go down, you must say: 'Please demonstrate this slavish form of prostration, so that I, a king unused to such attitudes, may see how one assumes such a posture of worship.' And when he is lying flat on the ground, strike off his head with a quick cut of the sword. In that instant, all the supernatural power that this sorcerer is trying to conjure from the sphere of the celestials will fall to you. And you will be a potent king indeed!"

The specter, with that, departed and the king proceeded freely on his way. The magician betrayed no impatience at having been forced to wait, but on the contrary seemed filled with admiration that the task should have been accomplished at all. He had used the time to complete the ritual arrangement of his magic circle. It was all marked out with a hideous material gathered from the immediate neighborhood: a kind of paste composed of the whitish meal of ground bones mixed with the blood of dead bodies. And the area was unpleasantly alight with the flickering of wicks burning with corpse fat.

The sorcerer lifted the burden from the king's shoulder, washed it, and decorated it with garlands, as though it were a sacred image, then set it in the center of the magic circle. He summoned the specter by means of a series of potent incantations and compelled it to enter into the prepared body. Then he undertook to pay it worship after the manner of a priest paying worship to a divinity which has been invited to take up residence within a sacred image as an august guest. The time came, presently, for him to make the king go down, first on his knees, then on his face; but when he pronounced the command, his noble acolyte required to be shown how to take the posture. So the terrible monk got down on his knees. The king watched and waited. The monk fell forward, pressing his hands, shoulders, and face to the ground, and with a quick slash the king struck off his head. The blood gushed. The king rolled the body over and with another expert blow split the chest. He ripped the heart out and offered it up, together with the head, as an oblation to the specter in the corpse.

Then a mighty sound of jubilation arose out of the night from every side, from the host of surrounding spirits, souls and ghouls, lifting a tumult of acclaim to the victor. By his deed he had redeemed the supernatural powers from the threat of the necromancer, who had been on the very point of reducing them all to slavery and enchantment.

The specter in the corpse lifted its uncanny voice, but now in joy and praise. "What the necromancer sought was absolute power over souls and ghouls," it said, "and over all the spiritual presences of the supernatural domain. That power now shall be yours, O King, when your life on earth is ended. Dominion over the whole earth, meanwhile, is to be given you. I have tormented you; I shall therefore now make atonement. What do you wish? Announce your desire and it shall be granted."

The king asked, in compensation for his toils during this strangest of all the nights he had ever known, that the twenty-four riddle tales told him by the specter, together with the story of the night itself, should be made known over the whole earth and remain eternally famous among men.

The specter promised. "And furthermore," the voice stated, "not only shall the twenty-five tales be universally celebrated, but even Shiva, the Great God, Overlord of all the Specters and Demons, the Master-Ascetic of the Gods, will himself do them honor. Neither ghosts nor demons shall have any power, whenever and wherever these tales are told. And whoever re-

215

cites with sincere devotion even a single one of them shall be free from sin."

With this great promise the specter abruptly departed; and immediately Shiva, the Lord of the Universe, appeared in glory, attended by a multitude of gods. He gave greeting to the king and serenely thanked him, with high praise, for his deliverance of the powers of the spirit world from the impure hands of the aspiring ascetic. The divinity declared that the cosmic powers now were placed in the service of the king in return for his having prevented their misuse by the black magician who had been working for universal dominion, that the king would come into full possession of them at the close of his earthly career, and that during his lifetime he would govern the earth. Shiva bestowed upon him, with his own hand, the divine sword "Invincible," which should give him the sovereignty of the world; and then he lifted the veil of ignorance that had been concealing from his consciousness the immortal essence of his human life.

Blessed with this illumination, the king was free to take his leave of the gruesome proving ground. The dawn was breaking as he returned into the spacious halls of his lordly palace, like someone awakening from a night of troubled sleep. The tales of the specter in the corpse had been like a succession of tortured dreams, seemingly endless, yet comprised in a comparatively brief period of time. And the victim, caught in the interminable sequence, walking to and fro across the burning-ground, across the scene of bygone life, had been like a sleeper tossing restlessly in his bed. And just as one may discover, on awakening, that what had been obscure the day before now is understood, and was very much more intricate and profound in its obscurity than one had supposed—as obscure as the riddle of life itself— so this king came from his night of experience full of knowledge and transformed. During the following years the miraculous fulfillment of the splendor promised came to pass, and his earthly life was enlarged in virtue and glory.[1]

3

Dreams of significance are recalled after waking; similarly, these stories, gruesome yet lovely, have lingered in the memory of the folk. What is it about this king that so enthralls? What is the meaning of this curious fairy story of the human soul?

A man has pledged himself to pay a debt that he incurred by accepting gifts, though at the time he had been ignorant of their value. He is prepared to do whatever may be required of him. And because he is both generous and brave—a kingly man—he goes through with his horrible task. Yet, in venturing upon such an obscure enterprise with a stranger, was he not a trifle rash? He seemed very certain that no untoward calamity would befall him. He was possessed of an immense self-confidence. But his insight was not particularly acute; nor was he as prudent as a man in his position should have been. This deficiency in circumspection was the fault in the coat of mail of his personality, through which the shaft of fate could drive into his inner existence. It was through this chink in his apparent perfection that he was to be laid open to the influence of life—laid open, acted upon, and, through the contact with an alien element, transformed.

[1] Five Sanskrit versions of the *Twenty-five Stories of the Specter in the Corpse* (*Vetālapañcaviṅśati*) are recorded: Somadeva's *Kathāsaritsāgara,* 75-99; Kshemendra's *Brikatkathāmañjari,* 9, 2, 19-1221; Jambhaladatta's version, edited by M. B. Emeneau, American Oriental Series, vol. 4; Sivadāsa's version, edited by H. Uhle, Sächsische Akademie der Wissenschaften, Berichte, Philologisch-historische Klasse, Bd. 66, Heft 1, Leipzig 1914, and an earlier anonymous version, also edited by Uhle. Versions exist in almost every Hindu vernacular, as well as in Tamil and Telugu. Translations in other languages also are current. The king in the story is the Hindu hero-king Vikramāditya ("The Sun of Valor"), who may have flourished about 50 B.C., and of whom innumerable legends are told.

How strange the behavior of that pertinacious beggar, day by day, for the period of ten years! And how inconsiderate the response of the king, who accepted his modestly offered gifts, permitting him to come and go, year in, year out, without so much as an attentive word! Yet ourselves, every day, do we not, each of us, receive from the unknown beggar an apparently unimportant fruit, only to disregard it and cast it heedlessly aside? Does not life itself, every morning, stand before us in ordinary workaday garb, like a beggar, unannounced and unexplained, unexacting and unostentatious, waiting upon us with its gifts of the day, one day upon another? And do we not generally fail to open its common gifts, the common fruits from its common tree? We should certainly ask: "What does this hold?" We should suspect some seed within, precious and essential; and we should break the fruit to discover it. We should learn to separate the radiant, imperishable kernel from the part that has ripened only to fade, the part that rots and is soon in the keeping of death. Yet we permit the fruit, jewel and all, to be tossed away. And the valuable fruit is not only continually presented to us by the patient hand of outer life, with each successive day, each passing moment; it is also offered from within. Each of us is a fruit of the precious kind of this parable: yet do we manage—do we try—to release from the pericarp of our everyday personality the brilliant jewel of our essential seed?

Everything that the story recounts of the inadvertent king upon his throne and the silent beggar coming daily to the hall, offering the same fruit, year in, year out, never complaining, never revealing his purpose, only effacing himself among the crowds of exacting and ceremonious figures, disappearing among them and departing—all this is simply ourselves and our inscrutable life. We accept indifferently the fruit of our existence and discover nothing particularly noteworthy about it. We take it for granted, blandly and blindly, and hand it over to the one who stands behind our throne.

For we have a number of egos, who administer the various departments of our life. We are not wholly or perpetually the kingly personage whom we present to the gaze of official circles, but a number of sometimes extraordinarily various personalities, according to the aspect of our nature momentarily summoned into play. One of these egos is the "royal treasurer," the administrator of the riches on which we draw. He stands just behind our throne and produces, on demand, the wealth that we distribute with such a royal air, the bounty that we live by, the treasure that makes us the great or the little kings we are. According to the parable, however, he is no more concerned than the king to investigate the simple fruits that each day so mysteriously brings. He does not even unlock the door of the treasure house for such ordinary things, but only tosses them into the dark, through an open window. And there they lie, neglected, rotting, distributing their precious beauty over the unattended floor.

But we have among our numerous egos yet another—perhaps our ninth or tenth ego—which we permit to play when we require relaxation from our attitudes of importance, our duties and privileges, our pomp of state. We have our monkey. And he does not belong within the throne hall; he is out of place in the chamber of our kingliness. His gentle keepers are sheltered in the inner apartments of our being, those pleasant seraglios where we enjoy ourselves in royal idleness with our women and our games. Nevertheless, the wheel of life turns and turns, and, ever turning, mingles all with each and each with all. In due time even the monkey breaks loose and comes bounding unceremoniously into the chamber of state, leaps on the throne and thrusts its grotesque little face into the affairs of the king.

The monkey receives the unimpressive gift of the beggar. The

219

king is above it, but the monkey is avid for its taste. With un-bridled impetus and dainty-mouthed curiosity, this monkey-readiness to grasp at things and play with them until they break cracks open the fruit at last and discloses its secret to the eye. Curiosity, the ordinary desire to tamper with things, to consume and destroy them, releases the jewel at the core. But the playful animal cannot understand what it has done. Its act has been one only of amusing innocence. Having disclosed the gem, it simply abandons it, bounds away to the next monkey somersault—and so leaves the tale.

Our fate bursts open in just this way, at a mere playful touch, at some little trick of chance, and reveals to our astonished eye its internal store. Then we perceive that by a long, hitherto unnoticed history of our own fashioning, we have unwittingly committed ourselves to a crisis of consequences. The seeds of all our thoughtlessly accomplished deeds have quietly accumu-lated in a dark and hidden treasury—the subsoil, so to speak, of our life of consciousness. And it is as though a thread of destiny that we had long been spinning had slowly entangled us with-out our knowing, and now, by some accident, were suddenly jerked taut. We discover that we are trapped in an inescapable net into which we have thoughtlessly delivered ourselves. We are implicated in an adventure of unknown proportions. And even if we meet it with self-confidence and the best of faith, it will inevitably prove to be something very different, very much more complicated, dangerous, and difficult, than we expect. Since we permitted it to escape us in its entirety, it cannot but astonish us now in its details.

The sanctimonious mendicant with his well-concealed cer-tainty of an ever-growing claim to the services of his harmless, heedless victim has permitted the ripeness of time, the click of circumstance, to bring his sinister purpose to pass. And he is there, at last, at the rendezvous, when the hour of the sacrifice has come. Who is this "Rich in Patience," able to wait for a year, two years, three years, ten, cherishing his secret design with an unrelenting power of endurance?

The wardrobe of Destiny is filled with all kinds of costumes in which to confront us, and just this one had to be selected for the meeting with the king. The king had elicited it; indeed, he had woven and tailored it himself. Out of the invisible substance of his own interior he had woven it, as a spider its web—as Abu Kasem his slippers. Out of the negative silk of his unkingliness— the failures of his judicious eye, the contentment that he felt for the pompous aspect of his public character—the robe of this impostor had been shaped. The unmonkish monk comes before the king as an incarnate analogy to his own counterfeit of omniscient wisdom, comes before him day after day, and by so doing gives proof to his own and to the general deception. The challenge is of threatening dimensions in proportion to the number of years of the kingly failure. Precisely this terribly deceitful sorcerer had to confront this all too guileless king: the two were one. It was the king himself who had brought this figure into being. It was he who had produced him, created him as the counterpart of his own spiritual blindness.

As William Blake has put it: "my specter around me night and day." Wherever we look we discover our own inescapable selves. Wherever we step, a portion of our unknown self steps before us significantly, mysteriously fashioned and projected. Our destiny, our environment, our enemies, our companions— we have built them all. They stalk out of our depth, essential and self-produced. That is why to the enlightened person everything encountered is a manifestation of the initiating priest, a spiritual guide able to bestow the key. The shapes of the initiating power change, but always in accordance with our own need and guilt; they reflect the degree of our spiritual nescience or maturity.

221

And they prefigure the transformations required of us, the tasks we have yet to solve.

Seemingly in the service of another, the king discovers himself obliged to fetch a corpse: and so do we. The living soul is forced to go wandering through a kingdom of death in search of something dead. There is no moon in this twice-black night of smoke to shed its mild and comforting light; all the devils and ghouls of hell are loose, horrible, threatening, and mocking; and only the flickerings of the dim flames of smoldering corpses are there to illuminate our weary wandering, with their smell of hot, decaying flesh. Similarly, Dante wandered through the hell pits of the dead, having "lost the way." He, however, was comforted. Dante, though aghast and deeply shaken, yet knew himself to be secure in the hands of his guide, the saintly Virgil, the pious master of the master poets, who had been dispatched to him by an act of heavenly mercy. The king with the corpse, on the other hand, was alone. And so are we. For which of us today can claim such heavenly guidance through the labyrinth of the past of our life and soul?

To fetch a dead body: what a curious task! To cut down the corpse of an unknown hanged man, and then to bear the body of the criminal on one's back! The work of the king was performed in the service, apparently, of another; yet actually his burden, his task, was his own. For he had been bound to that other by an involuntary indebtedness, yet not without a certain blame; just as we are all personally responsible for the prodigious burden of the dead years that have become heaped over the life of our lives. And which of us would not welcome, if only once, the opportunity to retrieve some moment lost, to exhume secretly and by night—even with the flaming orgies of the hell ghouls roaring around us—something dead, something buried, something already rotting away?

Within the recovered corpse there is a ghostly life. An uncanny

222

vitality, a demoniacal insolence speaks out of it, mocking, threatening. The sorcerer is not the only tyranically commanding figure in the night world of the inadvertent king; between the moment of his submission to the summons and that of the consummation of the sacrifice, this other equally inescapable presence becomes known to him. And it lays its grip, its ghost hand, at his throat.

Who would ever have thought that a dead body, strange fruit of the graveyard tree, could give harbor to such a talkative seed? Yet each of us carries on his shoulder such a load, such a dead weight from the past. This corpse, this decaying thing, is another one of our egos (how many the fullness of their number? who knows?), and therefore a portion—a forgotten, moribund, broken-off portion—of our own being. And the ghost inside is still another, the strangest ego of all. It dwells behind, beyond, within the kingly "I" that we consciously consider ourselves to be, and, making its voice echo from the dead forms around, threatens sudden death to us should we refuse to obey its whims. It sets us tasks and pricks us to and fro, involving us in a hideous game of life and death.

The ghost, to pass the time, to dupe us, and perhaps to prove us, begins recounting enigmatical tales. And we are compelled to propound replies. But if we know an answer, the recovered corpse escapes us; we are compelled to retrace our steps. If we know and yet hold our peace, we are made to explode. The kingly ego of our daytime, that noble, powerful personage whose word, whose wish is law (he can command all to go or to stay, to depart or remain), now is bound to an elusive superior power and forced to wander wherever this extraneous possessing-spirit orders, to and fro, back and back again to the gallows of the hanged man. He must discover ever anew, fetch again, and bear the burden of that dead thing, that incubus of life undone.

The night seems endless, as though time had stopped to give place to the timeless rhythm of this strange Sisyphus-damnation.

223

When shall we be free again? When will this purgatorial night of our purification end? How many tales the terrible night holds for us—tales enticing and appealing, ominous and piteous, crowded with astonishing event! They unfold, as the specter in the corpse on our back talks on and on. And after each there comes the challenge: "Find the answer to the riddle that life here puts to you. Split the pericarp that conceals the brilliant seed."

Guilt and innocence are rarely obvious. They are unapparent, interwoven intimately with each other in a marvelously convoluted design. For example, who was to blame when the parents died heartbroken over the fate of their slandered and abducted daughter? Not the lovers, or their clever adviser, but the king who was duped by the sanctimoniousness of a mock ascetic! That had been a king very like the king who now was working out his problem with the corpse, very like this governor of the people who had accepted fruit after fruit, without examining them, from an impostor beneath a gown of virtue. The obvious is only the semblance; beneath lies something hidden, the real. And whoever clings only to the semblance will become entangled in it before he knows. He will discover himself engulfed in a hell of inexplicable fiends, harried hither and thither without result. And like a corpse the weight of his omission will mount his back, shriek in his ear, and mock him with ghost laughter, taunting him with having failed to discern the real when it stood before him in the light of day.

The man who, satisfied with his own appearance, presumes to consider himself right and whole, a hero, a king in the seat of judgment, is at fault. He is at fault, and his own failure steps before him, presently, in a disguise of blamelessness, but with an uncanny demand. The seemingly harmless figure (corresponding to his own good judgment of himself) conducts him into a night that is the exact contrary of his day, and there sets him the task

224

—unkingly and impure—of carrying corpses like an outcaste. The fine and kingly one is commanded to do the work of the pariah, not only once, and to good and speedy purpose so that he may quickly forget the humiliation, but again and again—as often, indeed, as he had sinned, as often as he had neglected to search the proffered fruit and had discarded the core. This fruit must seem to him, at last, very horrible and bitter, as bitter as a night of hell in contrast to the sweetness and grace of a kingly day.

The ordeal cannot be evaded. The time of outward semblances is past. The king's problem is to become truly and entirely himself. It would do him no good to protest that all the weird confusion pouring from the mouth of the corpse had nothing to do with him; for it already had stood and waited before him many times, in the comely daylight of his throne hall, where, as the omniscient governor of his realm, he sat in judgment. All this inferno and confusion is the confusion of his kingdom, the kingdom of his own life—and it is equally ours.

Nothing is far from us. Nothing can be treated as alien. When we put distance between ourselves and another, we are at fault, and the consequences will be ours. So now go back, go back again; fetch down the corpse of the past from the gallows tree to which you yourself condemned it. And listen to the voice of the persecuting imp: there will be no other voice to talk to your night, no other voice to teach or save. For, somehow, all the heroes, villains, and heroines in the convoluted histories recited to us by our hell dream are ourselves; and, somehow again, we are the sole resolution to the riddles it will pose. The corpse is a concretion of our own past—the neglected, the forgotten. Unfulfilled, unsatisfied, yet not quite dead, it must needs haunt us, until, in the night of seeming endlessness, we shall have accepted, recognized and satisfied, the hitherto unadmitted aspect of our own existence.

The quality that finally saves the kingly personage—the

225

*sincerity
helps to
endure —*

Ariadne-thread that guides him through the labyrinth of the interior night—is the sincerity of his willingness to endure the enterprise, his courage in the toils of the demon powers let loose upon him. This sustains him against the enigmatic questions. And because he is pure and true and able to transcend the limitations of his kingly ego, even curbing it to the service of the powers of the dark, what an exaltation, what a magnificent consolation is in store! The path of our initiation leads through the hell of the undesired yet self-inflicted trial, through the cremation ground of our moribund omissions, to a transfiguration into that higher reality which all the while was immanent within us and potent to be fulfilled. Our mistakes, our very culpabilities, are the wings to bear us aloft to the seat of the zenith powers; and these then invest us with our mission. But between those powers and our present selves, between our victory and the banality of our complacency, there stand to be met and absolutely satisfied the false ascetic and the specter in the corpse.

*The unexpected
voice can lead
to thoughtfulness
/ insight*

The latter is the defender, the guide, though only a ghost in a dead body, not a master poet such as guided the steps of the poet Dante, or a protecting angel such as might have attended the paces of a child. For this king is neither a poet nor an innocent. Nevertheless, the unexpected voice is enough: the moment it speaks, the man who was thoughtless suddenly gains the thing he lacked. He is awakened to thoughtfulness. And as its tales unfold, old yet ever new, the king is initiated into a broad and penetrating insight. The once careless, guileless one becomes a match for the cunning, crooked, perfectly hidden enemy. Taught to comprehend reality in its fullness, the tangled web of light *and* dark, made capable of distinguishing the hidden character behind the mask, he is at last in a position to outmatch the archdissembler at his own game of cynical dissemblances; for never did the cunning one ·imagine that the guileless one might become more cunning than himself. The hero is made actually what he formerly only imagined himself to be—a king. The real king can annihilate the shadow of himself wherever it may arise to intimidate and slay. But a personality is not whole and real, the king not a valid king, until he has recognized the antagonist, discovered the corpse, that gallows-fruit from the tree of his own life, and learned the lesson of the hellish interior voice.

the personality is not full, not complete — until it recognizes its own corpse

The specter in the corpse represents the high judge within ourselves who keeps record of everything, and, in deep wisdom, foreknows all. By a hint this power can pull us back from that brink of calamity toward which, with all the energy and one-pointedness of our conscious nature, we are blindly striving. It is a wiser ego than the one we know. It is a more powerful power than the king we wish ourselves to be. In the moment of our need it comes, comes to us, and warns with a laugh of scorn, then disappears. And once again we are alone in the night of ghouls and corpses, the night that yielded the enigmatical voice. We can do nothing to bring it back to us. We had no defense against it when it chose to plague us; we have no knowledge now of how to compel its return.

Nevertheless a certain relationship was established between the king and the specter during this night with its endless series of enigmas and its wandering to and fro in the field of death. That was a communion of only a few fleeting hours, yet a timeless encounter. The two came as close to each other for that hideous period as they ever would or could have come in the blood-warm realm of life. Even as a living "I" and "You," they were interwoven with each other by a common danger, welded by one doom. Each saved the other, and by virtue of that mutual rescue the entire universe was given redemption, including the spirit world on high.

The bodily king and the bodiless specter, the tangible and the invisible realms, the kingly "I" of daylight and the ghostly voice

227

of the dark depth of our night (full of wit and intuitive wisdom), belong together. Neither can exist without the other; separated, both would be totally impotent; together they form a single living unit. And, furthermore, had their activities not been synchronized, they would have been equally lost. It was for the king to perform the deeds, but the inspiration came from the ghost of the hidden depth. And in this wise each redeemed the other. The specter rescued the king from the doom toward which he was being dragged by the blindness of mere consciousness, and the king released the ghost from the decaying past. The relationship was the same as that of Prince Conn-eda to the voice of his enchanted alter ego within the shaggy horse.

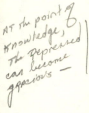

When, finally and suddenly, the voice was satisfied that the king had reached the point of knowledge, then it became gracious, indicated the mortal peril toward which he had been heading, and taught him what he must do, at the very last moment, in order to be saved. For the hell-fate prepared for us is really more terrible than we rightly deserve. But, on the other hand, the officiating devil is not very difficult to trick. A stratagem is suggested, the simplest possible, yet it is enough. The master of sham is annihilated, the ordeal is converted into a festival of joy, and the king comes into the fullness of his strength.

It is important to observe the manner of the rescue. Following the instructions of his guide, the courageous king slashes off the head and rips out the heart of the malignant black magician. Then these are offered to the specter, who is temporarily deified and made resident in the set-up corpse, like a divinity in an image. Therewith, the enchantment that binds both the king and the specter is dispelled. The former, no longer forced to wander in the night of his being over the execution ground and burial place of his past, is allowed to return to his stately palace; and the latter, no longer condemned to haunt the corpse of the life beyond recall, or to mock with riddles and whims the kingly consciousness, is released, permitted to quit the field of death. And the effect is achieved because with this oblation the part of the personality that had been proud and hostile was humbled in sacrifice—through a deliberate act of the conscious ego—and submitted to a higher, invisible, inner authority. The head, that is to say, was precisely the center of the royal fault, and with its perversion it had involved the heart. Both infected centers now were sacrificed and given in offering to the mysterious authority which at last had reasserted itself and pointed the way to the violent yet requisite act of release.

Thus, in the end, the ghost, who had seemed no less uncanny and revolting than the corpse itself or the magician, proves to be the savior, the oracular spirit who wishes us well. This elusive, invisible quintessence of our unfulfillment, vocal specter of our unconsciously amassed guilt, turns out to be the only one in the whole world, the only guide in the darkness of the night of our being, who can save us from the magic circle of our own self-created evil. And it is because we have finally submitted to its whim and will that it can save us. It can save us because we have patiently performed the tasks that it laid upon us, in trial and in scorn. Of all those components of ourselves that come bursting out of our being and in many and varied shapes then surround us, it is the wisest. It seems, indeed, to know everything, everything that has ever happened not only to ourselves but to all beings whatsoever, kings, beggars, criminals, and women ever fresh and lovely, in far distant realms. With the compelling convincingness of dreams, which are vague yet exact, the ghost voice draws to us these figures, lifts them casually out of the well of the past—the well wherein nothing is lost, the deep well of forgetfulness and remembrance—and tosses them mockingly on the glassy table surface of our consciousness. There we are forced to consider them. There we are forced to regard, analyze, and reunderstand.

229

A significant transformation of the ghost took place the moment the king passed the test of the enigmatic questions. The two having discovered each other, and having been united by the long dialogue in the common work of mutual self-salvation, the specter took its leave of the corpse and permitted the king, who had been tethered to the task of the tree, to go his way. Then, with altered character, the specter returned when the corpse had been set up in the center of the magic circle, and there abode as a kind of deity, entitled to prostrations and to the highest sacrifice of all, the oblation of a human being. Furthermore, the corpse, too, had by then become transformed. It had been converted from gallows fruit on the tree to anointed image in the center of the place of worship, set about with flickering wicks. Turned from something contemptible into something entitled to adoration, the abomination was now a divinity, radiant with power, eloquent with blessing.

"It is a significant trait of many fairy tales," observes the German poet-philosopher Novalis, in one of his inspired and inspiring aphorisms, "that the moment one impossible thing becomes possible, simultaneously another impossible thing becomes unexpectedly possible: the hero overcoming himself simultaneously overcomes nature. A miracle occurs that grants him the contrary agreeable thing the moment the contrary disagreeable thing has become agreeable to him. For example, the conditions of the spell on a prince changed into a bear cease to exist as soon as the bear is loved for its own sake. Perhaps a like transformation would take place if a man could become fond of the evil in the world. The moment he could bring himself to cherish illness or suffering, he would hold in his embrace the most charming delight, the most voluptuous positive pleasure would pervade his being."

This view, as daring and paradoxical as profound, displays a very deep trait of our psychic make-up. Novalis here touches upon a truth, an obscure yet verifiable truth, of human life. And this is the truth revealed in the Indian tale of the king and the corpse. A decisive triumph on the inner battlefield of the soul bestows an essential and thoroughgoing metamorphosis. The king takes upon himself both the specter and the corpse; he shoulders the twofold burden. And he shoulders thereby the apparently endless task of solving the riddle questions put to him by this dual phantom of his inner night. Accepting them, he has paid them their due heed; and they are transformed for him into a sacred image and a savior. The moment they change for him, he too is changed. Even the darkness around him is transformed into a dawn, glowing with light from the Light of the World.

The landscape in this story undergoes three radical transformations, in reflection of the spiritual states of the king. For we are, each of us, our own world: the world we know flows out from us, faces round at us, and shines back upon us from without. The pompous throne hall of the king, and all that went on there, was a reflection of the kingly consciousness, the weakness, blindness, and apathy of the self-complacent ego. The dark burial ground was the rotten core of this brilliant shell. Just as the murderous magician was the true core of the sanctimonious ascetic, "Rich in Patience," so was this night the core of delusive day. It was a night through which the king was forced to grope and falter. There was here none of his fine assurance. Spellbound, life-threatened, faltering back and forth, he was blundering unsuspectingly toward a treacherous death. But all the fell threats and apparitions dissolve at the glorious break of the New Day: the day of the dawn of the superworld of the Highest God.

Change yourself (that is the lesson), and you inhabit a renovated world. Whether stately in the room of splendor, tortured among the ghosts and corpses of one's past, or communing with

231

the supreme powers of existence, one never goes even a step beyond the pale of one's own circumference and self. The world and all the worlds up to the heavens and down to hell are but ourselves: spheres, externalized, of our own being; productions. outbursts, of the creative, all-powerful Māyā that brings about our existence-form and holds us spellbound within the precincts of our life. The king's way leads from royal earthly pomp, through the realms of death, to the summit of glory. The empty attitude of kingly splendor—brittle and doomed—contained within itself the seed of death; but the way of death is itself the way of initiation. The fiends of the grave reach out with a ghostly grip at the throat, and the life forfeited to death is broken on the rack; nevertheless the end is life reborn, with exemption from death forever, self-entirety and consecration.

Who among us, then, is the prince elect, graced by fate, of whom the fairy damsels sing:

> "Were I to yield my thought to love,
> This youth alone should move my heart";

and to whom among us does the "Queen of Night," clad in her starry mantle of the firmament, present the Magic Flute that conquers the wrath of fire and water, and banishes all peril? Who—like Tamino, as described by Sarastro—is "rich in virtue, discreet and charitable"? Who "wishes to draw the veil of darkening night from his eyes and look upon the shrine of supreme light"? Or, who among us is worthy to be welcomed by the high priest of Isis and Osiris in the temple halls—the mystagogue who by divine right wears upon his breast the radiant Sevenfold Solar Circle of the One Who Knows?

In this magnificent fairy tale of the twenty-five stories of the king and the specter in the corpse, the king's way of transformation carried him out of the world of mere semblance into the reality of his kingly being. He learned to integrate into his life

232

what he had hitherto ignored. He confronted and gave satisfaction to the whole of life's claim upon him. And, as a consequence, whereas he had formerly only worn the diadem, while sitting upon life's throne enjoying the privileges of royalty, he now merited it. He had become the authentic king, the all-penetrating eye of wisdom, the administrator and true representative of the power of justice. That is why he was given the sword "Invincible," the counterpart of the Arthurian "Excalibur" of the Lake.

4

The supreme revelation, which brought to a climax the initiations of this mysterious, horizon-breaking night, was the one that the king received when Shiva, the Supreme God, lifted for him the veil of ignorance. He was shown that he was of a higher nature than he had supposed. A spark of the empyrean fire had descended to earth and become incarnate in him, so that he was an "avatar," a manifestation in space and time of Infinite and Immortal Being. After he had enjoyed his period on earth, he would proceed to dominion over the realms of the gods, and in the end return to that supreme fire-source of life and power from which he was originally sprung; for though of human form, he was in essence divine, and he was, therefore, beyond all human bondage. Shiva, the Lord of the Cosmos, abided in him. In his ultimate deep he was eternally one with the Supreme. This is the truth of truth. This is the interior, ultimate, most intimate fact, which centers and gives both beginning and end to all the other facts of the king's existence and experience of existence. The brilliant jewel of price within the fruit of the body —enveloped in the enclosing sheaths of the flesh, feelings, reasoning faculty, and power of understanding—is the identity of the essence of mortal life with Immortal Being.

233

Shiva is the Lord of Destruction: lord of the disintegration of the pulp of the fruit, and the revelation of the imperishable seed. Shiva is the Lord of Creation: lord of the manifestation within the frame of space and time of the power, majesty, and serenity of the Transcendental. Shiva is the Master of Yoga: the master of meditation, self-recollection, and the discriminating eye; his sword cuts through the veils of life, through the disguises of the mystagogue, the false appearances of Māyā, to the Quick of Being. Shiva is King of the Dance: the worlds of action and event are the flashes of his flying limbs, as, in an ecstasy of self-delight, he dances the cruel, ruthless, delirious and sublime dance of the universe.

And the human king is an avatar, an incarnation, or coming-into-visible form, of the essence of this god. The two are separate—apparently—in space; the king is limited in stature, the god unlimited; the king is mortal in his existence-form, the god immortal; the king is bounded in knowledge, the god unbounded; the king is human in his character, the god divine. Nevertheless, the space that separates the two is itself only the illusion prerequisite to the ephemeral spectacle of creation. Beyond it there is no place for twoness. The mortal and the god, the knower and the known, the worshiper and the sacred image, then are one.

Like the king, we must become masters over the terrible world of the spirits, for they are within us as well as without. Everything outside ourselves, whether we know it in its proper relationship to us, or whether it remains for us apparently without significance and unrelated to our mind and heart, actually reflects and mirrors our inner selves. This we are meant to learn. And we are meant to approach through this way of learning to the ultimate, the last and highest possible realization—the realization vouchsafed, in the end, to the king: that of our own divine identity with the substance, the consciousness, and the bliss that we know as "God." This is the realization of the absolute nature of the Self. This is the discovery of the jewel at the core. This is the last experience in the long course of initiation-integration. And with it there comes the immediate knowledge that we—not only we, but all the "thou's," also, of our surrounding night and day—are so many avatars, disguises, masks, and playful self-duplications of the Self of the world.

This is the awakening to joy.

But the king, with the fulfillment of his enlightenment, did not immediately give up the prison of his flesh. On the contrary, he returned to the worldly throne within the palace of the kingly "I." Conn-eda, similarly, hero of the Irish tale, after becoming a member of the Fairy Realm, returned to his appointed role on earth. The prince, through his initiation, was made potent to govern wisely among men; likewise this Hindu king. Through knowing himself as an incarnation of the immortal—light of the supreme, spark or beam from the celestial, central, life-giving solar fire of the universe—he was made bearer among mankind of the sword "Invincible." And the two heroes were set at peace with respect to the transiency of the forms of the phenomenal world; for though the bodies, the disguises, the masks, and costumes of the spectacle, may come and go, appear on the scene, remain but a moment, and vanish forever, yet the Self, the adamantine core and seed of their being, was never born—nor will it die.

PART II

FOUR EPISODES FROM THE
ROMANCE OF THE GODDESS

I. THE INVOLUNTARY CREATION

THE involvement of the gods in the web of their own creation, so that they become, like Abu Kasem, the harried victims of their creatures, entangled in nets of not quite voluntary self-manifestation, and then mocked by the knowing laughter of their own externally reflected inner judge: this is the miracle of the universe. This is the tragicomic romance of the world. The gods, the fairy powers, are always in danger of self-enchantment. Like the self-hoarding merchant of the Bagdad bazaars, like the youth Narcissus, they become fixed to their own reflected images —momentarily reluctant to pass with the passing of time, and critically in need of the shocking, shattering blow of the redemptive catastrophe. Man is the little world creator; God, the great. Each, surrounded by the figments of his own mirrored depths, knows and suffers the cosmic self-torment. And the fatal power that enchants them both is ever the great goddess, Māyā, self-delusion, the supreme creatrix of all the worlds.

In the popular myths of India, three pre-eminent masculine personifications of the Godhead hold sway over the universe: Vishnu, Shiva, and Brahmā. The first, reposing in a transmundane yet world-embracing solitude, sustains the whole course of the history of the world, ensures its continuance, and periodically descends into its turmoil, as savior and deliverer, to re-establish justice and order. The second, in contrast, is the

239

divine in the state of absolutely withdrawn immobility. With his gaze turned inward and absorbed in the perfect void of his own being, he restrains his consciousness from the perpetual confusion of the world spectacle, declining to regard this self-engendering, self-entangled round of delight and anguish until the moment comes for him to dissolve it. And Brahmā is the creative countenance of the divine whole. In exalted labor he unfolds the play of the world out of the interior heat of his self-absorbed contemplation.

Brahmā

Vishnu can be regarded as the aspect that embraces the totality, tranquilly sustaining everything within himself, as a peaceful slumberer sustains the breathtaking incidents of a dream; while the other two divine figures then denote the opposed dramatic moments of dissolution and creation. Yet all three, since they are but aspects or manifestations of a single Unfathomable, are themselves finally the productions of Māyā—in substance one, yet in form and functions three, by virtue of the mirror trick that breaks the All into the Many. Māyā is the Mother. Māyā is the charm by which life is forever seducing itself. Māyā is the womb, the nourishing bosom, and the tomb.

A Hindu biography of this great Mother, Weaver of the World, is supplied by the *Kālikā Purāna,* a comparatively late document of the Indian tradition. The term *purāna* means "ancient teachings and tales handed on from immemorial times." There are many Purānas. They are sacred books, composed of materials that have floated down the broad and powerful stream of Indian wisdom from the early centuries of the Vedic singers and seers —hoary myths and oracular teachings brought into the river-flow from many tributaries. They are loaded with every sort of popular lore. And all begin by treating of the inexhaustible problem of the creation, though in various ways, from various points of view, and with various manifestations of the meaning. The title of the *Kālikā Purāna* is derived from Kāli, "The Dark Lady,"

240

India's supreme manifestation of the Mother Goddess. She is distinctly its dominant divinity. The compendious work unveils in its opening chapters a version of the creation and first days of the universe which, to anyone familiar with the general trend of the Hindu tradition, will come as something of a surprise.[1]

The Creator, Brahmā, the demiurgic, world-producing aspect of the Godhead, sat in serene meditation, bringing forth, from the enlivened depths of his own divine and all-containing substance, the universe and its multitudes of beings. A number of apparitions had already sprung into the sphere of time and space out of the abyss of his yogic state, crystal pure visions suddenly precipitated into embodied form. And these were disposed around him in a serene circle, as he continued in his creative trance. The group of his ten mind-born sons surrounded him—those supernatural priests and seers who were to become, later on, the ancestors of the holy Brahmins. And besides these, the "Lords of Creatures" stood there, ten lesser duplicates of himself, who were to assist in the later stages of creation and then supervise the natural processes of the cosmos. Brahmā, sinking still further into the limpid darkness of his own interior, struck a new depth: suddenly the most beautiful dark woman sprang from his vision, and stood naked before everyone's gaze.

She was Dawn, and she was radiant with vivid youth. Nothing like her had yet appeared among the gods; nor would her equal ever be seen, either among men, or in the depths of the waters in the jeweled palaces of the serpent queens and kings. The billows of her blue-black hair were glistening like the feathers of a peacock, and her clearly curving, dark brows formed a bow

[1] Curiously enough, though the Sanskrit text of the *Kālikā Purāna* was made accessible in 1892 by the Shrīvenkateshvaram Press (Gangāvishnu Khemarāja), published in Bombay from earlier manuscripts, it has failed, hitherto, to attract the notice of the Western scholars. The following pages present what is, apparently, the first published translation of this text in any European tongue. [Dr. Zimmer's manuscripts for the translation are in German.—J.C.]

fit for the God of Love. Her eyes, like dark lotus calyxes, had the alert, questioning glance of the frightened gazelle; and her face, round as the moon, was like a purple lotus blossom. Her swelling breasts with their two dark points were enough to infatuate a saint. Trim as the shaft of a lance stood her body, and her smooth legs were like the stretched-out trunks of elephants. She was glowing with little delicate pearls of perspiration. And when she found herself in the midst of her startled audience, she stared about at them, in uncertainty, then broke into a softly rippling laugh.

Brahmā became aware of her, arose from his yogic posture, and fastened on her a long and earnest gaze. Then, with his physical eyes still fixed upon her, the Creator permitted his spiritual vision to fall back again into his own profundity; and he searched to know—as did, also, the ten mind-born sons and the ten guardians of the ages, the "Lords of Creatures"—what the task of this apparition would be in the further unfoldment of the work of creation, and to whom she would belong.

When lo! a second surprise: out of Brahmā's inner search sprang another being—this time a youth, splendid, dark, and strong. His limbs were powerful and beautifully formed. His heroic chest, with its great pectoral muscles, was like a panel of mahogany; his hips were neat and trim; his sensitive brows came together at the bridge of his nose. He gave forth an aroma of blossoms, and he was like an elephant stung with vehement desire. In one hand he bore a banner emblazoned with a fish. The other hand swung a flowery bow and five flowered arrows. Thoughtful astonishment filled the ten mind-born sons and the ten world guardians when they saw him. Desire began to creep into them. Each felt himself beginning to be moved with a secret, burning longing to possess the woman. So it was that desire first made its way into the world.

The new arrival, charming and not the least bit shy, turned

242

his handsome face to Brahmā, bowed and inquired: "What am I to do? Please instruct me. A being flourishes only when performing the work for which he is designed. Assign to me an appropriate name. Give me an abode, and, since you are the creator of all things, a wife."

Brahmā remained silent for a moment, astounded by his own production. What had slipped from him? What was this? Then he gathered and constrained his consciousness, and brought his mind again to center. Surprise was conquered. Again in mastery, the World Creator addressed his remarkable creature and assigned to him his field.

"You will go wandering about the earth," he said, "striking bewilderment into men and women with your flower-bow and shafts, and in this way bring to pass the continuous creation of the world. No god, no heavenly spirit, demon or evil spirit, serpent-divinity or nature sprite, neither man nor beast, neither the flying nor the swimming creatures, shall be inaccessible to your aim. And I myself, as well as all-pervading Vishnu, even Shiva, the rocklike immovable ascetic, steeped in his meditation, We Three, shall be given into your power—not to speak of other breathing existences. You shall drive, impalpable, to the heart, and arouse there delight, in this way provoking the ever-renewed creation of the living world. For the heart is to be the target of your bow; and your arrows are to carry joy and intoxication to all breathing beings. This, then, is your task. It will perpetuate the moment of the world creation. Receive now, O Highest Being, the name that befits you."

Brahmā, turning to his ten mind-born sons, ceased in his speaking and resumed his sitting posture on the lotus. The ten read his countenance and understood. They knew, were unanimous in their knowledge, and spoke. "Since you churned the spirit of the Creator into excitement as you arose, you shall be known in the world as 'The Churner of the Spirit'; and your

243

name shall be 'The Desire of Love,' because your form awakens loving desire; you are to be called 'The Intoxicator,' since you suffuse intoxication."

Then the "Lords of Creatures" assigned to him an abode and a wife. "Greater than the power of the arrows of Vishnu, Shiva, and Brahmā," they recited, "are the arrows of your flower-bow. Heaven and earth, the profundities of the abyss, and Brahmā's empyrean shall be your abode: you are the All-Pervader. Wherever breathing creatures, trees, or meadows shall exist, even to Brahmā's throne at the zenith,[1] you shall abide. And Lord Daksha, the primary 'Lord of Creatures,' will bestow upon you the wife of your desire." Thus they offered their pronouncement and in silence then turned, with a respectful bow, to Brahmā's countenance.

Brahmā is the divine original consciousness of everything contained in the universe; hence he is capable of speaking only truth. Even when truth demands of him that he should point to himself as one of the victims of the God of Love, he does so without hesitation or constraint. He is sheer light, the light of the spirit—not a being of semihuman kind, like the Homeric divinities of Olympus, who fear risks and take prudent precautions. Brahmā is all divine, a personification of the creative light of consciousness, and remains so, even when overwhelmed by desire for the divine woman, who is the incarnation of irresistible charm.

Similarly "Desire," Kāma, the God of Love, is a sheer, directly operative force, heedless of possible consequences. Having heard the words of Brahmā, the ten mind-born sons, and the ten guardians, he lifted his flower-bow, which is set like the eyebrows of a beautiful woman, and made ready his five flower-shafts, which are named respectively, "The Exciter of the Paroxysm of Desire," "The Inflamer," "The Infatuater," "The Parcher," and "The

[1] Brahmaloka; cf. *supra*, p. 83, footnote 2.

Carrier of Death." Then he made himself invisible. "Right here, and without a moment's delay," he thought, "I will prove upon these holy ones, and upon the Creator himself, the supernal power that Brahmā has assigned to me. Here they all stand, and here is this magnificent woman, Dawn; they shall be made—every one—the victims of my weapon. For has not Brahmā himself just declared to me: 'I, and Vishnu, and even Shiva shall be given into the power of your shafts?' Why then should I wait for other targets? What Brahmā has made known, I will bring to pass."

Having decided, he assumed the stance of an archer, notched a flower-arrow to the flower-string, and drew the great curve of the bow. Then there began to blow intoxicating breezes, heavy with the scents of spring flowers; and these disseminated rapture. From the Creator to the last of his mind-born sons, the gods then were set mad, one after another, by the shots of the disorderer, their temperaments undergoing immediately a magnitudinous change. They continued to stare at Dawn, the woman, but with altered eyes, and the spell of love increased in them. The beauty itself of the young female only worked to continue and to heighten the precipitated intoxication. They were all set wild together, and their senses thickened with lust. Indeed, the entrancement was so strong that when the Creator's pure mind apprehended his daughter through this aggravated ambient, his awakened susceptibilities and compulsions directly opened themselves, with all their gestures and spontaneous physical manifestations, for the world to see. And in the meanwhile, the woman was exhibiting, for the first time in the long romance of the universe, the signals of her own agitation. Affectations of shyness were alternating provokingly in the dim dawn light of this morning of the world with overt efforts to stimulate amorous admiration. Struck profoundly by the arrow of the God of Love, she stood and quaked before all the eyes there gazing with growing desire upon her body—now in shame hiding her face in her arms, but now lifting the eyes again to flash glances. And a shudder of emotional tumult ran over her, like the ripple of waves along the course of the divine river Ganges. Brahmā, beholding her performance, broke into a steam; desire for her conquered him entirely. And the ten mind-born sons, as well as the ten "Lords of Creatures," were raked within. Thus it came to pass that emotions were brought into the world, together with their appropriate gestures and natural signs.

The God of Love took note of everything, and was satisfied that his gift of power was adequate to his mission. "I can accomplish the work that Brahmā has assigned to me," he decided; and a wonderful satisfaction with himself pervaded his being.

But still another great surprise was to break upon the company. While the love spell had been holding the Creator, the Goddess, and the whole assemblage in its thrall, and the Love God had been congratulating himself on the efficaciousness of his power, Shiva, the sequestered and remote arch-ascetic of the gods, had been aroused, unbeknown, from the quietude of his self-absorption. Seated still in his yoga posture, he came drifting through the regions of the air. And when he drew near to the place of the love constellation and beheld the predicament of Brahmā and his flock, he simply burst into a peal of contemptuous, echoing laughter. Again and again he laughed, and, as though this were not enough, shouted out derisively: "Well, well! Well, well!" Then he put them all to shame with a rebuke: "Brahmā, just what is going on here? What has brought you to this pretty pass? The sight of your own daughter? But it hardly becomes the Creator to disregard the precepts of the Vedas: 'The sister shall be as the mother, and the daughter as the sister!' That is what the Vedas declare—the laws revealed by your own mouth; and have you forgotten all this, in an excess of desire? Brahmā, the universe is founded on constancy. How can you lose your balance in this way, merely because of a miserable desire? And all these fine yogīs, your mind-born sons and the 'Lords of Creatures,' the holy ones who are capable of beholding the Godhead itself without derangement of their faculties, have they too been overwhelmed by the sight of a female? How did the God of Love ever do this to you all, indolent and destitute of discernment as he is? A curse on him through whose power the beauty of woman is made to purloin integrity, and the spirit is delivered to the billows of desire!"

When Brahmā heard these words, his mind immediately split in two: on the one hand, his original nature again asserted itself, but on the other, the person overcome by concupiscence remained. Waves of heat streamed down his limbs. A longing to possess the incarnation of his desire groaned in him, yet he conquered this passionate modification of his character, and let the image of the woman go. At which moment, a burst of perspiration broke over his entire body, for the desire could not be destroyed, even though expelled. And from these drops then were born the so-called "Spirits of the Departed."

The Spirits of the Departed were to become the progenitors of the human race, the ancestral presences who devour the offerings made to the dead. They sit on straw. Their bodies are as black as eyelash dye, and their eyes like dark-blue lotuses. They are the Fathers, whose fleshly forms are destroyed in the pyres of the cremation ground. Yet, they remain, longing for funerary offerings, because without these and the filial worship of their descendants they would fall out of existence altogether, suffering the second death, forfeiting even the pitiful shadow semblance of a fleshly life to which they so tenaciously cling. Their longing is for mere maintenance; yet their birth, out of the drops of the perspiration shed by Brahmā when he crushed his desire, denotes that though this longing is the meanest and most humble manifestation of the universal urge for life, nevertheless, it is of

247

one substance with the mighty force that sends lovers to each other, brings the stallion to the mare, and inspires even the supramundane gods.

When the Creator, Brahmā, the Four-Headed One, was pressing his passion out through his pores, the other divinities were striving to reclarify their senses too. From Daksha, the Dexterous One, the oldest of the "Lords of Creatures," perspiration streamed to the ground, and from it arose a splendid woman, gleaming like burnished gold, radiating beatitude, and with slender limbs. Six of the mind-born sons of Brahmā succeeded in mastering the play of their senses without event, but from the others perspiration poured; and this changed into further varieties of ancestral presences: those, so-called, "who died when their hour came," and those "who eat the offerings." With them, the whole range of created creatures, deriving from Brahmā and filling out the world, was made complete. Properly speaking, it was by the love-shot woman, Dawn, that they had been called to life, and their production had been without premeditation. By an involuntary process, creation had been pressed another step, and the whole range of beings predestined to fill the world had been made complete by the addition of a host of creatures hitherto unthought of—the host of the dead. Their number is greater than the number of the living. They are "the great majority."

Brahmā was cleansed of his lust, but the sting of Shiva's words had made him angry. His brows contracted, and the irritation was projected against the divinity of the bow. ·Swift to comprehend, and in awe both of Brahmā and of Shiva, the blithe young god quickly set aside his arrows. Brahmā, however, was already cursing him in a voice made terrible by a profundity of wrath. "Since the God of Love, with his flower-arrows, has disgraced me before your eyes, O Shiva," Brahmā said, "let him reap the consequences of his act. When his excessive spirits shall one day increase to such monstrous proportions that he lets loose a shaft at you, penetrating your impenetrable calm, he shall be blasted to ashes by a glance of your middle eye."

At a critical moment in a later chapter of the world romance this curse was actually to be brought to pass, precipitating further surprises in the development of the unpredictable plot; but for the present it remained only a terrible threat. The God of Love was in no mood to test it. Execrated by the Creator himself, and before Shiva, the flood of whose hair is the broad expanse of the ether, he was really frightened; and, in order to master the situation, he made himself visible again. "Why do you curse me," he protested, "with such a curse? Is it not true that anyone who follows your divine ordinance is innocent of guilt? All I have done is what you declared was my proper work. You announced that You, and Vishnu, and Shiva, were to be victims of my bow; I only proved your words. You cannot justly blame me. Therefore, mitigate your terrible curse."

The Creator was moved to mercy. "The maiden, Dawn, is my daughter," he explained. "I have cursed you because you chose me for your target while I was in her presence. Now my anger has burned itself out and I shall tell you how your curse is to end. Shiva's eye will convert you to ash with a lightning glance; but you shall acquire another body when Shiva, the arch-ascetic, takes to himself a wife." Brahmā vanished from before all eyes. Simultaneously, Shiva, quick as the wind, went back to his place of meditation. Daksha pointed to the splendid woman who had sprung from the sweat of his own access of emotion, and bestowed her upon the young God of Love to be his mate. Then he told the first husband in the world his woman's name; her name was Rati, "Delight."

Luminous, she was, as the lightning; and her eyes were those of the timid gazelle. The God of Love beheld the arch of her brows, and in a moment of uncertainty he asked himself: "Did the Creator place my bow, 'Exciter of Madness,' above her eyes?"

249

Then he perceived that her movements were quick and her glances penetrating, and he no longer thought his own arrows very swift or keen. The sweetness of her breath took from him his belief in the power of the perfume-laden spring breezes of the south, which arouse in the heart the yearning for love. And her breasts projected like a pair of golden lotus buds; the dark points were two blue-black beetles perching upon them. From midway between, beginning imperceptibly and forming a thin line down to the navel, ran a luster of delicate hairs that made the god remember the string of his bow, which was composed of a row of sharply buzzing insects. Her legs were as trim as the shaft of his lance. "What!" thought he. "Is she dazzling me with my own weapons?"

Riddled, thus, with the fire of his own arrows, senses beguiled, he forgot the terrible curse that Brahmā had laid upon him. "With this woman as my consort," he said to Daksha, "this woman whose form is totally entrancing, I should be able to infatuate Shiva himself, the paragon of composure—not to speak of all the other creatures of the world. Wherever my bow is bent to a target, this Māyā, this 'Illusion'—called 'Woman,' or 'The Ravisher'—will disclose her beautiful countenance. And whether I mount to the abiding places of the gods, descend to the earth, or go down into the ultimate abysses of the underworld, everywhere and forever this softly smiling one will be with me. She shall be my companion, holding sway over all the creatures of the universe—just as Lakshmī, the Lotus Queen, is inseparable from Vishnu, and as the golden lightning-serpent is bound to the being of the cloud."

The Love God took to himself the Goddess—as Vishnu drew to himself the beautiful Lakshmī, when she first emerged from the waters of the Cosmic Ocean. Joined with her, he shone like an evening cloud low on the horizon and blazing with the light of the sun. Precisely as a yogī draws to himself the potency of his knowledge, so the young God of Love, full of exalted joy, took Rati to his breast; and she was joyful in the powerful embrace of his magnificent love.

And so it is that creation proceeds, according to this remarkable myth: by surprises, involuntary acts, and abrupt reversals. The creation of the world is not an accomplished work, completed within a certain span of time (say, seven days), but a process continuing throughout the course of history, refashioning the universe without cease, and pressing it on, every moment afresh. Like the human body, the cosmos is in part built up anew, every night, every day; by a process of unending regeneration it remains alive. But the manner of its growth is by abrupt occurrences, crises, surprising events and even mortifying accidents. Everything is forever going wrong; and yet, that is precisely the circumstance by which the miraculous development comes to pass. The great entirety jolts from crisis to crisis; that is the precarious, hair-raising manner of self-transport by which it moves.

The interpretation of the world process as a continual crisis would have been rejected by the last generation as an unwarranted and pessimistic view of life; the state of world affairs, however, almost forces such a conception on our minds today. Calamity is the normal circumstance, supporting both our struggle for order and our heartening illusion of a possible ultimate security. "This was sometimes a paradox, but now the time gives it proof." Yet the Hindu myth could not be said to be pessimistic. On the contrary, though presenting its uninterrupted series of critical and mortifying junctures as a matter of course, the myth, in its way, is vastly optimistic. Brahmā, in his all-inclusive knowledge, must have been aware of the risk that he was taking when he apprised the Love God of the power of the flower-bow, letting him know that it was capable of overwhelming even Shiva, Vishnu, and himself, the World Creator. Nevertheless, he was

251

absolutely outspoken. He could not have been otherwise, for qualifications were not in his character. Truth is the Creator's very being. Brahmā (Transcendental Reality and Truth Incarnate) was, therefore, true not only to truth but to himself when he made known the dangerous secret of the bow. Desire and humiliation might redound upon him as the unpremeditated consequences of the revelation, yet the possibility of such eventualities was not enough to restrain him; for, just as unpremeditatedly, something would occur to bring him rescue. That is to say, there is some secret safety even in the disorderliness of natural occurrence, some hidden power that creates surprising balances which keep the car of destiny from being finally overturned or smashed. Throughout all the pommeling that they suffer while creating the world and sustaining it through its ever self-renewed re-creation, the divine forces remain always true to their essential nature. That is why they are never ultimately frustrated by the startling, puzzling, and breath-taking violence of events.

As personified in the divinities of the Hindu myths who exhibit their manner of operation, the powers that shape the world are represented as relying on their wits and as being fair losers when their time comes, always trusting that the unexpected, which for the moment seems to be setting them at a loss, presently will come to their rescue and put its weight in the other balance of the scale. But, though ultimately they are to be rescued, meanwhile they are subjected to the most arduous tests and charged with excruciatingly difficult tasks, compelled to endure the most startling realizations about themselves, even to suffer the shattering of their cherished personalities and sacrifices of their visible bodies; or they are forced to take on tasks hitherto unfamiliar to them, some, even, that would seem to be totally at variance with their universal role. Brahmā, for example, is required to realize and admit that he is not wholly what he at first imagined himself to be, namely, divine and universal insight, clear as

252

crystal, pure spiritual force of vision, and all-pervading wisdom. In fact, the power out of which he shapes the world, and which becomes projected from himself, is quite the opposite. Suddenly it reveals itself to be the bedazzling charm of sex, libido incarnate in the enticing form of Woman. Brahmā is made conscious, thus, of his own profound, utter surrender to the blind force that propagates existence and that makes mock of the pure spirit steeped in quiescent meditation. The god accepts this revelation, this surprising fact concerning the nature of his own being, this part of himself, unforeseen, which arises out of his own depth. He is reconciled with the God of Love. And, though that divinity too must suffer harrowing consequences, even death —whereas he had thought himself entirely life—nevertheless, he, as well as Brahmā, is to be restored.

The ironical interdependencies of the powers, and the surprising paradoxes of their effects both upon each other and upon themselves, come to a vivid statement in the immediately subsequent adventure of the romance. Though reconciled with the Love God, Brahmā was still burning under the sting of Shiva's righteousness. Brahmā had disappeared from view, but, even so, the spiritual sore could rankle. "Before the holy ones, my sons, Shiva reviled me when he beheld me filled with desire for the woman," Brahmā mused. "But is Shiva himself so far above such desire that it would be impossible to create a woman who could move him? What woman image is his spirit holding in its depth —the one female to teach him disdain for his yoga, to work confusion upon him, and to become his bride? Who can she be, when not even the God of Love can upset his equilibrium? The word 'woman' is incompatible with his immeasurable yoga, and yet— how is the world to go forward in its development, come to fulfillment, and move along to the dissolution that no one but Shiva himself can bring to pass, unless he takes to himself a consort? Certain of the great ones of the earth are to be slain by my hand, certain by the powers of Vishnu; many, however, by the act of Shiva. Should he remain aloof and free from every passion, he would be fit for no work whatsoever, except his yoga."

Brahmā, musing in this fashion, gazed down from his zenith to the earth, where Daksha and the others still were standing, and there he could see the young God of Love, joyfully united with the beautiful and blissful Rati. Brahmā descended to the lower sphere, let himself become visible again, turned to the passionate couple, and addressed himself ingratiatingly to the god.

"How you beam, united with your consort, and how she, too, together with you! Like the moon and the night, like the night and the moon, is your luminous union. Magnified in this union, you are to be the standard-bearer of all the worlds and of all beings. For the good, therefore, of the whole universe, go now to Shiva and set him frantic with desire, so that he may take to himself a wife and find in her his bliss. Go and unsettle him, render him infatuate, in the verdant wilderness, among the mountain crags and the cascades, where he lives alone. No one but you can do it. Renouncing women, he has won the mastery over self. Yet if the mood to love should ever awaken within him, he would permit the inclination to grow. And then the curse that is upon you would end."

The Love God replied: "As you command! I will go to Shiva, and he shall be troubled with desire. But the principal weapon is woman; create me a woman that will interest Shiva, once I have aroused him. Though I may quicken in the god a maddening longing, nowhere do I behold the female so ravishing as to consummate the enchantment. Produce her whom we need."

Then the patriarch of the Cosmos, Brahmā, thinking to himself: "I will create the ensorcelling She," lapsed again into his own interior and sank into another state of productive trance. It was, however, not a goddess, but a youth who was condensed from the breath that came streaming from his nostrils—the youth called "Spring," and to the accompaniment of a blossom-laden wind. Bees buzzed around him. He was bedecked with burgeoning mango shoots and with lotus buds. He was majestic. His face was radiant as the moon, his hair blue-black as night, his physique was sumptuous and powerful, his hands were ruthless. And the moment his form had sprung into the light, like a burst of blossoms, fragrant winds blew in all directions, all the trees broke into bloom, the ponds and lakes became appareled in lotuses, and the birds began to sing.

Brahmā, becoming aware of the new presence, regarded him with a feeling of good will, and spoke in a friendly way to his earlier son, the God of Love. "He shall be your friend and companion forever, and, like you, shall throw the world into a state of passion. With him go these two others, South Wind, perfume-laden, and Amorous Mood. With Rati are to go all the Gestures of Love, Provoking Coolness, Involuntary Allure, and the rest, and they are at your command. With this little army you will overcome the Great God, and by that victory bring about the continuous creation of the world. Go where you will. And I, meanwhile, shall plunge again and summon the woman to life who is to consummate the work of your enchantment."

The eldest of the gods having spoken, the God of Love, together with his little army of assistants, bowed respectfully and departed to scout for Shiva; but Brahmā, in some anxiety, took counsel with Daksha and the other "Lords of Creatures," and with his ten mind-born sons. "Who," he asked, "can Shiva's future consort possibly be? What possible woman will ever wile him out of the profundities of his absorption?" Then he lapsed into thought, and after a time concluded: "Dawn! No other! Dawn! Māyā: the World-Illusion of Vishnu himself, who supports both me and the cosmos! She is the motive principle of the universe.

255

She is the one who will beguile him. She it is who is the intoxication even of the deepest vision of yoga. She is the genetrix of all being. Daksha, you must go and with proper offerings and gifts persuade the blessed All-Mother to consent, first to be born as your daughter, and then to become Shiva's bride."

Daksha recognized the wisdom of the decision, and was ready to play his role. He betook himself to the other shore of the divine Milky Ocean, the infinite and immortal sea of Vishnu's bliss—that timeless water upon which the supreme god, Vishnu, sleeps and dreams the dream of the world. And there he made himself ready to bring offerings to the goddess who is the sum and substance of Vishnu's dream. First he fixed her image in his mind and heart. Then he settled down to a period of protracted and severe ascesis, in order to generate and concentrate the spiritual heat that should make it possible for him to animate the image and behold the goddess bodily before his eyes. For thirty-six thousand years, and three thousand years besides, he remained there, in prodigious concentration, absolutely one-pointed, building heat around his vision of the goddess, and into it; but nourishing his own body, meanwhile, on only water, leaves, and air. Completely wrapt, he sat through the long millenniums of the first miraculous ages of the dawn of the world.

In this myth, the unexpected constitutes the form-building principle of the plot.

The Creator, whose spirit is properly a crystalline sea of contemplation (a divine mirror, perfectly still, not the slightest breath of creaturely impulse stirring its surface), becomes suddenly turbulent with desire. All the moods of feeling abruptly well up out of him—simultaneously with their compulsive physical expressions on the surface of the body; and these round out the fullness of the world he is creating—but in a manner that he did not foresee. They give the jolt that starts into motion the wild romance of his involuntary creation.

Not Brahmā, apparently, but a beautiful and amazing young lord of blind impassioned impulse—the God of Love—Brahmā's production, yet a distinct shock to him—holds mastery over every being, even over the Supreme Being from whom he sprang. Can it be that he is the incarnation of the productive energy of that being? Was he the power secretly at work in him all the time, while the Creator, according to the eternal plan, was bringing forth the world as a mirror reflection of the contents of his own interior? [1] But then why has the youth appeared as an adversary? Simply—as Brahmā himself immediately conceives—to bring about, by means of the interaction of the sexes, the continuation of the creation of the world?

The God of Love would have been powerless (indeed, would never have broken into the light) had it not been for the divine woman who just preceded him—Dawn, the first bloom of the universal day. She was the beginning of the Involuntary Creation. She was the first surprise. Can it be then that she, not the youth, is the visible form of the productive energy of the God, the power he serves, the power that sustains him during his work of creation? Variously beckoning, scintillating seductress, she is the primal power of existence, the world-tholing mother, from whom everything is born. The mere sight of her, and Brahmā unknots himself automatically from his yoga posture, rouses from his concentrated equanimity, comes quivering to his feet, and, self-questioning, seeks the explanation of the enigma within. For where else should he find it, if not in his own crystalline, gloaming bottomlessness? The reply that he receives is the God of Love, the allure that attends the female form, the blind desire that knits all beings into her subtle web:

[1] [Kāma, the God of Love, is called the "first born" of the seeds of mind: *Rigveda* 10.129.4.—AKC.]

257

A quell' amor che è palpito
Dell' universo intero,
Misterioso, altero,
Croce e delizia al cor.[1]

Boundless infatuation, apparently, is the elementary manifestation of the only possible manner of relationship to the feminine form divine.

The projecting genius of Creative Wisdom has adventured, thus, hardly a moment beyond the bounds of its own ordered image, when it finds itself face to face with the reverse—unconsidered impulse under the spell of the beautiful image of femininity—the incorrigibly unintentional; the spontaneously charming; enchantment enchanted by the wonder of its own nature and the inevitability of its own allure, enchanting in turn all who conceive and are in the act of bringing forth. And this impulse cuts across the Creator's plans for the world, like a shuttle across the stretched-out threads of a loom. But this is the way the taut threads are to be woven into a cloth. The flying zigzag supplies the material and design. Continually driving across the projects of the plan-projecting spirit, it is to weave the world surprisingly. The interlacing of the two irreconcilables will constitute the basic warp and woof of the tapestry of all events.[2]

1 *La Traviata*, 1, 5.
2 Apparently the Creator Brahmā does not know the depths of his own being. Neither has he the naïve self-assurance of the Old-Testament World Creator, who separates, in the neatest order, light from darkness, dry land from water, and then brings forth in due progression vegetation and the animals: first, the fishes and birds, then the hippopotamuses, giraffes, and other quadrupeds, and, finally, as the crowning glory, man in his garden. On the seventh day Jehovah calls out: *Plaudite amici, comoedia finita*, and sits back well pleased with his work, only to discover soon enough, *incipit tragoedia*, everything is going wrong. The lonely Adam is bored in Paradise; and Eve then is bored with Adam in the Garden; only the Serpent brings a bit of stimulating society. But just how much of all this had been intended? Two trees—and, of course, it is the bad one from which the couple plucks the fruit. Things go from bad to worse; God Himself destroys His Paradise, and His anger is boundless, tempered only by a remote eschatological

The course of the world runs awry, but therewith it goes directly to its goal. The catastrophe of the previously unforeseen is what breaks the world progression forward, and the moment the catastrophe has come to pass it appears to be what was intended all the while. For it is creative in a deeper way than the planning creative spirit supposes. It transforms the situation, forces an alteration on the creative spirit, and throws it into a play that carries it beyond itself, carries it, that is to say, really and properly into play, and into a play that entrains the entirety of creation. The planner, the watcher, is compelled to become the endurer, the sufferer. Such a metamorphosis into the opposite, into the absolutely alien, is what throws the knots that reticulate the net of the living whole and mesh the individual alive into the fabric.

The alien element among the powers—already embodied with Brahmā and creatively effective within him, but resting and working deep in shadow, unsuspected and averted—suddenly bursts, unwanted, into the sphere of studied operations, there to dominate the scene. Yet the response of Brahmā—Wisdom—to this intoxicating force, which threatens to overwhelm him with dizzy blindness, remains magnificent; Wisdom has all the power of knowledge on its side. Wisdom announces to the impulse what it is and just what it can do, for the impulse is in this respect impotent. It knows nothing about itself, indeed is not yet itself; it is no more than an impulse to its own self-fulfillment. And it would be incapable of grasping and realizing this potential, were it not pointed out, and were a name not given to it that cir-

---

promise—the silver lining of the terrific cloud. Then He withdraws in a state of pique, only to burst back into His creation, with still further storms of wrath, every time it reveals some further fault of its inherent imperfection. Really, a grotesque old myth! full of human appeal, but nothing quite concords with, or follows from, anything else. Its discrepancies cost it, in the end, the respect of a considerable and rapidly multiplying unchurchly circle. But in the Hindu myth things are different—much more consistent.

cumscribed its power, a name that therewith initiated the power, the name by which it might be summoned and honored, addressed and adjured. Brahmā's wisdom assigns to the Love God his name, frankly lets him know what he must do to become effective from the very roots of his being, and does not take refuge, by the slightest defensive prevarication, from the might of this surprising birth. Fear, such as is felt by every creature, is unknown to Brahmā's wisdom. No defense goes up against the sorcery and the disgraceful decline into voluptuous enfeeblement that is to menace both himself and his whole creation. Brahmā's utterance neither cheats the other nor dictates bounds to him, for pure knowledge is intrinsically fearless. It is a white flame of light, a firm fire tongue that burns in perfect quietude, not quivered by any breath of wind. Wisdom is the light that enlightens itself and pours illumination round about into the crowding dark. Fear of the truth that he himself radiates and produces is incompatible with Brahmā's fundamental character, even as pity is incompatible with the nature of the bow-weaponed genius of desire, who can be prevented only by fear from loosing his flower-shafts at the Highest Being. Brahmā announces the whole truth, and can do nothing to hinder its fulfillment on himself and his world. He is able to extol the very force that is to set his own character in question and threaten it with annihilation. He is even able to bring that force to a consciousness of itself by virtue of his unprevaricating words, instead of limiting it with a decree. And this is the mark of Brahmā the Creator's greatness.

In this mythological situation the two great antagonistic principles, Wisdom and Desire, stand against each other in the full simplicity of their elemental inhumanity, not yet modified into such literary personages, mingled of godlike traits and human motives, as Zeus and Aphrodite of the Greek, Wotan and Freya of the Germanic systems. Each of the potencies is here rooted in itself, the ban of its own nature supplying both its unconditioned motive and its own set of narrowing bounds. Like primitive elements, they are remote from all the measures of common sense, political advantage, and divided interest, that govern the conduct of creatures compounded of these two principles, and in whom the unmitigated energies come to expression only through collision.

Brahmā, the Creator, broods the world of matter out of himself by spiritual means, by sinking into his own depth in a state of yogic meditation; but he cannot control or determine the apparitions that he then produces. They surprise, stun, and disconcert him. Nevertheless he faces them, and he holds his own against them by selflessly fathoming their depths; for those apparitions are, finally, the productions of his own substance, antagonistic and alien though they may appear—the woman standing there before him as an everlasting seduction to the continued generation and unfoldment of the world, and the God of Love, who is the incarnation of her spell. The two figures arouse their own train of effects—a wild horde of feelings and agitations, together with all the concomitant expressions of countenance, compulsions to gesture, and forms of carnal, spontaneous display.[1] Perhaps Brahmā had been thinking the world complete without these things; but he would not have been pure and selfless spirituality, all-suffusing clarity, had he not grasped immediately their significance for the continuance of the cosmic play, and made them cognizant of their own nature, their fields of action and laws of being. He is able to recognize in the totality (compounded though it is of contrarieties, but of

[1] Brahmā's yoga is the clarified spiritual form of the same desirousness that, in the denser, duller spheres of the world of nature, streams into expression through the generative urges of the animals and plants. The life power that moves all things is one, whether here in the bliss of desire-ridden lovers, or there in the crystalline vision of the saint and sage.

which he himself, unwittingly, is the creative primal ground and, involuntarily, the producer) a plenitude of elements richly significant in their mutual counteractions and destined inevitably to run the course of the world.

This involuntary creation opens unhindered in the direction of the future. It does not exist as a constellation of facts, arranged for all time according to certain fixed, interior laws. It lives on its own self-surprises. For Creation is a continuous process threading the permanence of the universe, accompanying the world action from beginning to end, impelling it with onsets ever new. Creation and Preservation are, therefore, not two distinct phases of the world biography, written each in its peculiar style. The brooding effort of the beginning, the surprise that abruptly cuts across it, and the meaning-bestowing understanding that links the unintended back into the plot by assigning it its proper place, are elements playing into the style of the whole continuity of the cosmic course, the cosmic "permanence," which is "continuous creation." Every couple smitten by the arrows of the Love God renews the "continuous creation of the world"; that is why the feelings of lovers, at certain moments, are so solemn, fervent, and deadly earnest. The everlasting beginning pulses throughout the forward-developing course.

But, on the other hand, the entire course is already present in the beginning: the divine woman and the God of Love are, from the first, impalpably alive in Brahmā's depth. They are, indeed, his creative power, and they stand tangibly before him to disturb the repose of his self-absorption only when precipitated into shape out of the crystalline world-lake of his yoga. Everything has been down there all the time; things only come to view, assume, and shift their forms. What had reposed within the God like a dream, self-enclosed and all-comprised, arises, steps into shapes, and variously confronts itself, to work effects upon itself. That is the continuous creation, that is the play of the world.

The spell of the Love God is broken by Shiva—with a laugh. This laughter of the great uncaptured one shatters the turgid silence of the world-generating powers caught in their impulse to beget. Shiva is the self-absorption of the transcendental principal, beyond all event and possibility of event. Averted from the world, he broods on his own sublimity; as the unagitated plenitude of the uncreated, which is the pristine Void, he gazes into motionless infinity, and, like a stone, rests in the contemplation of the interior sea of perfect stillness. Only for a moment does he disengage himself, when the creative powers in their plunge awry have become caught in a moment of excessive pressures; and having set things right, he again withdraws.

The really wonderful thing about Brahmā's power is that he can discover infinite meaning in every one of the forms and events that foam out of his depth—the Love God and his assault, the horde of feelings that overwhelm him and strip him of his majesty; even Shiva's scorn and rebuke he knows how to value. But he understands also that the dizziness that befell him must touch the great Solitary too, if the "continuous creation" is not to stagnate. He realizes that the highest task and function of the God of Love is to involve Shiva, the superbly isolated one, in the general round, the maddened dance that conquers all and weaves its patterns out of every god and creature. He finds it easy to win the divinity of the arrows to his great purpose: the young God of Love would have gone of his own volition, so intoxicated was he by the possession of his passionate goddess, Desire. But where—and this is now Brahmā's paramount problem —where will the woman be found to absorb and perpetuate Shiva's yearning, once it has been aroused?

II. THE INVOLUNTARY MARRIAGE

The old story goes on to say that while Daksha was sitting, strenuously meditating in the mountain crags beyond the Milky Ocean, glowing with interior heat, and subsisting only on water, leaves, and air, mighty Brahmā betook himself to the holy mountain Mandara, there settled likewise to the terrific task of one-pointed meditation, and for thirty-six thousand years remained in perfectly collected mindfulness, praising with potent syllables the nourishing Mother of the World. He called to her as the one whose quintessential being is both life-redeeming world-transcending enlightenment, and the world-beguiled life-tormenting ignorance of every creature, the Queen who wants no rest yet remains unmoved for all eternity, the Lady whose body is both the tangibility of the world and the supersensuously subtle material of the heavens and hells. He named her "The Everlasting Divine Drunkenness of Dream," that is, the cosmic stupor out of which the matter of the whole living world derives, as the dream matter of the slumbering, consummate existence, Vishnu; and he named her: "Whatever Reposes Beyond the Form-assuming Realm of Life." "Thou art pristine spirit," he prayed, "the nature of which is bliss; thou art the ultimate nature and the clear light of heaven, which illuminates and breaks the self-hypnotism of the terrible round of rebirth, and thou art the one that muffles the universe, for all time, in thine own very darkness." This was the manner in which he gave praise to the enchantment of Māyā—the world illusion that is operative in all creatures, prisoning them in their flesh and binding them by the shackles of birth and death to the wheel of agony and delight—the enchantment that compasses the "continuous creation" of the world.

The ray of knowledge that dispels the enchantment of Māyā is known only to the spiritual eye of the initiated individual, and

264

even to him only in the rarest, most extraordinary moments of his life. Its flash transports him aloft and alone into the crystalline spheres, while the world meantime plays on in the general thralldom of the trance that holds within itself all the areas of space and all the creatures of the world, as the world and population of a dream. This dream power—this cosmic stupor, the everlasting divine drunkenness of the dream of the universal organism—suffusing all and everything, brings about the unfoldment of the cosmos, as well as its perpetuation and, at last, its end. This, in fact, is the power that is effective in the Trinity—Brahmā, Vishnu, and Shiva; for all opposition, as well as identity, stems from Māyā. Great Māyā is wisdom and increase, stability and readiness to assist, compassion and serenity. Queen of the World, she is alive in every nuance of feeling and perception; feelings and perceptions are her gestures. And her nature can be sensed only by one who has comprehended that she is the unity of opposites. This queen produces the round of mortal delusion; nevertheless the same power throws open the way to release. She is wisdom and ignorance in one—self-illumination in intrinsic luminosity. And all women are her self-manifestations, but especially the two great goddesses, Lakshmī, consort of Vishnu and the patroness of fortune, and Sāvitrī, goddess of the glowing words of the wisdom of the divine revelation and tradition—the latter is Brahmā's spouse. Brahmā, alone and praying to her, having practiced his devotions for one full century of heavenly years (each heavenly year corresponding to three hundred and sixty years of human reckoning), and not having let his mind once waver from the difficult meditation on the nature of the great Māyā that envelops Vishnu in the stupor of sleep and lives in Vishnu's sight as the dream of the world, the goddess at last bodily appeared to him, dark and slender, hair hanging free, and standing on the back of her tawny lion. He gave her greeting. And Kālī, "The Dark One," addressed him with the voice of a cloud of thunder: "For what reason have you called? Make known your wish. Though it were unattainable, my appearance would guarantee its fulfillment."

Brahmā said: "The Lord of the World, the Lord of Spirits, Shiva, remains a solitary. No yearning is in him for a wife. O do thou beguile him, so that he may be moved to possess a woman. There is no woman capable of ravishing his poised intellect but thyself. As in the form of Lakshmī thou dost constitute the joy of Vishnu, so do thou now, for the salvation of the world, enrapture Shiva. Should he take no wife, how is the world creation to continue in its course? He, the unimpassioned, is the cause of its beginning, its middle, and its end. Vishnu's power does not suffice to involve him. Neither can Lakshmī, and the God of Love, and I, together, bring him into play. Therefore do thou, O thou Mother of the Universe, bewitch him. And as thou art Vishnu's beloved, so bring thou also Shiva in thy thrall."

A reply was pronounced by the magic-powerful Kālī: "What you say is true. I am the only woman who can disturb that paragon of peace, and even for me this is not going to be easy. But just as Vishnu does with me as he will and is in my power, likewise shall it be with Shiva. I, in the figure of a beautiful woman, the guise of the daughter of Daksha, shall set myself for him and make him my own. Therefore the gods shall name me— me who am the Māyā and dream drunkenness of Vishnu, and who henceforth am to become the bride of Shiva—'The Woman of the Paragon of Peace.' Just as I trap the newborn babe into life at its first drawn breath, so also shall I take this God of gods. And as all the children of earth are susceptible to the charm of the beautiful feminine, so also shall it be with him. For when in his meditation he splits the inmost kernel of his heart, there he shall find me melted into it, who am amenable to all beings and worlds; and, bewitched, he shall then gather me to himself."

She vanished from Brahmā's perceiving eyes, and he supposed

himself to have arrived at the goal of his endeavor. Overjoyed, he proceeded to the God of Love, who was still engaged in the long campaign around Shiva, and informed him that the divine Drunkenness of Yogic Dream was now prepared to fascinate the impregnable objective. The God of Love desired to know, however, what kind of being this new ally was, and asked how she was to accomplish the impossible task. Brahmā, thereupon, became suddenly depressed. "Alas!" he deeply sighed, "Shiva, perhaps, cannot be moved at all."

The breath of Brahmā's sigh condensed into a troop of terrifying figures, with elephant heads and horses' heads, lion and tiger jaws. Others wore the faces of dogs or cats, bear heads, or donkey snouts, frog mugs and parrot bills. Gigantic and dwarfish, gaunt and bellied, many-limbed and footless, they presented themselves, with cow faces and serpent forms—every construction of animal existence, showing the most reckless crossings of shape and limb: many-eyed and eyeless, human-physiqued with crocodile jowls, centipedal and birdlike, a superabundant spew of blind life-compulsion, gargoylish and bumptious in unpredictable fecundity. Beating drums, flourishing every sort of weapon, these armies, whose strength lay in the divine drunkenness of dream, were shouting: "Kill! Fight!"

Brahmā wished to speak with them, but the God of Love broke in with a series of questions: "What are these for? What may these be called? Whereabouts in creation shall you assign these work to do?" Brahmā replied: "Since they were shouting 'Kill!' already, and they hardly born, they shall be called 'The Killers,' 'The Bringers of Death'; and they shall kill the beings that lack the respect for them that they deserve. Let them be added to your troupe. They will set people crazy who are the victims of your shafts. And, furthermore, anyone seeking redemptive illumination they will block, barring the difficult way. You are their commander. Who will measure their force? They have neither wives nor progeny; loveless, they have resigned from life." [1]

Brahmā began, then, to describe to the God of Love the wonderful might of the Enchantress of the Universal Dream, who holds sovereignty over Vishnu as his Māyā; how she takes into her power every creature as it comes from the body of its mother, causing it to cry for nourishment and squirm with greediness and rage; then rousing it to love so that day and night it is goaded with desire and bitted with apprehension, racked with anxiety and delight. "Her deceits are myriad. All shapes are her production. She keeps Vishnu cajoled, the sustainer of the world, and inveigles every being with her decoying figurations of the feminine. She is now prepared to beguile Shiva. So hurry with your bride, Desire, and the wonderful divinity, Spring, and these your armies; move him to require the goddess to wife. We then shall have conquered, and the romance of creation will continue without interruption."

The Love God confessed that his exercises around Shiva had remained, so far, without result. The delights of Spring, with all the delicate loving couples who deployed their tender dalliances and ecstatic joys before the eyes of the solitarily absorbed one—transfigured heavenly couples in embraces everlasting, gazelles, love-kindled dancing peacocks—had simply failed to touch in him the slightest spark. Senses controlled, he persisted, blind to

---

[1] This is the army with which the God of Love and Death (Kāma-Māra) went against the Buddha (*cf.* pp. 77-78, *supra*). This tempter and his queen-wife, "Delight," correspond to the Lord and Lady who put Sir Gawain to the test. As Brahmā tells, the Highest Gods of Creation (Brahmā, Vishnu, Shiva), not to speak of all the creatures of the world, are defenceless against this master god of the continuous creation. By withstanding him, the Buddha (the supreme initiate) surpassed not only creation but the Highest Gods of Creation, and won redemption from the everlasting round. It is possible that the celebrated incident of "The Temptation of the Buddha" was influenced by the present, almost forgotten myth. The great Vedic archetype is the conflict of the god Indra with the titan Vritra.

their delicious madness. "Never could I discover any chink or fault in him through which to send my arrows home. Your discourse, however, gives me heart. Anything that these armies of death-threatening devils cannot accomplish, the cosmic dream delusion will certainly be able to achieve. I shall have another try at Shiva." With that he took his leave of Brahmā, who had advised and instructed him to devote the night and one quarter of the day to all the other creatures in the universe, but the remaining three-quarters of every day to the work of the great seduction.

Daksha, meanwhile, in the remote fastnesses, had been bending his powers, in prodigious exertion, to the worship of the goddess; and she at last had come to him also. Very dark of body and with mighty breasts, she appeared upon her lion. In one of her four hands she exhibited the lotus, in another a sword, a third was in the "fear-not" gesture, the fourth lay open in the posture called "bestowing gifts." Daksha bowed, and, full of beatitude, gave praise to the great Māyā, who, blissful in her essence, enraptures the world and bears up the earth. The primordial force, whose inflorescence is the universe, bid him announce his wish, and, when he had done so, left her promise: "For the well-being of creation I shall become your daughter and Shiva's love. But if, for even a single instance, you should lack for me proper reverence, I will quit my body immediately, whether happy in it or no. Shiva I shall allure. And this I will do, so that he may be brought into the plot of the world romance."

She disappeared from Daksha's vision, and he returned happily to his home. He set himself to producing creatures, without the device of intercourse with women, by shaping forms in his deep meditation, which then stepped out of the profundities of his spirit into the world—sons by the thousand, sagacious Brahmins, who were to wander about, even to the rim of the earth, time

269

without end. After that, he took a wife to himself, in order to beget on her another brood of creatures. Vīranī her name was, and she was the beautiful daughter of the fragrant grass that is called Virana. When Daksha's first wish-vision fell upon her, out of his soul, she conceived, and the child was the Goddess Māyā. Daksha knew, and he was elated. The day the daughter was born a rain of flowers descended from heaven, fresh waters streamed from the clear firmament, and the gods rumbled their thunder drums. Vīranī did not realize that her husband, in devout fervor, was greeting in their child the Mistress of the Universe, the "Mother" whose body is the world. And the Great Goddess so deluded all there present that her new mother and the visiting friends heard nothing when she lifted her voice and spoke to her father. "Daksha," she said, "the wish for which you worked to win my grace is now fulfilled." Whereupon she resumed, by craft, the shape of the newborn child and rested crying on its mother's bosom. Vīranī arranged it, and offered it her breast.

The little goddess grew up quickly in her parents' hut, filling out with all the virtues that were pouring into her; and she was like the sickle of the young waxing moon that from night to night swells out perceptibly toward its fullness. Her great delight when playing among her little friends was to draw Shiva's picture for them, day after day, and when she sang her childlike songs the little rhymes were about him, always, out of the devotion of her heart. Daksha gave to his daughter the name Satī, "She Who Is." [1] Brahmā spied her one day at the side of her father, and she perceived the god and made obeisance properly. Then he pronounced to her his blessing. "Him who loves you and whom you already love as a husband, you shall possess as spouse—the omniscient Lord of the World. He who neither has

[1] [Cf. "He Who Is" as the truest name of God: *Katha Upanishad,* Damascene, etc.—AKC.]

possessed nor is to possess any other woman will become your husband—Shiva the Incomparable."

Her beauty, when she had passed the years of childhood, was ravishing, and Daksha considered how he was to marry her to Shiva. She herself knew no other thought and, at the suggestion of her mother, began to offer special devotions to her lord. She went off to meditate alone, and dedicated herself to great austerities. Twelve moons passed. According to her vow, she had fasted, watched through the night, proffered offerings, and meditated continually, devoting herself in full ardor to the god. Brahmā then, when this period of her surrender approached its close, betook himself, together with his goddess wife, who was the divine incarnation of his power, to the place of Shiva's peace, far aloft in the heights of the Himālayas. Vishnu, too, with his consort Lakshmī, made himself manifest in that rugged abode. And miraculously, when the god-ascetic became aware of the presence of the two bliss-radiant couples, the slightest taint of a trace of a desire for woman and the state of marriage made itself perceptible in the spirit of the agelessly solitary one. He greeted the two power-duads, and asked the reason for their visit.

Brahmā replied: "For the sake of the divinities, for the sake of all creation, we have come to you. I am the creating cause of the world; Vishnu is the cause of its continuance; you, however, are the one who brings to pass the annihilation of all beings. Conjoined with the two of you, I am continually capable of consummating the act of creation, just as Vishnu finds in me the ground and support for his function of preservation. Correlatively, without the two of us, you would never be in a position to bring about the end. Hence, in the counterpoise of our powers we are dependent on each other, mutually, and must perform our several works in co-operation; otherwise, there can be no world. A number of the titans and antigods who are forever contending with the deities for control of the cosmos, threatening to veto our su-

271

pernal order, I am to kill; some are to fall victim to Vishnu, others
to you. Sons of ours, portions and physical embodiments of our
potencies, are to subjugate still others of the diabolic swarm; and
others still are appointed to be killed by the Goddess Māyā. But
now, if you remain for all time aloof from the course of history,
yoked in your yoga, clean of every gladness and grief, it will not
be possible for you to play your necessary part in the development of the picture. How are creation, preservation, and destruction to mesh, if the absorbing diabolic powers are not perpetually
held in check? And if we three, with our several three gestures,
are not working against each other, for what reason have we then
three sundry bodies, differentiated out of the Goddess Māyā?
One we are in the primitive essence of our being, separate only
in the contexts of our action. We are an identical divinity distinguished in triplication; and so likewise is the godly force that
moves in us divided threefold into the goddesses, Sāvitrī,
Lakshmī, and Dawn, each according to the work she is to accomplish in the exfoliation of the world.

"Woman is the root out of which need germinates; blossoming out of possession of the woman appear desire and wrath.
Where the need that makes for this desire and wrath prevails,
creatures bestir themselves to get rid of it. World-attachment
is the fruit of the tree of passion, which is the provoker of desire
as well as of wrath; freedom from that tree and release from the
world, therefore, either follow as a reaction against suffering or
else are present of themselves, the individual being in the latter
case absolutely averted from every facet of the world and attached to nothing at all. He then is full of mercy and peace of
soul. He injures no created being. Ascesis and the path of faultless mindfulness are his call. You, O Shiva, have your root in
such yoga-quietude; you are attached to nothing, suffused with
mercy. Forever, your portion is to be peace of soul, which inflicts
no hurt on any being. And you are not compelled to concern

yourself with existences, so long as you withhold from desire its share. Nevertheless your delinquency, if you persist in refusing to co-operate in the work of the world unfoldment, will be as I have just described. For the salvation, therefore, of the universe and the gods, take to wife a glorious woman, one such as Vishnu's consort, lotus-throned Lakshmī, or such as Sāvitrī, who is mine." [1]

A smile drew back a corner of Shiva's mouth and he granted reply. "Everything is as you say. But were I to withdraw myself —not for my own sake but for the salvation of the universe—out of the stillness of this flawless contemplation of ultimate reality, where would be the woman capable of absorbing my incandescent power, shock by shock, the feminine yogī, shaped to my desire, who could be my wife? Within my own crystalline spirit, forever I will view the supreme, imperishable eternity of True Being, which is testified by the sages; forever fixed in its meditation, I will keep it actual in my consciousness; and there shall be no woman hindering me in my dedication. We three are in essence no other than this One Existence Supreme. We are its members; therefore, we must abide with it in mindfulness. Therefore, show me the woman who is consecrated to my work and who partakes with me of my highest vision."

Likewise smiling, Brahmā was elated. "The woman you are asking for," he said, "exists; she is Satī, Daksha's daughter. For your sake she burns with immeasurable austerities." To which Vishnu added: "Do as Brahmā has advised." And with that the two, together with their wives, departed: while the Love God, together with his goddess Desire, and full of a new confidence (for he had overheard Shiva's words), drew nigh. And he ordered Spring to begin preparatory operations.

[1] In this great statement of Brahma the Creator to Shiva the Destroyer, the destructive element is recognized as indispensable to the works of creation and preservation; perennial death is acknowledged to be the precondition of continuous birth and being. Briefly stated, we three, Birth, Life, and Death, are one—limbs and gestures of the One.

The Autumn Moon of Satī's vow was approaching its full. On the eighth night of its waxing, she was in her fast and with un-flagging devotion paying worship, one-pointed, to the Master of the Gods, when Shiva appeared. The moment she realized that he was physically before her, jubilation flooded her heart; she bowed her head modestly and paid her worship to his feet. She had carried her extreme vow through to its conclusion, and the God was not unwilling to take her to wife. Therefore he spoke: "Your vow has pleased me; I will grant what you ask." Very well he knew what was in her heart; nevertheless he said to her: "So now, speak"; for he wished to hear her voice. But she was overcome with shame, and could not bring herself to declare what had moved her heart since the years of her infancy. Humility kept her secret veiled.

This was the instant when the God of Love spied a chink in Shiva. The High God was not indisposed to seek a wife, and he had been moved to cause Satī to talk because he desired to hear her voice. The God of the Bow let fly the arrow that arouses agitation. Shiva looked on the maiden and shuddered; he forgot then the spiritual vision of Supernal Being. The Love God let fly the arrow that inspires ardor.

The maid, meanwhile, had got the better of her shame. "Grant me the boon, O thou bestower of boons . . ." she began. But the god, in whose banner is the emblem of the bull, could not delay now to hear how the petition would conclude. He suddenly shouted: "Be my wife!" She heard and with great excitement in her heart at this thundering fulfillment of her wish was again struck dumb. Only a smile of sweetness and a devoted gesture disclosed her feelings to the divinity who was standing before her, inundated with desire. And the two were moved and suf-fused by love. Satī stood; and before Shiva she was like a cloud, dark in yielding condensation, under the crystalline brilliance of the moon. "You must go," she said, "to my father, and receive me from his hand." She bowed—was preparing to leave; but he, stricken with the fire of the burning arrows, remained, repeating: "Be my wife!"

Satī said no more. With her deepest obeisance, she took her departure and hurried home to her parents, quivering with happiness. Shiva returned, thereupon, to his hermitage; and pained by the separation from her, he yielded his mind to the contemplation of her image in his heart. Shiva remembered Brahmā's exhortation to take a wife. He directed a thought to Brahmā, and immediately Brahmā, with his spouse, Sāvitrī, was before him. They had arrived, swift as thought, transported through ethereal space in the chariot drawn by heavenly wild ganders. Brahmā felt that his deepest wish was on the point of fulfillment and he wanted to do what he could to bring it to pass.

"Your suggestion," Shiva confessed to him, "namely, that I should take to myself a wife, now seems to me full of sense. The pious daughter of Daksha has been worshiping me with ardently dedicated devotion. And when I appeared before her, to grant to her a boon, the God of Love caught me with his shafts. Māyā, since, has completely tricked me of my senses, and I am powerless. With Satī's heart as it is, I know that I shall become her husband. Therefore, for the good of the universe, and this time for my sake too, have her father invite me to his home and give me her hand in marriage. Make haste, and do what you can to end my separation from her." He glanced at the wife of Brahmā, and the pain of his solitude increased in him at the sight of the united couple.

Brahmā promised to accomplish the charge, and flew in his swift chariot to Daksha. The latter had heard everything already from his daughter, and was trying to think how he could most discreetly manage the somewhat awkward preliminaries. The Great Solitary once had paid him a visit and graciously departed; would he come again for the maid? Or could Daksha send the

High God a messenger? That would be somewhat improper; for wooing was supposed to be initiated by the male. Well, then, should Daksha now himself begin to invoke the great divinity by means of strenuous meditations, preliminary to craving of him the boon that he should take Satī to wife? It seemed, however, that the God already wanted nothing more than to possess the girl.

This, then, was the quandary in which Brahmā found Satī's father. The swift chariot surprised him. Brahmā told him delightedly of the radical change that had overcome Shiva. "Drilled through by the fire of the arrows, he is letting meditation take care of itself. All that he can think about is Satī. And he is as riddled with the tumult of feeling as some poor creature in the throes of death. Holy Wisdom, which is the most intrinsic thing to him, has altogether fled his consciousness, and all that he can say, no matter what he may happen to be doing, is: 'Where is Satī?'—filled thereby with the agony of yearning. What I and all of us have long been hoping for, at last has come about; your daughter has found Shiva's heart; he wants only her; he wants to make her happy. Just as she, true to her vows, brought to him her worship, so now Shiva worships her. Therefore give her to him, for whom she was intended and prepared."

Daksha agreed, as filled with joy as though torrents of nectar were streaming into his being. Promptly Brahmā speeded back with the happy tidings to Shiva, who was looking out for him impatiently from the Himālayan height. The instant Shiva spied him, he cried out to Brahmā from afar: "What did your son say? Speak! or this God of Love is going to split my heart! The ache of desire of all the creatures of the universe has come pouring out of them into me, and I alone, uniquely, am filled to bursting with their pain. I think everlastingly of Satī, no matter what I turn to do. Therefore help me to possess her very soon."

Brahmā delivered the news to Shiva, and then, by means of a

thought, summoned Daksha, who arrived just as quickly, and
was immediately prepared to escort the bridegroom to his home.
Clad only in the tiger-skin loincloth of the yogī, and wearing
a live serpent, instead of the normal Brahminic thread, over
his left shoulder and across his body to the right hip, Shiva, the
mighty god, mounted his magnificent bull. The sickle of the
young moon that rested in his hair cast a gentle glow over his
person. And the host of his spirits (lesser and grotesque duplica-
tions of himself, precipitated into the atmosphere by the prodigious power of his electric presence), jubilantly tumultuous,
blasted trumpets of shell and flutes of reed, thumped kettle-
drums and tambourines, clapped hands, beat time, and careened
with piercing shrieks of joy in their big wagon, away through
the air. All the gods, in festival parade, arrived to give the bridegroom convoy. Divine musicians and the heavenly dancing girls
made the air round about melodious. The God of Love became
visible with his attendant Feelings, delighting Shiva and maddening him. The whole firmament was gay and brilliant, blown
with sweet-scented breezes, all trees stood forth in blossom, every
creature in creation breathed the air of health, and the halt and
the ailing were healed, as Shiva, celebrated thus by all the gods
with their music, made his way to Daksha's home. Swans, wild
geese, and peacocks, uttering dulcet cries of joy, winged ahead.

Daksha busied himself with the immense reception of his distinguished guests, bidding them to be seated, offering water for
the washing of the feet, and presenting gifts to entertain them.
He consulted with the ten mind-born sons of Brahmā, the Holy
Ones, and, following their judgment of the stars, settled upon an
auspicious hour for the wedding. Solemnly, Shiva received the
hand of his beautiful daughter. Whereupon the gods gave praise
with stanzas, proverbs, and melodies from the holy Vedas; Shiva's
host let loose their tumult, and the heavenly dancing girls began

to whirl; gathering cloudbanks let fall a rain of flowers from the sky.

Vishnu and his consort Lakshmī now arrived from the remotest ethereal distances, rapidly born on Garuda, the golden-feathered Bird of the Sun. And Vishnu greeted Shiva: "United with Satī," he said, "who glistens blue-black, like a dark ointment for the eyes, you now constitute just such a couple—only reversed—as myself, dark blue, with the fair Lakshmī. United with Satī, be a protection to the gods and to men; be of good augury to all creatures trapped in the circling stream of birth and death. You will slay the enemies as they arise in the course of history. But if anyone should ever let his desire repose on Satī, you will strike him dead, O Lord of Beings, without an instant's thought."

"Amen," said Shiva jubilantly, "so shall it be." And with merry eyes he smiled at the happy god.

At this, Satī laughed a charming laugh, and it attracted to her face the eye of Brahmā. But the God of Love had gotten into Brahmā's veins, and he lost his gaze in the beauty of Satī's countenance, dwelling there somewhat overlong. Thereupon a disturbing influence threaded his system and he found himself moved to the root. He had no control over what had begun to happen. An incandescent glow of his powers shot from him; creative energy streamed out of his body and, flaring with flames, flowed to earth before the eyes of the entire saintly assemblage. It became transformed into a thundering black cloud, mighty with rain, like the clouds at the end of the world, which are to collect, for the cyclone of the ultimate destruction, into a blue-black, lotus-dark, heavy mass that pours out rain as though from buckets. Thundering, this lifted and spread out across the heaven-tent, even to the rim of the world.

Shiva, also filled with emotions by the Love God, looked at Satī and was remembering Vishnu's word. He suddenly lifted his spear; he poised it for a fling at Brahmā. The Holy Ones cried

278

out in horror, and Daksha quickly stepped between. Shiva shouted angrily: "Vishnu's dictum has become my own: 'If anyone lets his desire repose on Satī, I will strike him dead.' Precisely this was my vow, and I will bring my vow to pass. Why has Brahmā allowed himself to stare upon Satī with the stare of desire? For that, I am about to strike him dead!"

Vishnu hurriedly rushed before him and pressed back his arm. "You shall not kill the Creator of the World," he said. "If you are in possession of Satī, it is because he prepared her for you. Brahmā exists for the unfoldment of the cosmos; if you murder him, there is no one else capable of unfolding the lotus of the universe from its seed. Creation, Preservation, Destruction—how are these three to be perpetuated without the three of us? Any one of us dead, and who will take up that one's share?"

Shiva, however, insisted on his vow. "I can create creatures myself," he shouted, "or I can create you another creator out of my own incandescent heat, and he will open out the universe—I shall teach him how. But I will not be kept from my vow. I shall create you your Creator. Let me go! Take away your hand!"

"Now, now," soothed Vishnu, "take a little thought." A knowing smile illuminated his benign countenance. "You would not wish to execute your vow upon yourself!"

"How so, myself? Is that Creator over there myself? Why, before all eyes, over there he stands, and I am here, and he is clearly a different one from me!"

Vishnu laughed, and made open mock of Shiva before all the Holy Ones. "Brahmā is no more distinct from you," he said "than I am from you and him. You and he both are portions of myself, who am the pristine and supreme Light of Heaven; and I who stand before you am also a portion of that Uttermost. Three hypostases of the Unique Godhead are we, and we function variously: create, preserve, and destroy. Seek that Godhead in your own divinity and repose your faith and trust in it. As the head and limbs are one in the life of a created body, just so are we three one in me, who am the Supreme Existence, Light, uncreate and immaculate. In that one Supreme Being we three are not distinct."

Shiva, of course, knew well enough about the one Supreme Being, devoid of all distinctions, but deluded as he was by the fascinations of Māyā, he had lost sight of the truly Real; something else had come into possession of his thought. And that is why Vishnu forced him to see again both the One and the Manifold, the deep secret of Reality, wherein the Three are identical while retaining their several mutually antagonistic functions of Unfoldment, Support, and Termination. "Sink into your own interior," Vishnu said, "and behold, within, that mighty Self, the Supreme Existence, pure and everlasting Light. You have been tricked from it by my Māyā, the spell that opens out the world. Entranced by the beauty of a woman, you have forgotten that supernal Light, and have become charged with anger. You can no longer discover within your own being the Being Universal."

Shiva's visage became radiant with joy. In the presence of all the Holy Ones he lapsed, absorbed, into introverted vision. Then he permitted himself to sink to the floor, legs crossed, shut his eyes, and sank into his being to the depth of the Being Sublime. His body began to glow, so that the eyes of all the Holy Ones present became dazzled. And the moment he reached quietude in this immersion, Vishnu's Māyā fell away from around him, and his entire body burst into such a radiance that even his own hosts were unable to bear the blast. Vishnu passed into him, poured into him as the pure Light of Heaven, and disclosed within Shiva's body, to the eye of his inner contemplation, the whole lotus-spectacle of creation and the procession of the world. Blissful and serene, beyond the senses and their universes of distinctions, alone and pure, beholding everything, the abstracted one experienced within his own being the Being Supreme, that Substratum of all Unfoldments. He beheld, riveted in contemplation, how the One Substance exfoliates into all the delectations of the world.

What he saw first was a darkness, and it was all-filling and empty of all creatures, and it was impenetrable, traitless, like a dreamless sleep, showing no difference of day and night, or of firmament and earth, no light, no water, no element. Only one presence stirred; immaterially, imperceptibly delicate: pure consciousness, as yet uninflected; and there was no other thing. Precisely, it was as though the two eternal first presences, original Matter and original Man, lay fused by indissoluble intertanglement, perfectly in one. Yet Time was there: the formal cause of all that lives, the primordial substance of the Highest Being. And souls were shooting out of it ceaselessly like the flying sparks from a tremendous fire. Through the multifariousness of these, the Highest Being was offering Itself to Itself for the sake of the enjoyment of pleasures and pains. Time unfolded; it differentiated; it compassed Creation, Continuance, Consummation. Time took form as the Māyā of all the gods; and it became Sāvitrī, the active energy of Brahmā, Lakshmī, the companion of Vishnu, and Satī also. In the person of "Delight," it joined the God of Love.

The Cosmic Egg took form and grew amid the waters of the abyss, enveloped in winds, in flame, and in space. Then Shiva beheld the Creator within his own interior, white as a white lotus, streaming light; and the Creator was opening out the world. The Creator's form was one, became three, and yet remained as one, the topmost personality with four heads and arms, white as the corolla of a lotus, being Brahmā; the middle, dark blue, with a single head and four arms, Vishnu; but the undermost had five faces set upon a body crystalline and possessing four arms, and this was Shiva. The three grew out of each other and flowed together into one. The middle, Vishnu, melted now into the upper, Brahmā, now into Shiva below, and now Brahmā disappeared

281

into Vishnu, Shiva flowing into him; then again it was Brahmā and Shiva that commingled. This was the fashion of the playing of the triune figurations, various in their unity, and they remained both three and one.

By the waters cradled, by the waters rocked about, the Cosmic Egg burst open. The World Mountain towered out of it, and around this the earth extended, floating, and surrounded by seven seas; the shell arranged itself into bounding mountains. Shiva became distinct from Brahmā, and beside the two was Vishnu, soaring on the golden Bird of the Sun. Shiva discerned the Love God and he saw all the deities and the Holy Ones, beheld the sun, the moon, and the clouds, turtles, fish, and the monsters of the sea, saw birds and insects, meteors and men.

Then a beautiful woman became visible to his inner gaze, and she was embraced by arms. Shiva saw the creatures originating, flourishing, disappearing. Laughing ones he saw, ecstatic in love. but mourners, too, and others in precipitous flight. Many were magnificently garbed, made beautiful with their garlands and aromatic sandal-paste, and these were pleasantly engaged in games. Many others were sending up prayers to Brahmā and to Vishnu, or bending in the worship of Shiva. Still others sat absorbed in ascetic meditation along the banks of rivers or in consecrated groves. The seven seas Shiva viewed, as well as the rivers, lakes, and mountains. And he discovered how Māyā in the figure of Lakshmī was enchanting Vishnu, even while he was beguiling himself in the delectable form of Satī. Shiva recognized himself alone with Satī on a lofty mountain pinnacle. They were enlaced in rapturous love. The godly grove was pungent with the aroma of their desire.

Thus the great God gazed into the future. He saw Satī put off her body and disappear; but then she was born again as the daughter of Himālaya, the Mountain King; and Shiva found her again, after long separation. He murdered the titan named "The

Blind One" for desiring her with lust; and their son, the War God, came into the world to slay the titan tyrant Taraka. All this Shiva beheld in minute detail. And he watched Vishnu, as the Man-Lion, tear to pieces the great titan Golden Garment, beheld all the brilliant battles between the titans and the gods; and he saw the romance of the world alternate, through the course of these interminable conflicts, between the buoyancy of divine victory and the dreadful impotencies of defeat.

Again and again, and still again, he viewed the creatures of the world, saw all the phenomenal forms unfolding in accordance with their distinct intrinsic qualities, and watched himself, in the end, come to sweep them all away, taking them into, and powerfully annihilating them within, himself. There remained only Brahmā, Vishnu, and Shiva—nothing more, not another existence. The world again was empty. Brahmā moved into Vishnu's form and melted. And Shiva then watched himself flow into Vishnu and dissolve. But Vishnu finally disintegrated and was subsumed into the Supreme Divine, which is perfect Light, beatific Consciousness.

The simultaneous oneness and manyness of the universe in the Highest Being was what Shiva had seen, and he had seen it inside his own body. Creation, Preservation, Destruction: all three had been there. These were nothing more nor less than his own existence, which was at one with itself and full of stillness. Who is Brahmā? Who Vishnu? Who is Shiva? Shiva pondered; there was no inkling of reply. He himself was the Highest Being—and that was All.

Having exhibited in this manner the unity and multifariousness of Reality, Vishnu withdrew himself from Shiva's body, and the meditating bridegroom emerged from his deep trance. Māyā crowded immediately about him again; he became discomposed within, actuated by her craft, and his thoughts flew directly back to Satī. Then he looked upon her, and, as though waking from the depths of a dream, gazed at her blossoming lotus-countenance. His eyes, marveling, traveled to Daksha, then reviewed the surrounding company of the Holy Ones, rested on Brahmā, rested on Vishnu, and stared astounded.

Vishnu smiled. "And so now," said he, "you have seen the unity in multiplicity that you were inquiring about, have discovered Time and Māyā in your body, and have rediscovered what they are. You have watched the unique Being in eternal stillness and have seen its way of florescence into the multitudes of the world."

"I have, indeed," Shiva replied. "That One in its silence and infinitude have I looked upon, and beyond that there is nothing. The world which you support is not distinct from it. That Being is the wellspring of all creatures and gods. And we Persons of God are the triune parts and forms of it, made manifest to contrive Creation, Duration, and End."

"That is the truth," Vishnu responded. "We are three, but in that substance, one. And this is why you are not to murder Brahmā with your spear."

And so that is the tale of how it came to pass that Shiva, recognizing the identity-in-essence of the separate-in-form, withheld from Brahmā the annihilating blow.

The peculiar and wonderful virtue of the Indian gods is that they are continually doing, and being overwhelmed by, perfectly impossible things, which, from the standpoint of the Christian drawing room, would be (and are) extremely shocking. For all their supernatural dignity, they are still entirely Nature—personifications of the elemental principles of the cosmic play—not such urbanized formulations as the Olympians of the Greeks. The profoundly essential verity of Indian mythology derives from the fact that it operates exclusively in terms of such astonishing uttermosts, alternately entirely filling and completely emptying its lungs, and thereby both compelling and enabling ourselves to do the same. Reaching, driving always (no matter what the direction) just as far as it possibly can, it is continually bringing together the remote extremes of symbol—as in the above depiction of the wedding festival of Shiva. A huge, far-reaching pendulum stroke to the furthest distances of reality swings through these wild adventures, precipitating counterplays of opposites from the poles of being.

Furthermore, in all the intemperances of the Great Gods it is the overpowering play of Māyā that is depicted. So long as the world runs on, the divinities who bring to pass the Unfoldment, Maintenance, and Conclusion of it all are caught in the net of their own self-delusion. Caught in it, they weave it—that is the sublime paradox; seeing and knowing all, knowing better, nevertheless they suffer and act because threaded with the magic. That is the great comfort presented to the mind by the mythical pattern, the great model for the understanding and the living of human life. The High Gods, in their relationship to the spell of Māyā, are exemplars, on the one hand, for the released sages and yogīs, as well as, on the other, for the Children of the World who are still captured in the toils of hope and fear.

III. THE VOLUNTARY DEATH

Amid the thundering boom of the cloud-drums Shiva took his leave of Vishnu. He lifted Satī, radiant with joy, upon the back of his mighty bull, and while the whole assemblage of the gods, demons, and created beings raised an immense uproar of jubilation, the couple started on their way. Brahmā and his ten mind-born sons, and the Lords of Creatures, and the gods, and the heavenly musicians, together with the dancing girls, all accompanied them a short stretch of the road, before releasing the two with a great farewell, and scattering to their innumerable habitations. The whole of creation was jubilant, Shiva having finally taken to himself his consort.

The couple arrived at Shiva's abiding place among the fastnesses of the Himālayan peaks, and the god took his bride down from the back of Nandī, the bull. Then he dismissed the bull and also the tumultuous company of his host. "Leave the two of us alone now. But when I take thought of you," said he, "be immediately at hand." And so, then, the god and goddess consummated their festival in the secrecy of their solitude, and they dwelt long in love with each other, night and day.

Shiva would gather wood flowers for Satī and place them in a wreath about her head; and when she then studied her features in the glass, he would step behind her, and in the mirror the two faces would be merged in one. He let down her night-dark hair, let it stir about and play, and then himself was also stirred to a rollicking play. He knotted it up, let it loose again, and convoluted himself endlessly in that occupation. Her pretty feet he painted with scarlet lac, in order to hold them, while doing so, in his hands. He whispered into her ear what he could just as well have spoken aloud, only to bring himself close to her face. And if he stepped away from her for a moment, as quickly as possible he hurried back. Wherever she turned herself to some task, he constantly followed with his eyes. By means of his arts he made himself invisible, then suddenly startled her with his embrace, and kept her dizzy and excited with fright. He set a spot of musk on her beautiful lotus-breasts in the form of a sucking bee, then lifted off the necklaces of pearl and set them back again in some different arrangement, just to touch her lotus-softness. He drew the bracelets from her wrists and arms and opened the knots of her clothing, tied them again, and put back the ornaments. "Here is a wasp," he said, "as dark as you; that is why he is pursuing you. . . ." She turned to see, and he gathered up her breasts. Heaps of lotus blossoms and wood flowers he piled on top of her in the frolic of love, blooms that he had plucked for her delight. And wherever he walked, stood, or reposed, he would not be happy for an instant without her.

The bridal couple had scarcely arrived in the Himālayas when the God of Love came, in a gala mood, together with Spring and Desire. Majestic Spring worked magic: all the trees and vines broke into blossom, the water surfaces were covered with lotus chalices swarmed about by bees, aromatic winds blew from the south, and dizzying fragrances went out to unsettle the senses of the steadiest matrons and disconcert the beatitude of saints. In bowers and by the banks of high, torrential mountain streams, Shiva and Satī tasted each other; and Satī's desire was so powerful that Shiva was never without great delight in her. When she gave herself, it was as though she were melting into his body, drowning in his fire. He decked her whole person in chains of flowers and studied her; he joked and laughed and conversed with her; he lost himself in her, as a yogī in full self-collection submerges in the Self, there deliquescing totally. Shiva swallowed the nectar of her mouth, and, as though it were the divine liquor of immortality imbibed from the cup of the moon, his body became filled with unflagging desire and knew nothing of the exhaustion known to men. The scent of her lotus-countenance, her grace and her nuances of allure, linked him, like powerful cords around the ankles of a bull elephant, so that he never could break away from her. With such changing delights, the godly couple, in the remote mountain solitudes of Himālaya, went on for nineteen heavenly years and five (nine thousand two hundred and forty human years) among the bowers and in caves, knowing only the ravishment of love.

Once, when the dry season was approaching, the goddess complained. "It will be getting hot," she said, "and we have no house to shelter us." Shiva smiled. "I have no home," he an-

287

swered, "but roam through the wilderness without any special place to stay." So they passed the season together under shady trees. And then the rainy time drew near. "See there, the clouds are heaping," Satī said; "they are like an army accumulating in a multitude of colors, and they shut out the round of the sky. The winds are beginning to storm, their force terrifies the heart. The cracking thunder of the clouds that soon will be sending down the rain in sheets, flinging lightning like a terrible pennant, quails my joy. The Sun God is not to be seen, nor the Lord of the Night, for they are blocked from our sight by this heavy crowding of the thunderheads. Day and night are one. The heavens boom on every side. Lashed by the tempest, the whole world seems about to be brought down around our heads, and big trees, uprooted by the blast, dance through the air. This is a difficult time of year to bear. Please, I beg you, build a hut for us, where we can find a bit of shelter and repose." But Shiva smiled again. "I have nothing of my own," he said, "with which to build a home. A tiger's skin covers my loins, and, instead of ornaments, live serpents decorate my arms, my neck, and head." Then Satī sighed. And this time she was ashamed of him. She kept her gaze fixed to the ground, and answered impatiently: "Am I supposed to spend the whole rainy season here, burrowing for shelter under the roots of trees?" Shiva laughed. "The rainy season will pass," he said, "and you will have been sitting far above it, untouched by a drop of rain." He lifted her high upon the back of a cloud, and went up and united with her in love; and there they stayed until the clear bright days of the sunlit autumn arrived, when they came down and lived again among the mountains of the earth.

The next time the rainy season threatened and Satī again pleaded for a house, Shiva answered gaily, and his face was luminous with the light of the moon in his hair: "Where we are going, my beloved, to enjoy our love, there will not be any clouds. Clouds reach only to the hips of the great mountains; the mountain heads are zones of everlasting snow, untouched by the seasonal rain. Which pinnacle do you choose? Shall it be towering Mount Himālaya, where Menakā is expecting you, the Queen-Wife of the Mountain King, who will greet and take care of you like a mother? The wild animals there are made tame by the holy presence round about of all the meditating hermit saints and sages. You will meet heavenly maidens there and pinnacle-daughters, with whom to while away the time in companionship, the saintly wives of the blessed, and serpent-princesses. But then, on the other hand, we have also to consider the World Axis, Mount Meru; its sides are brilliant with precious stones, and its peak supports the palaces of the Kings of the Gods and the Guardians of the World. There Indra's wife would be your friend. Or would you prefer, do you think, great Mount Kailāsa? There the God of Wealth sits throned among the earth genii that guard the treasures of the mines."

Satī replied: "I should prefer Mount Himālaya." And they proceeded directly to its summit, whither no bird can fly, no clouds come, and where the wives of the blessed play. Shiva and Satī dwelt there for three thousand, six hundred years. Frequently they went for visits to Kailāsa; once they went to Mount Meru and enjoyed each other among the gardens of the world-warding King of Gods. Shiva's heart was wholly held by Satī, and he was indefatigable in his offerings of love. Day and night he knew no other joy, knew nothing now of the serene Essence of Being, never gathered consciousness to the ardent vivid point of self-submersion. For Satī's gaze held to his countenance, and his eyes, in turn, never left the loveliness of her features. The inexhaustible fountain of their passion watered abundantly the roots of their tree of love, and the tree continually grew.

But now Daksha, Satī's father, began preparations for a prodigious sacrificial ceremony, which should redound to the well-being of all the worlds and creatures. He commissioned eighty-eight thousand priests to proffer offerings, sixty thousand sages and saints to chant magical incantations, and again sixty thousand saints and sages to intone, in a low, uninterruptedly muttering rumble, proverbs and aphoristic stanzas of potency. Vishnu himself took charge of the overseeing of the event and Brahmā supplied advice on all the finer details of holy Vedic law. The divine World Watchers, who keep lookout over the Four Quarters from the slopes of the World Mountain, were the Door Guardians at the entrances to the consecrated compound. Earth stretched herself out, to be the altar of the offering. The Fire God apportioned his body to a thousand sacrificial pyres. And the holy personage, "The Sacrifice," was personally present to be offered up for the salvation of the world.

Every living thing in all the reaches of space was invited to attend, gods and seers, men, birds, trees, and grasses. They began to arrive—wild and domesticated animals, all the inhabitants of the upper regions, saints and sages, and all the denizens of the depths, rich subterranean demons and magnificent serpent kings and queens. Clouds and mountains were invited, rivers and oceans; monkeys and all beings came to partake of their share of the feast. The kings of the earth arrived in state with their sons, and followed by their counselors and troops. All living existences in all the regions of the universe, whether moving or fixed in place, made their appearance; both the conscious creatures and the unconscious were invited. And Daksha paid out everything he owned in fees to the priests. Throughout all the vast, wide-reaching, lofty and abysmal reaches of the world, there was only one being whom Daksha did not invite, and that was Shiva, his son-in-law, together with Satī, the daughter whom he loved. They were not invited because they were judged to be ceremonially impure. "He is a beggar ascetic and not fit to be present at the sacrifice," said Daksha; "he meditates among

corpses and carries a skull for a begging bowl. Neither is Satī
qualified; she is his wife and contaminated by association."

Vijayā, the daughter of a sister of Satī, visited the mountain
retreat just when the creatures of all the worlds had begun to
stream from their far-flung places to the precinct of the universal
festival. She discovered Satī alone, Shiva having gone off on his
bull, Nandī, to perform his evening meditations on the shore of
Lake Manasa, up on the summit of Mount Kailāsa. "You have
come alone?" said Satī. "Where are your sisters?"

Vijayā made it known that all the women in the universe were
on their way to the great party being held by her grandfather,
Daksha. "I have come to fetch you," she said. "Are not you and
Shiva coming?"

Dumbfounded amazement brought a glaze to Satī's eyes.

"Have you not been invited?" exclaimed Vijayā. "Why, all the
saints and seers are coming! The Moon and his wives! Everyone
in all the worlds has been invited. Haven't you?"

Satī was struck, as by a bolt of lightning. Anger began to burn
in her, and her eyes hardened. She had understood immediately,
and fury increased in her beyond bounds. "Because my husband
bears a skull in his hand for a begging bowl," she said, "we have
not been invited." She thought for a moment, in order to decide
whether to blast Daksha to ashes with a curse, but then she
suddenly remembered the words she had uttered to him, the
time she had mercifully granted the great boon of becoming
flesh in the earthly status of his daughter: "If, for even a single
instant, you should lack for me proper reverence, I will quit my
body immediately, whether happy in it or no." And with that, her
own eternal form became visible to her spiritual eye, complete
and incomparably terrible, the form out of which the universe
is made. She submerged herself in the contemplation of this,
her primary character, which is Māyā, known also as "The
World-Creative Dream-Drunkenness of the Sustainer of the

291

Cosmos," and she meditated: "The world period of the universal dissolution has not yet arrived; that is true; Shiva has not yet a son. The great wish that agitated all the gods became fulfilled for them: Shiva, caught in my spell, found his joy in woman. But what good did it do them? There is no other woman in all the worlds who could arouse and satisfy Shiva's passion; he will never marry another. That, however, is not going to stop me. I will quit this body, just as I declared I would. Some later day, I can reappear for the redemption of the world, here on Himālaya, where I have dwelt so long in happiness with Shiva. I have come to know dear Menakā, the pure and kindly wife of King Himālaya. She has been as sweet and good to me as any mother could have been. I have grown very fond of her. She shall be my next mother. And I will grow up playing with the pinnacle-daughters, a little girl again, and be Menakā's delight. I will marry Shiva again, dwell with him again, and complete the work that all the divinities have in mind."

Thus she meditated. Then her wrath overcame her. She closed the nine portals of her senses in yoga, stopped her respiration, and braced all of her powers. The life breath ripped through the coronal suture of her skull, out the tenth portal (the so-called Brahmā-fissure), and shot upward from her head. The body slumped inanimate to the ground.

When the gods above beheld the wind of her life, they lifted a universal shout of woe. Vijayā threw herself across the lifeless form and wept with agony. "Satī, Satī!" she cried, "What has become of you? Where have you gone? O lovely sister of my mother, did you quit your body only because you heard something that hurt you? How shall I ever live, whose eyes have witnessed such a terrible thing?" She stroked the dead cheeks, kissed the mouth, and wet the bosom and face with her tears, let the dark, glossy hair run through her fingers, and gazed continually into features now gone motionless. With both her hands she began to beat her own chest and head, shrieking with a voice half drowned in weeping, throwing back her head in a fit of mad grief, and dashing it forward against the ground. "The pain," she cried, "will shatter your poor mother, and she will expire of the affliction. And how will your heartless father ever survive for another minute, after he learns that you have died? Oh, the distress, the remorse that will come to him, when he realizes how rudely he has treated you! Learned in the proprieties of the sacrifice, jubilant in its routines, how will he keep his mind on the details of his immense sacrifice, when faith in all his wisdom will have collapsed? O lovely Mother, speak one more word to me. I am crying like a little child. Do you remember the way I annoyed Shiva with my teasing, that time, and you became vexed with me? O Mother, Mother! Why do you not reply? Here is your face, these are your eyes, and this your mouth: has all the play of life gone from them? How is Shiva going to stand it, to see your dancing eyes mute and stark, and your face without a smile? Who will ever greet me again with loving and helpful words, sweet as the dews of night, the way you used to when I came into the hermitage? Where will there ever be another so thoughtful of her spouse and endowed with all the favors of joy? Shiva without you will be racked with sorrow, eaten out with pain; every power to act will be taken from him, and all capacity to feel!"

Vijayā cried out in her misery, stared at the inert corpse, threw her arms up with a cry, and collapsed.

Delusion, enchantment, Māyā everywhere, among the gods as well as in the world of creatures—otherwise there would be no world moving on at all, no continuous creation. The same Daksha who had exercised himself to bring Satī into the world and marry her to Shiva, drives her out of it again and destroys the very union that had cost him so much head-breaking concentration. Furthermore, all the other gods and creatures who had taken part with the greatest enthusiasm in the celebration of the universally desired, happy but arduous consummation of this union, join Daksha in his immense ceremony of sacrifice, and do not even ask where the Great God can be—little thinking that his absence is about to cause the withdrawal of the Goddess from the phenomenal scene, and the dissolution of the marriage on which the whole world-continuity depends.

The sequence, Involuntary Creation, Involuntary Marriage, Voluntary Death, would seem to suggest that in this, our great theater of Life in Space and Time, the only gesture of free will possible to any actor—whether he be man merely, or the highest god—is that of quitting the stage. From time to time individual performers may imagine that they are exercising their powers voluntarily; but they did not themselves determine what those powers should be, nor have they any inkling of what is to appear in consequence of their actions. And the situations, furthermore, that compel the actors to act, always break with such force out of nowhere into the immediate Here, that they smite the mind with the categorical impact of a blow. Responses then ensue, not as elected measures, but in spontaneous reaction. And though long periods of lull may extend between the world-creative, great crises of irrevocable act and bound-shattering decision—permitting, for a time, a gentler dalliance of liberal human intercourse, and thus fostering the illusion of a certain freedom—nevertheless, whenever the catastrophic instant finally matures and at last bursts, men, gods, and demons are blown by a mighty wind.

Even that one recourse, the Voluntary Death, is finally nullified. Satī, the snubbed and insulted goddess, quit the scene; but her disappearance was of no real cosmic consequence. Another female—Pārvatī—would be born to take up the role, and she would be in essence the same as Satī, though in name and beauty different. And the situation, together with its task, would gradually build up again—slowly and deviously, by irresistible progressions of event. So that the willful act would at last appear to have been only a momentary, blind, and impetuous explosion of emotion that short-circuited the currents of life and precipitated all around it confusion, difficulty and distress, but left nothing either damaged or resolved. Who died? Who was it that passed away?

Suicide and murder are the motions of a Māyā-bewilderment, gestures of an abject absorption into ego. To shatter the carnal shell, either of one's self or of another, under the delusion that by this violence something decisive is accomplished, is to be really and utterly tricked by the shell. For concrete human circumstance, no matter what its physical explanation may be thought to be, primarily is the projection of a constellation of inner, psychological complications—the world responding in meaning to the madness of its inhabitant. The desperate sufferer fancies he can eliminate the dark labyrinths of the interior walls of fear by an exterior, arbitrary cut of wrath. But he would do better to unknot himself from his turbulent ego and, thus coming to a changed perspective, slip from the thing that has been holding him, simply by realizing that it is unreal.

Sati's pique and demise are the signs of her entanglement in the net of her own delusion; and yet—her net is the fabric of paradox. She knows that she is going to have to return. She will be born as Pārvatī, daughter of the Mountain King, and through long and difficult austerities will win again her beloved Shiva. And this time, when the Love God sends his darts into Shiva's heart, the great god of yoga will open his middle eye at him, the orbit called "The Lotus of Command," and the buoyant, self-delighted, handsome divinity of the flower-bow will be burnt, as by a lightning bolt, to ashes. Thus, the primeval prophecy of Brahmā will be fulfilled; or, in other words, the calamity and all that led up to it will be disclosed to have been predestined all the while. And so the question will have to be balanced in the mind, as to whether the Voluntary Death was voluntary after all. Where is the beginning or the end of the playfulness of Māyā's play?

IV. SHIVA MAD

Satī had died; Vijayā had collapsed in grief. The old story goes on to narrate how Shiva, having rounded off his evening meditation with a bath in the radiant waters of the beautiful lake Manasa, mounted Nandī again, his white and splendid bull, and went riding at an easy canter along the skyways back toward his home. And when he was still some distance away, he heard a shriek that chilled the marrow of his bones. Vijayā had revived, and her lamentations were coming out from the high Himālaya peak, like signals, through the stillness of the evening air.

Quick as thought, Nandī increased his pace, and he carried Shiva to the hermitage with the velocity of wind. There the god discovered Satī, his beloved, dead. And because of the power of love, he was at first unable to believe what his eyes beheld. Stooping, he gently patted and stroked the unresponsive cheek. "You are asleep?" he asked. "What has sent you off to sleep?"

Then Vijayā told him what had happened, beginning with the news of Daksha's sacrifice to which had been invited every god and created thing in all the worlds. "There is not a single living thing," she repeated, "who has not been asked!" And she broke down with that, weeping heavily. She described to Shiva, through her sobbing, how she had arrived to call for Satī and himself, and how his wife had received the news of the sacrifice. She declared that Satī had understood immediately why her father had withheld his invitation. "Satī's face," Vijayā told him, "grew hard. I never knew she could look so terrifying. A frightening color came into her features and she was so angry she could not speak. Her brows pulled together, and her face grew tight; it became as dark as a sky filled with heavy smoke. Then, after she had sat that way a little while, suddenly her body burst, and Satī seemed to have broken through the top of her own head, leaving the corpse to collapse."

Shiva lifted himself in anger. Listening to the girl talk, he let his anger become prodigious. It was converted into an all-consuming, interior conflagration: flames started shooting from his mouth, ears, nose, and eyes; rocketing meteors shot out of him, whistling, and streaming death, like the seven suns at the end of the world. An instant, and he had transferred himself to Daksha's place of offering. At the edge of it he stood, and with terrible eyes surveyed the populous compound. A wrath unbounded overcame him then, seeing the entire creation there assembled—invited guests from every corner of the worlds, every quarter of the sky—gods, plants, beasts, saints, every conceivable sort of existence, high and low; fish, worms, the seasons, the ages of the world, all in their physical forms; men and plants, each in its apportioned position, according to their various parts fulfilled in the constitution of the world. Shiva, seeing them all so solemnly gathered, each following the progress of the ceremonial and playing reverently his apportioned role, let suddenly break forth from him a horrible monster, born of the bursting of his wrath: Virabhadra was its name: and it was a frightfully lion-headed "Lord of the Hosts." Virabhadra would soon enough discomfit the decent procession of the rite.

With a sheaf of arrows in one hand, a stocky bow in another, his club in a third, and a long pike in the fourth, Virabhadra easily pushed one of the Door Guardians aside, and broke with a roar and an angry streaming of the lion mane into the center of the sacred place. The gods and all the kings of the earth arose

297

with a great glittering of their weapons, but the monster frightened them back with the swiftness of the dense volley of his arrows. Then he plunged for the altar where the priests and sages were in the act of pouring out the offerings. They abandoned hurriedly the sacrificial vessels and took refuge in Vishnu, who was standing at the center, supervising the whole affair. Vishnu stepped forward, and there now began between the Universal God and Virabhadra a battle of the most astonishing proportions. Each assailed the other with weapons of magic, and they continually were surpassing each other in miraculous inventions, feints, and blows. But Vishnu finally seized the warrior servant with his naked hands, whirled him through the air, dashed him to the ground, and then stamped on him with bare feet, until the blood broke from his head. Streaming blood, Virabhadra gathered himself together and returned in misery to his master.

Shiva came into the arena in person, wrathful and with red eyes, and all the saintly ones went stiff with terror. Vishnu vanished; he had made himself invisible. And Shiva, ranging in his fury where he would, overturned the sacred vessels, kicked the altars apart, and scattered debris on all sides. The entire cosmic assemblage drew back in fear; many broke away and fled, screaming for their lives. One indignant god made bold to face the Destroyer with an angry glare; Shiva struck both his eyes out with the back of his hand. The Sun God, with immensely outspread arms, then attempted to hold the wild divinity back, smiling at him, meanwhile, with brilliantly friendly teeth. But a quick jab of Shiva's fist sent the bright teeth down the Sun God's throat. Shiva took him, rattled him as easily as a lion would a young gazelle, and whirled him overhead until the blood shot from the tips of his fingers and his sinews cracked.

When Shiva let the Sun God drop, broken and wet with blood, the gods and the creatures of the universe turned and fled. They fled with cries and tumult, dispersed in all directions, and darted to hide wherever they could. Many were killed by the glance of his eyes. Those eyes consumed the entire offering-ground to ashes, laid it waste, and exploded all the fires. "The Offering," scared nearly to death, transformed himself into a gazelle, and scurried desperately away into the skies. Shiva pursued, with arrows and bow. The gazelle bounded into Brahmā's realm to hide; but even there Shiva followed. The frightened animal doubled back, made for the earth, and there darted for cover, Shiva still in steady pursuit. The hiding place that the animal finally discovered was the corpse of Satī, into which it disappeared: all Shiva knew was that it was suddenly gone, and that he was standing before the body of the dead Satī, his love. When he saw her, he forgot the gazelle. He stood perfectly still. Then a great cry of grief broke from his throat. Her beauty, her goodness, roared in his mind as he gazed at the lotus-miracle of her countenance, the line of the perfect brows, the lips. And he was overpowered by the pain of bereavement; and he broke, like any common mortal, into a convulsion of grief.

The Love God heard the wild, heavy sobbing, and approached, together with Desire and the God of Spring. Coming on Shiva, broken with emotion, weeping as though his senses had disintegrated, he smiled, notched an arrow to his bowstring, drew, and sent all five of his bewilderers into Shiva's heart. The god was galled by a hot infusion. Shattered by grief, he yet discovered himself insidiously roused, and the madness increased in him until his wits broke and he flew wild with a terrible passion of loss and need. He flung himself to the ground. He got up and ran. He returned and crouched, staring, beside the corpse. Gently he smiled and he reached out to the body and embraced it, calling into it to rouse the emptiness. "Satī, Satī, Satī, Satī! Come out of your sulking-corner, Satī, Satī!" The body was stiff and stark. And he caressed the forehead and the cheeks. He began to tinker with the abundant ornaments, playing, removing them, piece by piece, and putting them back again, but differently arranged. He lifted her and clasped her to him, let the corpse drop from his arms, fell on his back, and wept.

Brahmā and the worlds of divinities were very anxious and afraid when they beheld the flow from Shiva's eyes. "If those tears get to the earth," they said, "it will burn. What can we do?" Then they hurriedly summoned the Slow Wanderer of the heavens, the planet Saturn, the son of the Sun God, on whose banner is emblazoned the Vulture. This power once had rescued the earth from a deluge by sucking the rain up and swallowing it as fast as it fell—and this for a period of one hundred heavenly years. "No one but you can stop those tears before they touch the ground," the gods said to him. "If the earth catches fire, the heavens will go too, and then all the gods." But the Slow Wanderer was reluctant. "If Shiva notices what I am doing," he protested, "he will shrivel my body to a crisp." The gods consulted. They quickly promised to keep the pain-mad Shiva distracted by their crafts, so that he should not notice the Slow Wanderer when he drew close to him and began to catch the burning tears in the cup of his hands.

Shiva was still on his back. The Slow Wanderer found the tears so hot he was unable to hold them. They had begun to gush in abundance. What he did was to cup the flood in his hands as it fell, but then sharply fling it to the remotest mountain of the universe, far, far away, at the outer rim of the world, where the Void yawns, and where that-which-is comes against that-which-is-not. The mountain was no less mighty than the mountain of the gods, Mount Meru, at the center of the world, yet it was inadequate to withstand the heat of Shiva's tears. It cracked and split through the middle, so that the burning flood poured down into the Cosmic Ocean that supports and encircles the world. Mixed with the waters of the ocean, Shiva's hot tears lost a little of their fire, so that the universe was not ignited; but they did not completely mingle with the waters. They circled eastward in a smoking current that is flowing to this day: the stream that is called Vaitarani, "Not to be Crossed"; and it borders the kingdom of the Lord of the Dead.[1] Where it passes the high portals of the castle of the King of Death it is two miles wide, very deep, and rough with mighty waves. No boat, no ferry, can cut across its burning flood. And the gods do not dare to pass across it in their chariots, even far aloft in the air; for, by the terrible turbulence, the tears are spurted to the highest reaches of the sky.

Shiva lifted himself from the ground; he was blind with agony. He stooped, lifted the corpse to his shoulder, and, wandering madly, vaguely, without aim, headed eastward, babbling to himself crazily. The gods observed this, and again were troubled. They called to each other, back and forth. "Sati's corpse will never decay," they cried, "so long as it is in contact with the body of Shiva." So they began to follow him. Brahmā, Vishnu, and the Slow Wanderer, having made themselves invisible, by virtue of their Māyā-craft got themselves inside the corpse. And then, while Shiva stumbled along in his blind bewilderment, they dismembered the body, letting the pieces, one by one, drop to the ground. The two feet fell on the "Mountain of the Goddess," the two ankles a little farther on; still farther eastward, in the land called Kāmarūpa, "The Form of Love," her womb fell on the "Mountain of the God of Love," and close beside it the delicate cup of her navel. The two breasts came, together with a golden necklace, and after that the shoulders, then the neck. The whole course of Shiva's walk was left scattered with the remains of the blessed body; and this road of his sorrows the peoples of those eastward lands regard as sacred ground. Wherever a por-

[1] Compare the river crossed by Lancelot on the "sword-bridge."

tion of the body fell, a shrine is standing, and Satī is revered there under one or another of her many names. She is called upon to exercise, for the happiness of mankind, one or another of her miraculous powers. And thus the terrible dismemberment has redounded to the benefit of the children of the world.[1] Brahmā, Vishnu, and the Slow Wanderer cut certain parts of the corpse into minute shreds, and these were carried away by the winds through space, and transported upward to the fields where the Heavenly Ganges flows among the stars. There they fell into the sacred stream. Where her head dropped to the earth, however, Shiva stopped in his witless passage, stood and stared, got down on his knees, and broke into a groan of pain.

The gods drew around him. They wished to bring him consolation, but were still afraid. They remained at a distance, but presently he saw them. The moment that happened, he was so ashamed that he transformed himself, before their eyes, into a lingam of stone, solidified, stark and prodigious, in the torture of his love. The gods bowed in reverence. They gave praise in unison to the Everlasting. They sought by this praise to recall Shiva to his reason. They wished to renew in him the realization of the nature of his True Being, that he might come to know again the light of his eternal consciousness. "Thou art abundant with the nectar of Illumination," they prayed. "Thou art the Highest Being in this, thy form of the lingam. Wisdom, thou; thou dost understand the impermanence of the things of time. O thou, mid-point of the sea of annihilation, prime cause at once of continuance and decline, light of all light, brilliant in the radiance of thine existence, thou art the Highest Being, in this thy form of the lingam. All the gods quail when in the fury of thy grief thou dost make thyself before them manifest. There-

---

[1] This legend, well known to the popular lore of India, accounts for the wide distribution of the so-called "Fifty-two Sacred Places"—shrines of pilgrimage erected to Satī, the paramount model of traditional Indian womanhood.

fore be thou unto them most merciful, and let this moment of thine anguish pass."

The god, during the course of their prayer, resumed before them his familiar form, but reeling still with pain. Brahmā spoke gently, to assist him to a recollection of his being.

"O thou, God, those desiring deliverance from the world's sorrow turn to thee in worship, and are delivered. Those also that are greatly wise—clean of lust, malice, and all passion, that have averted their faces from the fields of sorrow, and repose beatifically in quietude—meditate on thee. They continually contemplate, with their inner vision, the third eye in the middle of thy forehead, for it is exalted above the five elements, akin to the sun and to the moon, and makes luminous the passage to enlightenment. That eye is reality supreme and immaculate, the flawless blossom that crowns the magnitudinous, variously branching tree of thine existence; and its nourishment is the liquor of untroubled contemplation that is sealed within the glow of ascetic fervor. This yields to thee thy might, forever.

"O thou, God, in the lotus of thy heart behold, immovable, the flame of immaculate light; serene it is, far beyond the confusion of these passions that now, like a cloud of dust before the sun, envelop and obscure it. Invisibly visible to the apprehending yogī, that supreme, indestructible, one Eternal, is, has been, will always be, thy Self. It is impalpably delicate; nevertheless, it pervades the cosmos. It is gravid with power, and the wise are in quest of it. It is at once the path and the end of the path. No one guards it, no one steals it away. It is thy treasure; it is without tangible form.

"O thou, God, bewildered by the plausibilities of Māyā, thou dost not now see what lives in the chamber of thy heart. Only realize the specious character of the ubiquitous allure; shatter it; dissolve it. Collect thyself; unite with thine own quintessential being; and join thyself therewith to the Highest, and remain

303

there, fast, thy self the Self. All this pain—let it go. It does not touch the kernel of thy being."

Shiva listened in silence. He remembered the Highest Self that had always been the theme and object of his meditation; but he was now unable to collect himself and bring his powers to focus, so disordering was his grief over the loss of Sati. Head bowed, he remained for a time without a word. Then he turned his eyes to Brahmā. "What am I to do?"

Brahmā replied. "Almighty God, detach thy mind from the billows of thy pain, and turn thy whole thought to the Highest Being. The center of thine existence lies beyond this sea of torment. Because the agony of time now fills thy consciousness, the gods are amazed and at a loss. Thy passion pulverizes the universe; the heat of thy wrath scorches every life; thy tears would have split the earth, but were caught by the Slow Wanderer, and turned him black. The magnificent mountain where the gods and saints dwell and the clouds of the air dip to drink was split by them, the fish of the universal sea were killed by them, and their burning river does violence to the body of the world. The torrid blasts of thy sighs have already uprooted mountains, withered forests, so that the tigers thus dispossessed, and the elephants rendered homeless and distracted, range the earth, at a loss to settle down. Every living creature has been made nomad by thine uncentering. And where thou didst travel with the corpse of Sati on thy shoulder, there the earth broke beneath thy feet, and it quivers yet. Through all the heavens and hells no creature exists that has not been harrowed by the teeth of thy despair. O do thou therefore relinquish this thy moment of despair and pain; permit thy wrath to go its way; bestow on us thy peace! For thou dost know—indeed, in thy proper being, thou art—the Supernal Being and Consciousness of Bliss; retain that Being and Consciousness, that Bliss, in the deep stillness. Three thousand six hundred years will pass (one hundred

304

heavenly years) and in the long-whirling round of time the goddess will be thy spouse again; meantime . . ."

Shiva, head bowed, remained in silence, inward plunging,
totally abstracted. Presently one heard the sound of his voice.
"Till the pain has left me—till I come up again from this, the
ocean of my loss of Satī—O Brahmā," said the god, "you must
remain beside me, and give me comfort. Wherever I go, you
must remain beside me, and give me comfort."

"So shall it be," Brahmā replied.

And when they prepared, then, to depart, the hosts of Shiva
came together all around them, and his magnificent white bull,
Nandī, came; Nandī waited for the god to mount. Serpent-kings
arrived and coiled up along Shiva's body, disposing themselves,
by way of ornament, about his neck and limbs. Attended, accompanied by all the divine figures of the universe, he made his way
back to Himālaya, his sometime home. And there the Mountain
King came to him out of the portals of the mountain palace,
making Shiva welcome.

The young girl, Vijayā, was there. She bowed before the returning god, and broke, when she saw him, into an agony of
weeping. "O where, Great God," she cried, "is thy beloved, Satī?
Without her, thou lackest radiance. Great God, if perchance thou
shouldest never again take thought of her, in my mind she will
dwell forever; from my heart she will never depart. Since the
moment she gave up her body before my very eyes, no other
image has existed in my spirit; the arrow of the pain transfixes
me, and I shall never know again the joys of joy."

Her face she covered with a corner of her veil and, breaking
with a sob, she crumbled senseless to the ground. When Shiva
saw her fall, his own memories assailed him, and he stood, rooted
by the pang. Tears swam to his eyes. The gods again became
anxious. Brahmā stooped to comfort the sorrow-shattered Vijayā,
then addressed himself benignly to the god.

"O thou, Yogī from before the beginning, pain does not become thee. The proper object of thine inward regard is the Light Supernal, Unmitigated Majesty. Why does that regard repose now on a woman? Thy Being is supreme stillness, strength indestructible undefiled by change, beyond the perception of the senses. How, therefore, is it touched by pain? The highest world-pervading peace is thy reality; comprehend it with the wisdom of thy soul. In the form of Vishnu the yogīs know thee as the Preserver of the World. The same Satī who beguiled thee is Māyā, the enchantress of the world. She takes from the unborn infant, while yet it lives in the mother-womb, all remembrance of its previous state of being; and she has similarly deluded thee, so that thou art racked with pain. A thousand times before hast thou been ravished of thy wit by Satī, and thou hast lost her in every eon precisely as now. But just as Satī has always returned to thee, so wilt thou know her again as thou hast known her, and again cleave to her. Collect thy recollection and behold the thousand Satīs, how they were snatched from thee by death, so that thou wert forsaken of them a thousand times; and then see how they are born again, and again attain to thee who art hardly accessible even to the meditations of the gods. Behold in thine inner vision how Satī is to be again thy bride."

Blind with his suffering, Shiva accepted the offered hand of Brahmā, and the two departed out of that city of the King of the Mountain. They went away westward, and disappeared into the solitude of the hills.[1]

[1] The Involuntary Creation, *Kālikā Purāna* 1:1-5:10; the Involuntary Marriage, *ibid.*, 5:11-13:53; The Involuntary Death, *ibid.*, 14:1-16:70; Shiva Mad, *ibid.*, 17:1-19:13. The description given in the next chapter, On the Siprā Shore, is abridged from *Kālikā Purāna* 19:13-33.

Bringing Shiva to the Siprā lake, the narrative of the *Purāna* then turns to other themes, largely the history of Vishnu's Incarnation as the Boar, but resumes with the story of Shiva and Pārvatī at the beginning of Adhyaya 42. The burning of the Love God to ashes is described in 44:125.

ON THE SIPRĀ SHORE

LIFE is much too horrible in its inescapable, unmerited and un-justifiable possibilities of sorrow to be termed "tragic." The "tragic" view is, so to say, only a foreground view, held by people who marvel still, unable to conceive that life is the thing it is. The Greek Tragedy itself, which has given its name to this view, is, paradoxically, above the reproach, for it delights in the monstrous. Yet the delight of the Attic Tragedy is that of turning the point against one's own breast, amidst a tumult of pity and terror, and remaining exultantly defiant of the monstrousness, even as the glowing barb drives hissing into the heart, to burn it to ashes—which is still a too sensational attitude. The only appropriate bearing is that of the solemn, ceremonial dance of Shiva in his madness, with the balanced wing-beats of the rocking arms and hands, and the inexorable pounding of the naked soles, to the rhythm of the tinkling ankle-rings, and therewith the masklike smile.

The word *mythos* is Greek; and in spite of all the vestiges of Celtic and Germanic mythology that remain to us, whenever the word is mentioned we still think primarily of the myths of Greece, as preserved and handed on by Homer, Hesiod, and the tragic poets. But these supreme productions of the creative imagination have been lifted away from the common flood of popular and priestly lore, and have been transformed into expressions of the peculiar personal and contemporary-historical problems of the Ionic, Boeotian, and Attic worlds. They do not

307

render the quality of their archaic sources of the older and irrevocably lost Orphic epochs, when the materials, still obscurely interfused, interlaced, and grandiosely muffled in their meanings, were passing along in the great general stream of the folk tradition.

That archaic, earlier manner of myth is what survives to this day in the great popular mythical traditions of India. That is why, for the pampered modern Western reader, who has been well trained in his classics, and who desires, as the platonizing Schiller remarked, to arrive "in the land of knowledge only through the sunrise-gate of beauty," the Hindu fare is sometimes a little difficult to relish. For though the priestly Brahminic tradition never scorned, in any period of its development, the techniques of the contemporary, highly sophisticated secular art of poetry, nevertheless the priestly stylists were a long way from being poets. By and large, their myths remain on the relatively crude popular level and are not transmuted into poetical images through the vivifying power of a new economy, structure, and consistency, in the service of a fresh and original reconception, as are the myths in the *Iliad* or in the tragedies of Sophocles. The "poetical" is employed, indeed, as decoration, and in high-flown rhetorical passages, but generally unsuccessfully and unattractively, without taste or measure, as must always be the case when people who are not really poets flap their wings. The result is that the mythical content often appears rather like an overpainted, tricked-out old beauty. Beneath all the frippery there is nothing of the reborn freshness of a youthful figure with radiant countenance, but only a shriveled, corrugated old thing with a rewritten face. Nevertheless, just such long-overripe old beauties are often the very ones to tell best the ancient tales of life; they are better at that, by far, than the young and attractive fascinators. The only problem is not to shudder at the look of them while we are listening.

In any case, the traditional form in which the myths of India have been handed down has the great advantage of anonymity. Here no singular individual is speaking, but an entire people—perhaps with the tongue of some sect, having particular prejudices in favor of this or that divinity, and with the coloration of a certain century and local landscape, yet a people always—a generality, extensively valid and recognized, and free from every pretension to special genius or sensibility. What we are hearing when we listen to these stories is not the voice of any personality, but a consensus of teaching Brahmins at numberless temples and shrines of pilgrimage, saints and sages in the hermit groves, and spiritual instructors in villages and homes. A great group, in the role of teaching class, is speaking through these stories to another great group, the pious, each continually controlling and depending upon the other. What the native listener is and feels, yet does not know, is told to him. He comes into a more abundant possession of the common depths and heights of the universal spiritual and religious life and culture, by virtue of the pictures, the celebrated personages, and incidents of the *mythos*.

Nowhere else can one come so close to drinking at the very source of the being of the culture, drinking the original essence of its sap of life. It is as though one had tapped the birch where the sap rises that builds out its limbs and crown—or better, had tapped the palm tree, the sap of which yields an intoxicant; for intoxication is one of the principal effects of the *mythos*. Cultures that no longer know it are prosaic and burnt out. And the hunger for myth is a hankering for an intoxicant that will stimulate and vivify, as the intoxicant of the sacramental soma drink stimulates the Hindu war and thunder god, who imbibes of it three times a day at the offerings of the Brahmins and becomes fortified thereby for his deeds of cosmic government, as well as for the work of clearing the way with his heavenly thunder bolts for the victorious marches of his chosen people, the Vedic Aryans.

The myth is among spiritual foods what the drink of the gods (soma, ambrosia) is in the myths themselves; through it one communes with the superhuman beings and powers. The myth disregards—does not even know—the individual. As all the members of the community participate in it in like manner, giving and receiving and subsisting thereby, so it links man to the being of the superman.[1] That is why the old myths of remote and unknown peoples have become so fascinating for us in recent times. With the dawn of Western critical thought, the link with the godly powers formerly woven for us by our own sacraments and dogmas lost its hold, and yet today a more primitive level of myth, abundant with timeless truth, which for nearly two millenniums was overlaid and disfigured by the dogmas and sacraments of the religion of the later revelation, suddenly seems to have something very deep to say to us.[2] This return of the long

[1] "It is not true," says Nietzsche, "that there is some hidden thought or idea at the bottom of the myth, as some in a period of civilization that has become artificial have put it, but the myth itself is a kind or style of thinking. It imparts an idea of the universe, but does it in the sequence of events, actions, and sufferings." This is why we may look into it as into a mirror or fountain full of hints and prophecies, telling us what we are and how we should behave amidst the bewildering sequences of surprising events and happenings that are our common lot. At least, this is the way in which Hindu people have always regarded the deeds and sufferings of the gods and heroes of their myths and legends.

Myth is the sole and spontaneous image of life itself in its flowing harmony and mutually hostile contrarieties, in all the polyphony and harmony of their contradictions. Therein resides its inexhaustible power.

[2] Ages and attitudes of man that are long gone by still survive in the deeper unconscious layers of our soul. The spiritual heritage of archaic man (the ritual and mythology that once visibly guided his conscious life) has vanished to a large extent from the surface of the tangible and conscious realm, yet survives and remains ever present in the subterranean layers of the unconscious. It is the part of our being that links us to a remote ancestry and constitutes our involuntary kinship with archaic man and with ancient civilizations and traditions.

In dealing with symbols and myths from far away we are really conversing somehow with ourselves—with a part of ourselves, however, which is as un-

lost to our contemporary comprehension and interest is a necessary compensation, on a world scale, for its simultaneous decline
in the Indian and other ancient culture lands under the impact
of the modern technological age. To be a match for the new development, even in our own limited sphere, we must seek to pene-
trate the mythical contents of every possible antique tradition;
for the change is so comprehensive that nothing of the more short-
winded kind, that has come into being in more recent ages, can
suffice to furnish us with strength to bear the force of our terrific
century and to support its fires of transmutation.

The Universal Goddess, the World Mother, is among the
oldest, "longest-winded," of the great supporting divinities
known to the myths of the world. She is represented everywhere
in shrines dedicated to local mother-goddesses; countless images
have been found from the Neolithic period, some even from
the Paleolithic; she was known to the cultures of the Mediterranean under many names—Cybele, Isis, Ishtar, Astarte, Diana;
she was the Magna Mater. And, if one inquires to know her
origin, the oldest textual remains and images can carry us back
only so far, and permit us to say: "Thus she appeared in those
early times; so-and-so she may have been named; and in such-
and-such a manner she seems to have been revered." But with
that we have come to the end of what can be said; with that we
have come to the primitive problem of her comprehension and
being. For just because she is the Great Mother, so was she there
before anything else. She is the *primum mobile*, the first beginning, the material matrix out of which all came forth. To question
beyond her into her antecedents and origin, is not to understand
her, is indeed to misunderstand and underestimate, in fact to in-

---

familiar to our conscious being as the interior of the earth to the students of
geology. Hence the mythical tradition provides us with a sort of map for explor-
ing and ascertaining contents of our own inner being to which we consciously
feel only scantily related.

sult her. And anyone attempting such a thing well might suffer the calamity that befell that smart young adept who undertook to unveil the veiled image of the Goddess in the ancient Egyptian temple of Saïs, and whose tongue was paralyzed forever by the shock of what he saw According to the Greek tradition, the Goddess has declared of herself: οὐδείς ἐμὸν πέπλον ἀνεῖλε, "no one has lifted my veil." It is a question not exactly of the veil, but of the garment that covers her female nakedness—the veil is a later misinterpretation for the sake of decency. The meaning is: I am the Mother without a spouse, the Original Mother; all are my children, and therefore none has ever dared to approach me; the impudent one who should attempt it shames the Mother —and that is the reason for the curse.

This, then, is the Goddess who sprang from the incubating world-creative self-contemplation of the Creator Brahmā. But that was not properly the creation of her; that was simply the story of how she stepped into manifestation. There can be no description or discussion of her creation; for it is out of her that everything has come into being, and it is in her spell that everything remains captive, and it is back to her that everything must return.

The point of the myth of the Romance of the Goddess seems to be that no one is long permitted to remain what he is. This is the circumstance through which the world moves forward as a continuous creation. None of the Celestial Ones can remain what he started out to be, what he thought himself to be, and what he would have liked to go on being without change.[1] Brahmā becomes ridiculous. Brahmā and Vishnu become suppliants. The

[1] This meaning, scarcely ever explained, yet unfolded and reiterated in the sequence of events, bears some resemblance to the main aim of analytical psychology, namely, at the cost of painful, startling, and even humiliating experiences, to throw into contact forces and spheres of our inner being which have been inclined to remain isolated from each other, crippled consequently, and frustrated, and by these crises to keep the energies of the psyche in creative flow.

God of Love finds himself in command of an army of Hate. And
Shiva, the removed, unattached ascetic, has scarcely declared
that he could never give up the contemplation of the Highest
Being, when he is rapt into the spell of Satī, and his supremely
concentrated powers are swept into lust and rage—rage at the
moment of Brahmā's indiscretion; wild despair after Satī's death.
The freest and most independent of the gods, a disdained and
insulted son-in-law, emotionally involved to such a degree that
he becomes disordered in his mind! This is a condescension of
the highest divine principle akin to that which St. Paul, in his
pastoral letter to the Philippians, recognized in Christ Jesus,
"who, being in the form of God, thought it not robbery to be
equal with God: but made himself of no reputation, and took
upon him the form of a servant, and was made in the likeness of
men: and being found in fashion as a man, he humbled himself,
and became obedient unto death, even the death of the cross"
(Phil. 2:6-8). The all-comprising Mother of the World, in a similar gesture of supreme humiliation, does not regard it as a dimin-
ishment to be brought into the phenomenal sphere as the daughter of a second-class demiurgic power, and then to exercise
herself in prolonged observances to win the hand of Shiva, who
has really belonged to her, as her immortal consort, from all
eternity, and moreover represents only a basic power, a major aspect, of her own being.

The simultaneity of the earthly, epical masquerade with the
distant interfusion of all the characters, who take form on the
scene beside each other and in mutual opposition, is the higher
import of this myth, the central force and figure of which is the
great Māyā, the self-delusion that masks and deploys itself in all.
That all that happens really need not have happened, or does
not happen, yet happens in dead earnest within the frame of
Māyā, and precisely in order to create continually this Māyā and
to press it on—that is the meaning, the great point.

313

The joke of the myth is the way in which the characters are all equally caught by the tricks of the world play; the story has hardly begun when every one of them is trapped, each in his own, but equally paradoxical, way.

Brahmā's hymn to the goddess (the *shakti* or "power" of him self and of the entire pantheon) accepts life as a *whole,* just as it is, in full surrender to all of the peace-disturbing opposites. "Thou art one *and* the other." He says always *"and";* which means: "Thou art all in its entirety, there is really nothing to be done." This amounts to a colossal acceptance, an almost incredible *laissez-faire* to life. Brahmā was equally wonderful when Kāma first appeared before him. To each the creative principle permits his rights and claims, recognizing the whole of creation as the incalculable sum of the multifariousness of the innumerable powers that here, necessarily and continuously, work against each other. Surprise, perplexity, catastrophe are the categories of all significant happening. The Involuntary Creation, the life process and generation, is in itself involuntary, accidental. And it triumphs ever and again over the planned. The making of plans, indeed, only serves to heighten its overwhelming effects.

The Myth of the Goddess shows with magnificent gestures how to adjust one's self to this universal circumstance—composedly, without fear, because accepting and in essential agreement. Hence this creation story knows nothing of the motif of the Fall of Man that goes contrary to God's will, knows nothing, indeed, of God's wrath. The individual—God himself—has to cooperate in continually new improvisations, and that is how the precarious evolution of the universe proceeds. The creation is made possible through the self-surrender of the divine and human actors to roles unfamiliar to them, but urged upon them by the ever new and surprising situations. Everyone, one time or another, is to be forced to realize that the "other fellow," who at first sight always seems to be disturbing the normal course of events, is really an indispensable instrument for the evolution of the world. What at first seems upsetting and bewildering proves in time to have been the beneficent and necessary factor. The main thing is that the process of the continuous creation should not grow rigid in any momentary posture. Always it is on the point of sticking; and the awaited next event is always the sinister, the surprising, and difficult-to-bear—like the changes and realizations of one's growing old. In the procession, however, the whole of the sublime form of the state of the Imperishable is revealed, which transcends, survives, and yet perennially reveals itself in the gains and losses of our phenomenal existence. In the recognition of this one and only living consciousness is the bliss and wisdom of the unending crucifixion.

Shiva, bereaved, distracted, was conducted gently by his *guru*, Brahmā, out of the gates of the city of his life's loss and away into the Himālayan peaks of snow. There, walking together, the two came upon a little lake of solitude, clear, and delightful to the mind. Brahmā perceived it first.

And seated here and there about the quiet shores were saints and sages in absolute meditation; two or three stood bathing in the cool crystal waters, sending ripples out across its mirroring of the blue and immobile, high, mountain sky. Many migratory birds, shrilly crying, were coming from all directions to flutter down into its lotus-bordered waters—pairs of splendid ruddy geese beautifully spreading out their great wings in exultation, cormorants with their hooked bills, gray-winged geese, and Siberian cranes, stalking about the shores, floating on the surface of the lake, peering into the waters, themselves beautifully reflected—and, occasionally, with a sudden thunderous beating of hundreds of wings, all lifting out of the lake into the sky, to circle in many companies, and presently return to settle, flutter, and preen. And beneath them, in the crystalline depths, were swimming fish of innumerable brilliant hues, visible as they darted in and out among the lotus stems. Lotus buds, lotus chalices, blue lotuses and white were abundant there; and the vegetation about the shores was luxurious and of cool shade.

When Shiva's eyes beheld this lake he was moved; and he beheld the river Siprā that flowed from it, as the Ganges from the disk of the moon. This lake never dries up in the summer heat. Those who have bathed in it and drunk of its waters acquire, according to the statutes of the gods, the boon of immortality, and, remaining young forever, pass through the years with undiminished faculties. Those who bathe in it during the night of the October-November full moon are borne in a brilliantly shining chariot to the heavenly abode of Vishnu. And those who bathe in it through that entire month go to the abode of Brahmā and then are released entirely from all the worlds of form.

It was beside the waters of this lake of peace that Shiva found again his repose and majesty, in the contemplation of the supreme, unchanging, all-pervading source and end of being, which is the substratum, life, and consciousness of all existence-forms. Thereby he released himself from his mad fixation, which had been threatening to unbalance the world process. He centered himself in the adamantine meditation. And thus he remained until the Goddess, having taken form again as the maid Pārvatī, daughter of Himālaya, the Mountain King, and Menakā his wife, moved him again from his high solitude, by dint of her long-sustained spiritual and physical austerities, and their life together was resumed.

INDEX

INDEX

A

Abraham, 52

Abu Kasem, 9–25, 145, 221, 239; *see also* attachment; fate; magic; rebirth; symbols; unconscious

acceptance, in Romance / Myth of the Goddess, 314–15

Achilles, 114

Adam, 170, 177n, 258n; old, 18, 37

Adonis, *see* Tammuz

Aeneas, 84, 132n

Aitareya Āranyaka, see *Brāhamanas*

Alexander, 131

alter ego: Balan as Balin's, 136–37, 145–48; Galahad as Lancelot's, 180–81; lion as Owain's, 118–20; Meleagant as Bademagu's, 173–74; shaggy horse as Conn-eda's, 28–32, 38–50, 63, 122, 228

ambivalence, *see* opposites, coexisting

ambrosia, 310; *see also* elixir

Amrita, *see* elixir

analytical psychology, 133, 312n

ancestor worship, origin in Hindu myth of creation, 247–48

ancient and medieval tales, 128–30, 160–62, 181

Andromeda, 20, 184

Anglo-Saxon invasion of Britain, 187

anima-archetype, *see* archetypes

animal, representing instinct: in Buddha legend, 78; St. John Chrysostom as, 56–58, 63–65, 116; and Christianity, 127–28; in

Conn-eda story, 38–50; in Gawain story, 87; in king and corpse story, 202, 219–20; in Lancelot story, 150, 171–72; Merlin and, 182, 183–84n; in mythology, 126–29; Nebuchadnezzar as, 65–66n, 116; Orpheus and, 134n; in Owain story, 98, 101,116,118–26; in Romance / Myth of the Goddess, 267–69, 275, 277, 282, 283, 285–86, 288, 289, 290, 297, 304, 306n, 315–16; *see also* birds; boar; dragon; horse; hound; lion; monkey; myth; Nandī; nature; opposites, coexisting; primitive man; serpent

animus-archetype, *see* archetypes

Aphrodite, 46–47, 260

Apocalypse, 186

apostolic succession, 61–62, 64

apotheosis: Conn-eda's, 48, 50; in king and corpse story, 233–35; *see also* transfiguration

Apuleius, *see The Golden Ass*

archetypes: anima, 133–34n, 159–60 (Guinevere); animus, 133, 159–60, 179 (Lancelot); Jehovah, 52; Marriage of Heaven and Earth, 26; savior, 177 (Jesus Christ, Lancelot); temptation, in conflict of Indra with Vritra, 268n; Wise Old Man, 39; women, realm of, 82; *see also* female; male

Argonauts, 194

Ariadne, 226

Artemis, 47

Arthur, King, 68, 80–81, 83, 86n, 88–95, 98–99, 106, 109–15, 132–34, 136–40, 149, 157, 162–63, 165, 171, 182, 185–196, 198–99; see also death; fate; initiation / integration; trials

Arthurian romance, 67–201, 233

Aryans, Vedic, 310

asceticism 282; St. John Chrysostom's, 53; as generator of spiritual energy, 256; see also beggar ascetic; Shiva

Assumption, see transfiguration

Astarte, 311

Astolat, see Elaine of Astolat

Astyanax (Francillon), 132n

Atalanta, 47

Atouts, in Tarot pack, ix, Pl. IV; see also Tarot cards

attachment: Abu Kasem's, 15–25; rebirth through liberation from, 17–19, 36, 78; see also ascetism; bondage; Shiva

Attic: Tragedy, world, see under Greek Tragedy and mythology respectively

Avalon, Arthur in, 188; see also Blessed Isles; death; initiation / integration; Mothers, the

avarice, Abu Kasem's, 9–25

avatars, see apotheosis; transfiguration

Axis, World (Mount Meru), 289, 300

B

Babylonia, tales of, 130, 177n

Bademagu, King (Death), 172–75; Merlin as, 183; see also death; Meleagant

Balan, 136–37, 145–48; see also alter ego; Balin; female

Balin (The Knight with the Two Swords), 136–49, 150–51n, 173n;

and chivalry, 148; and death, 143; and demonic possession, 136–37; Dolorous Stroke of, 136, 141–43, 149; ego of, 146–49; and female, 146–48; as ideal male, 148; and life, 147; and unconscious, 144–49; see also fate; initiation/integration; opposites, coexisting

ball, magic, Conn-eda's 28–30, 39–41, 63

balsam: in story of Owain, 116–118; see also elixir

Ban, King, 135

baptism, in St. John Chrysostom story, 53–65

Barabbas, 177

basket, Conn-eda's magic, 28

battle-ax, of Green Knight, 67–68, 77, 78, 85

bed, marvel: Gawain and, 86–87, 167; Lancelot and, 167

beggar ascetic: and king, in king and corpse story, 202–4, 212–16, 218–231; prince's friend as, in king and corpse story, 205–6

Benz, Richard, 60n

Bernlak de Hautdesert (Bernlak of the Lofty Desert), disguise of Green Knight (q.v.), 80, 172; Merlin as, 183

Bible, 128; see also Apocalypse; Daniel; Genesis; New Testament; Nicodemus, The Gospel of; Old Testament; Paul, St. (Epistle to the Philippians)

Bird of the Human Head, Conn-eda's visit to, 28–29, 39–41, 50

Bird of the Sun, see Garuda

birds, speech of: as angelic communication, 40n; in Kynon's tale, 99–100; in Owain story, 102, 110, 125; Siegfried and. 114; see also animal

birth, see life s.v. death implicit in; myth s.v. birth in; virgin birth

Black Knight, lord of the Lady of the Fountain: and Kynon, 100; in Owain story, 102–115, 147

Blake, William, 221

Blessed Isles, Arthur in, 188; *see also* Avalon; death; initiation / integration; Mothers, the

Blind One, The, titan murdered by Shiva, 282–83

blood: of Conn-eda's shaggy horse, 44; of Jesus Christ, 51, 61

boar, Vishnu as, 306n

Boeotian world, *see* Greek mythology

bondage: of fairy prince in Conn-eda story, 32; of Helen of Troy, 82; of Dame Ragnell, 90–95; of women in Arthurian romance, 81–83; *see also* attachment

Bo-tree, Buddha under, 77

bow and arrows of Kāma, *see* desire; Kāma

Brahmā, 239–85, 295, 299, 300–306, 312–16; *see also* female; truth

Brahmā-fissure, 292

Brahmaloka, 83n, 244n; *see also* death

Brāhmanas: Aitareya Āranyaka, 48n; *Jaimīniya Upanishad,* 83n; *Śatapatha,* 39n

Brahmins: ancestry of, 241, 269–70; priestly tradition of, 308–9

bride, ugly, 96n; Gawain's, 90–95

Brisen, Dame, and Lancelot, 151–54, 157

Britain: early culture, 82, 181, 184–85; early population, 181, 187; invasions of, 187

Broceliande, 195, 198; *see also* forest

Brown, A. C. L., 77n

Brünnhilde: enchanted sleep of, 114; self-sacrifice of, 51–52

Bruno, Giordano: *Della Causa Principio e Uno,* 40

Brun sans Pitié, defender of Fountain of Life, 184n

Brut Tysilio, 187

Bryan, W. F., 96n

Buddha, Gautama, 77–79, 166n, 268n

Buddhism: Mahayana, as universal religion, 52; in Tibet, 185

Buddhist art, 76–77

bull, Shiva's, *see* Nandī

Burton, Richard F., 13n

C

Caerleon upon Usk, 98, 109, 113

Caesar, 131

Cagliostro, 197

Calogrenant, 183–84n

Calypso, 200

Camelot, 153, 162, 174, 190, 195

cart, in story of Lancelot and Gawain, 164–66, 174–76, 179, Pl. II; *see also* symbols

Castle: of Abundance, Owain and, 100–101, 109, 121, 130, 173n, 183; of Bliant, Lancelot and, 158; of Case, Lancelot and, 151–52; of Death, Lancelot and, 172–75, 179; of Fountain of Life, 102–12, 122, 147, 151n; of Grail King, 142–43, 150–51n, 156; of Merlin, 182; *see also Château Merveil*

Cattle of the Sun, 86n

Celtic imagination, 127–30, 199–201; and Arthurian romance, 96, 150–51n, 181, 193–94; and prophetic protest, 186–87; *see also* Merlin; myth

Celtic Revival, 130

centaur, symbol of man's character, in Conn-eda story, 38, 43–48; *see also* symbols

Challenger, *see* death

chance, 13–15, 251–52, 314–15; *see also* fate; free will

charisma, 61

Charlemagne, 131, 187

Charles VII, King of France, 132*n*

Charon, 83; *see also* ferryman to netherworld

Château Merveil, Le (Marvelous Castle): Gawain in, 81–82, 86–88, 188; *see also* death; initiation / integration; Mothers, the

Chaucer, 96*n*

chess: as conflict, 35*n;* Conn-eda's game of, 27

Chevalier au Lion, Le, see Owain

childhood, as state of primitive enlightenment, 131, 134*n*, 185, 187, 192

chivalry, 97, 129, 130, 161, 193; Balin and, 148; in Gawain story, 67–73, 81, 85, 163–67, 173–74, 191–93; Lancelot and, 132–33, 161, 164–77; Owain and, 108, 110–13, 115, 119, 120–26; Perceval and, 114*n; see also* Round Table

Chrétien de Troyes, 81*n*, 82*n*, 83*n*, 97, 98*n*, 122–26, 161–62, 165, 168, 171, 174, 175, 176

Christ, *see* Jesus Christ

Christianity: and animals, 127–28; and archaic wisdom, 130, 181, 194; and belief in savior, 51–52; in *Golden Legend,* 60*n;* and Grail quest, 132, 151*n;* and Merlin, 184

Christmas, 67, 68

Chrysostom, St. John (John Golden-Mouth), 52–65, 116; as animal, 56–58, 63–65, 116; asceticism of, 53; and compassion, 53–54, 56–57, 59, 61; as hermit, 55–57, 64–65; humility of, 59, 62–65; initiation/integration of, 52, 61–65; and instinctual forces, 63–65; intuition of, 54–55, 61–65; poverty of, 54–55; rebirth of, 54–65; and redemption, 53, 59, 60*n*, 65; and sacrifice, 53–65; trials of, 54–65; *see also* opposites, coexisting

Circe, 200

Comfort, W. Wistar, 124*n*, 162*n*

compassion, 51–52; in St. John Chrysostom story, 53–54, 56–57, 59, 61; in Conn-eda story, 44

Conn, King, 26–27, 33; *see also* male, ideal

Connacht, Conn-eda's kingdom, 33

Conn-eda, 26–51, 62–64, 122, 128, 228, 235; apotheosis of, 48, 50; and compassion, 44; and death, 44–51; ego of, 36, 42–51; and evil, 34–38, 42, 48–49; humility of, 38–39; initiation/integration of, 36–38, 42–51; rebirth of, 37–38, 42–51; and sacrifice, 36, 42–51; transfiguration of, 44–45; trials of, 35, 38–45; and unconscious, 38–51; *see also* opposites, coexisting

Coomaraswamy, Ananda K., 39*n*, 43*n*, 76*n*, 96*n*, 102*n;* notes by, 40*n*, 48*n*, 77*n*, 79*n*, 83*n*, 166*n*, 270*n*

Coomaraswamy, D. L., 171*n*

Cornwall, 129–30

corpse of hanged man, *see* king, and the corpse

Cosmic: Egg, Hermaphrodite, Ocean, *see under respective nouns*

Council of Trent, and Merlin, 186

Countess of the Fountain, *see* Lady of the Fountain

creation myth: in *Kālikā Purāna,* 240–64; in Old Testament, 258–59*n; see also* Brahmā

crucifixion: of Jesus Christ, 151*n*, 177; unending, 315

Cuchullin, 40*n*, 79*n*

curiosity, role of, 220

Curoi MacDaire, 77*n*

Curtin, Jeremiah, 33*n*, 47*n*

Cybele, 311

Cyprus, 47

D

Daksha, 244, 249, 250, 254, 255–56, 264, 266, 269–71, 273–77, 279, 284, 289–91, 293–94, 296; *see also* sacrifice

Danaë, 184

Daniel, Book of, 65–66*n*, 116

Dante, 83*n*, 135, 149, 222, 226

darkness, *see* opposites, coexisting

David, 131

Dawn (Desire; Māyā), first woman in Hindu creation myth, 241–49, 255–58, 260–63, 272, 273, 287, 299; *see also* desire; female; Kālī; Kāma; Māyā

dead, kingdom of the, *see* Avalon; Blessed Isles; death; Mothers, the

death: and ancestor worship, 247–48; Arthur's, 188; Balin and, 143; in Conn-eda story, 44–51; fascination of, 199–201; Gawain and, 67–81, 85, 130–31, 163–67, 169, 173–74, 176–77; as God's name, 77*n*; green associated with, 76–77; implicit in life, 193, 253 (Kāma), 273*n*; in king and corpse story, 203–35; kingdom of, 165–79 (Guinevere), 301 (Hindu myth); in Kynon's tale, 99–100; Lancelot and, 164–79; in myth and epic, 77–88; in Owain story, 102–8, 130; as penalty for failure, 114–15; Satī's, 285–96; significance of Satī's, 294–96; in Tarot pack, 179, Pl. IV; *see also* Bademagu; Castle; *Château Merveil;* Green Knight; life; Meleagant; Mothers, the; Shiva; suicide

debt, *see* Karma

decapitation: in *Gawain and the Green Knight,* 67–68, 74–75, 76*n;* in king and corpse story, 210, 214, 229; of Lady of the Lake, 140; in myth, 76; significance of, 79*n,* 229; *see also Transposed Heads, The*

Delight, *see* Rati

deliverance, *see* attachment; ego; initiation / integration; rebirth; transfiguration

demon: in forest, 182; in king and corpse story, 203–4, 215–16, 222–34; Merlin as son of, 184, 185; pagan god as, 184; in Romance / Myth of the Goddess, 271–72, 285, 290, 294; as tempter, 78 (Buddha story), 267–69 (Shiva story); *see also* demonic possession

demonic possession: Abu Kasem, 16–25; Balin, 136–37, 140–49; death-wish as, 200; Lancelot (and Guinevere), 135, 159–60, 179; Owain, 129; Tristan, 135; *see also* demon; love-spell; magic

Dempster, Germaine, 96*n*

desire: in Buddha legend, 77–78; Francesca da Rimini and, 135; in Gawain story, 69–80, 84–88, 130; Lancelot and, 132–35, 167–81; in Owain story, 101, 130; Paris and, 135; in Romance / Myth of the Goddess, 241–316; Tristan and, 134–35; *see also* guilt; Kāma; Māra; Shiva

destiny, *see* fate

destructiveness, *see* evil; guilt; Shiva

Devil, *see* demon; demonic possession; Satan

Diana, 105, 311; as mother of Niniane, 194

dilettante, attitude of toward symbols, 2–6, 96–98

Divine Comedy, see Dante

Dolorous Stroke, of Balin, 136, 141–43, 149

Don Quixote, 194

dragon: Indra and, 119; Lancelot and, 136, 150; Merlin and, 185; in Owain story, 101, 119; Perseus

dragon (*cont.*)
  and, 20, 113, 119, 184; Siegfried and, 113–14; significance of, 49, 119, 134*n*, 184; Tristan and, 119; *see also* animal; Hydra; myth; serpent
dream, *see* myths; symbols
druids: and Conn-eda, 27–28, 32, 38–39; and Merlin, 134*n*, 186, 192, 194; and pre-Christian Britain, 185, 187; *see also* Wise Old Man
Dyonas, 194

E

East: attitude toward life, 129–30; myths of, 171–72
Eda, Queen, 26–27; as ideal female, 26, 34
Eden, Garden of, *see* Garden of Eden
Egg, Cosmic, 281–82
Egmont, 21
ego: Abu Kasem's, 15–25; Balin's, 146–49; Buddha's, 78; Conn-eda's, 36, 42–51; Gawain's, 79, 176–77; in king and corpse story, 213, 217–35; Lancelot's, 176–79; multiplicity of egos, 219–20; Owain's, 131; suicide as bewildered absorption in, 295; *see also* alter ego; beggar ascetic; rebirth; sword
Egypt, tales of, 130
Elaine, daughter of King Pelles, 151–58
Elaine of Astolat, 159
Eleanor of Aquitaine, 98*n*
elixir (All-heal, ambrosia, Amrita): Conn-eda's, 29–32, 37–38, 44; *see also* balsam
emotions, birth of, in Hindu myth of creation, 245–46, 261
encounters, *see* trials

endings, happy, in fairy tales and myths, 20
epics, 4, 77*n*, 79; *see also* Homer
Epiphany, 67
Ereshkigal, 177*n*
Erne, Loch, 29
Escalibor, *see* Excalibur
Eucharist, 62
Eve, 170, 177*n*, 258*n*
evil: in St. John Chrysostom story, 52, 56, 58, 60–65; in Conn-eda story, 34–38, 42, 48–49; and Round Table, 143–44; *see also* guilt
Excalibur (Escalibor), 86, 134*n*, 136, 139, 190, 233; *see also* sword

F

fairies, *see* demonic possession; magic
fairy city: Conn-eda's visit to, 30–33; as kingdom of God (eternal life), 38, 40, 43, 46–51
fairy tales, *see* myth
faith, Conn-eda's, 38, 40–51
Fall of Man, 314
Fata Morgana, *see* Morgan le Fay
fate: Abu Kasem and, 13–25; in Arthur story, 188–94; in Balin story, 136–49; Gawain and, 68; in king and corpse story, 218–35; in Lancelot story, 136–37; of Lancelot and Tristan, 134–35; Merlin and, 137, 184–86, 188–201; in Romance / Myth of the Goddess, 251–52, 294–96; in Round Table story, 190–94, 201; *see also* chance; free will; Karma
Faust, 82, 84
fear: freedom from, 78 (Buddha), 260 (Brahmā); in Gawain story, 72, 74–76, 78, 87–88, 130–31; in Owain story, 101, 130; in Siegfried story, 113
feats, *see* trials

female, 210; anima-archetype, 133–34n, 159–60; Balin-Balan and, 146–48; Brahmā and, 252–53; creation of, in Romance / Myth of the Goddess, 240–42, 244–49; Eda, as ideal, 26, 34; Gawain and, 81–95; Guinevere, as feminine life-giving principle, 170; Merlin and, 194–201; Owain and, 98, 101; Rati, as first wife, 249–51; Satī, as Indian ideal of, 302n; see also archetypes; Dawn; desire; intuition; Shiva

ferryman to netherworld, and Gawain, 81, 83, 87

fertility, see life

Fifty-two Sacred Places, 302n

Finn McCool, 47n

fire, as source of life and power: in Conn-eda story, 30, 36–37, 43, 46; in king and corpse story, 233, 235

flaying: of Conn-eda's horse, 30–31, 43; of Nemean lion, 127

Fled Bricrend, 77n

Foerster, Wendelin, 124n, 162n, 165n

folklore, see epics; myth

"Fool, The," in Tarot pack, 178, Pl. IV

foreknowledge, see prophecy

forest, as place of initiation, Merlin and, 181–82, 183–84n, 192–201

forgetfulness: Owain's, 108–109, 112–13; Siegfried's, 114

Fountain of Life, in Owain story, 98–113, 115, 118, 125–26, 128, 129, 131, 147; and Calogrenant, 183–84n; see also Lady of the Fountain; life; water

Francesca da Rimini, 135, 149, Pl. I

Francillon, see Astyanax

Frazer, Sir James George: The Golden Bough, 104–105

free will, as illusion, 295–96; see also chance; fate

Freya, 46, 260

fruit: forbidden, 49, 258n; gifts in king and corpse story, 202–3, 218–20, 224–25, 233, 235; see also gifts; symbols s.v. gifts

Furterer, Ulrich, 98n

G

Galahad, 133, 135, 149, 152–54, 156, 157; and Holy Grail, 143, 151, 180; see also alter ego; rebirth; redemption; symbols s.v. son

Ganges, 207, 246; Heavenly, 302, 316

Garden of Eden, 46, 49, 258n

Garlon, and Balin, 141–42, 144, 173n

Garuda (Bird of the Sun), 278, 282

Gaul, Arthur in, 187

Gautama, see Buddha, Gautama

Gawain, 68–97, 98n, 113, 122, 130–31, 136, 146, 149, 163–67, 169, 173–74, 188, 191–93, 198–99, 268n; chivalry in story of, 67–73, 81, 85, 163–67, 173–74, 191–93; combat with Owain, 110–11; and death, 67–81, 85, 130–31, 163–67, 169, 173–74, 176–77; desire in story of, 69–80, 84–88, 130; ego of, 79, 176–77; and fate, 68; and female, 81–95; as ideal male, 81–88, 133; initiation/integration of, 68–88; instinctual forces in story of, 69–75, 77–79; intuition of, 68; life as Death's bride in story of, 69–73, 76–77, 268n; rebirth of, 78–88; transfiguration of, 87–88; trials of, 68–95, 96n, 163–67, 173–74, 268n; and unconscious, 144; and water-bridge, 166–67, 173–74; see also cart; geis; opposites, coexisting; ring

Gawain and the Green Knight, 76n, 77n, 79–81, 162, 172

geis (condition): in Conn-eda's chess game with queen, 27–28; of fairy prince's bondage, 32; in Gawain story, 89, 91–94

gems, *see* jewels

Genesis, 46

Geoffrey of Monmouth, 182n, 184n, 186n, 187

ghosts, 67; in king and corpse story, 204–17; 221–35; *see also* Green Knight

giants, *see* Golden Garment; Green Knight; King of the Wood; titans

gifts, in king and corpse story, 202–203, 218–20, 224–25, 233, 235; *see also* symbols

Gilgamesh, 79, 84

girdle, green, in Gawain story, 72–76, 79, 85

Glewlwyd Gavaelvawr, 99

Gnosticism, 178

Goethe, 21, 82

Golden Age, 26

golden apples, Conn-eda's quest of, 27, 33, 46–48

Golden Ass, The (Apuleius): metamorphosis in, 66n; mysteries of Isis and Osiris in, 36n

Golden Bough, The, see Frazer, Sir James George

golden calf, 128

Golden Garment, and Vishnu, 127, 283

Golden Legend (Jacobus de Voragine), 60n

Golden-Mouth, John, *see* Chrysostom, St. John

Gordian knot, 20

Gower, John, 96n

grace, in St. John Chrysostom story, 56–59, 61–62, 64

Grail, *see* Holy Grail

Grail King, *see* Pellam, King

gravity, law of, Conn-eda and, 40–41

Great Mother, *see* Mother Goddess

greed, *see* avarice

Greek mythology, 284; adaptation to age, 307–8; archaic sources in Orphic period, 308; Herakles as lion-man in, 127; in *Iliad,* 308; sibyl's prophecies in, 186; in Sophocles, 308; sun-god in, 86n

Greek tragedy, 307

green, significance of color, 76–77, 79

Green Chapel, 67–69, 73, 79

Green Knight (Death), 67–81, 84–86, 172, 173n, 268n; *see also* death; life

Grimm, tales of, 60

Gringalet, 86

Gromer Somer Joure, 89–95

Guénon, René, 39n

Guest, Lady Charlotte: *Mabinogion,* 98n

guilt: Guinevere's, 156, 159–61; and initiation, 221; Kāma's, 249; in king and corpse story, 206, 224–29; Lancelot's, 132–35, 137, 158–61; Owain's, 114–15; Perceval's, 114n; Siegfried's, 114; Tristan's, 134–35; *see also* evil

Guinevere, 80–81, 98, 133–35, 149–56, 158–65, 170–80, 187, 190–91, 199, Pl. I; as anima-archetype, 159–60; in death's kingdom, 165–79; as feminine life-giving principle, 170; guilt of, 156, 159–61; as life-goddess, 165, 170, 175–80; love-spell of, 132–36, 149–80; Lancelot's redemption of, 170–77; transfiguration of, 159–61; and unconscious, 159–60; *see also* Lancelot

guru: Brahmā as, 315; Conn-eda's, 39; in Hinduism, 134n; Merlin as, 181–83, 186–94

H

Hamlet, 83–84
"Hanged One, The" (*Le Pendu*), in Tarot pack, 179, Pl. IV
Hartmann von Aue, 98n
heads: primacy of, 210; sacrifice of, 229; transposed, 210; *see also* decapitation; *Transposed Heads, The*
heaven, *see* rebirth; transfiguration
Hebrew religion, *see* Jewish religion
Hector, 132
Heinrich von dem Türlin, 81n
Helen of Troy, 82
Hellenistic interpretation of love, 161
Herakles, 79, 127, 194
Hermann of Fritzlar, 60n
Hermaphrodite, Cosmic / Dancing: as bisexual symbol of transcendence, 178–79; in Tarot pack, 178–79, Pl. IV; *see also* Shiva
hermit: St. John Chrysostom as, 55–57, 64–65; as life-stage, 18
hero, the, *see* trials
Hesiod, 307
Hesperides, 46
Himālaya: Mount, 289, 292, 296, 305; Mountain King, 282, 289, 292, 295, 305, 306, 316
Himālayas, 271, 276, 286–87, 315
Hinduism: *guru* in, 134n; as national religion, 52; sun-god in, 86n, 288, 298, 300; *see also Brāhmanas;* India; Karma; Māyā; myth *s.v.* archaic quality of; *Purānas;* Romance / Myth of the Goddess; symbols *s.v.* chariot; thread, Brahminic; *Upanishads; Vedas*
Hippomenes, 47
Hoffman, E. T. A., 188
Holy Ghost, 51–52, 61
Holy Grail (Sangreal), 51, 114n, 132–33, 143, 151n, 179–80; and Lancelot's cure, 157; in medieval story, 150–51n, 181
Homer, 4, 244, 307
horse, in Conn-eda story: Conn-eda's shaggy, 28–32, 38–50, 63, 122, 228; fairy king's, 27, 32, 46–48; *see also* alter ego; animal
hospitality, in Conn-eda story, 48
hound, of supernatural powers, in Conn-eda story, 27, 32, 46–48; *see also* animal
Hull, Eleanor, 40n
humility: St. John Chrysostom's, 59, 62–65; Conn-eda's, 38–39; in king and corpse story, 229
Hydra, killing of, 127; *see also* dragon; serpent

I

Ibn Hijjat al-Hamawi: *Thamarat ul-Awrak*, 13n
identification, *see* initiation / integration; rebirth
Igerne / Igraine, 186–87
Iliad, 308; *see also* epics; Greek mythology; Homer
images, *see* symbols
immolation, *see* redemption; sacrifice
immortality, *see* life; rebirth; transfiguration
Inanna, *see* Ishtar
incarnation, *see* apotheosis; transfiguration
Index, and Merlin, 186
India: chariot symbolism in, 166n; civilization of, 18–19; religion of, 15, 23, 52, 126–27; *see also* Hinduism; life-stages
individual, disregarded by myth, 310
Indra, 119, 184–85, 190, 268n, 289; *see also* archetypes *s.v.* temptation
Inferno, see Dante

Inglewood, 90
initiation / integration, 18–19, 194;
  in analytical psychology, 312*n;*
  Arthur's, 185–94; Balin's, 136–
  49; Buddha's, 77–79; St. John
  Chrysostom's, 52, 61–65; Conn-
  eda's, 36–38, 42–51; Gawain's,
  68–88; king's, in king and corpse
  story, 202–35; Lancelot's, 132–
  37, 149–81; Merlin and, 185–94;
  in mysteries of Isis and Osiris,
  36; Nebuchadnezzar's, 65–66*n;*
  Owain's, 100–31; Round Table's,
  190–94; and Tarot cards, 178–
  79; *see also* forest; guilt; *Magic
  Flute, The;* metamorphosis; rebirth; transfiguration
inner voice, *see* initiation / integration; instinctual forces in man; intuition; unconscious
innocence, transcended through experience: Conn-eda, 34–51; *see
  also* guilt; initiation / integration
instinctual forces in man: in St.
  John Chrysostom story, 63–65; in
  Conn-eda story, 34–35, 38–51; in
  Gawain story, 69–75, 77–79; in
  Owain story, 116, 119–20, 122,
  126, 128–31; *see also* intuition;
  nature; opposites, coexisting; unconscious
integration, *see* initiation / integration
intuition: St. John Chrysostom's,
  54–55, 61–65; Conn-eda's, 38–
  51; creative, 2–6, 85, 96–98; Gawain's, 68; in king and corpse
  story, 217, 227–28; and maternal
  womanhood, 83; Merlin's, 134*n;*
  Owain's, 98, 115–16, 119, 122,
  126, 129–31; *see also* instinctual
  forces in man; unconscious
invisibility, of Owain, 103
invulnerability: of Achilles, 114; of
  Siegfried, 114
Ionic world, *see* Greek mythology

Irish invasion of Britain, 187; *see
  also* Britain
Ishtar / Inanna, 84, 177*n,* 311
Isis, 36, 232, 311
Islam, 194
Isolt, 134, 150; *see also* love-spell;
  Tristan

J

Jacobus de Voragine: *Golden Leg-
  end,* 60*n*
Jaimīnīya Upanishad Brāhmana, see
  Brāhmanas
Jalal-ud-din Rūmī: *Mathnawī,* 79*n*
Jambhaladatta, 217*n*
Jehovah, 51–52, 258–59*n; see also*
  archetypes; Jewish religion
Jesus Christ, 51–52, 61, 64, 68, 131,
  141, 151*n,* 177, 184, 313; descent
  into Hell, 170–71
jewels, in story of king and corpse,
  202–3, 218–20, 224–25, 233, 235;
  see also gifts; ring
Jewish religion, 51–52, 127–28, 186
Joan of Arc, 132*n*
John Chrysostom, St., *see* Chrysos-
  tom
Jones, Owen, 187*n*
Joseph of Arimathaea, 150, 151*n*
Joyous Isle, Lancelot and, 158
Judith, 131
Jung, Carl Gustav, 210*n*

K

Kai / Kay, 93, 98–100, 109–10,
  163–64
Kailāsa, Mount, 289, 291
Kālī, 210, 240–41, 265–66; *see also*
  Māyā
Kālikā Purāna, see Purānas
Kāma (Love God): (Kāma-Māra)
  and Buddha, 77–78, 268*n;* in
  Hindu myth, 242–69, 273–78,
  281–82, 287, 295, 299, 301, 306*n,*

313, 314; *see also* death *s.v.* implicit in life; desire; guilt; Māra

Kāmarūpa, 301

Karma, 15, 23, 220–35; *see also* fate; free will

Katibah, H. I.: *Other Arabian Nights*, 13n

Kay, *see* Kai

king, and the corpse, story of, 3, 202–35; apotheosis in, 233–35; death in, 203–35; ego in, 213, 217–35; fate in, 218–35; guilt in, 206, 224–29; humility in, 229; rebirth in, 216–35; redemption in, 215–16, 227, 230; riddles in, 204–35; sacrifice in, 213–15, 220–23, 228–30; transfiguration in, 216–17, 221–35; unconscious in, 224–35; *see also* initiation / integration; opposites, coexisting; symbols *s.v.* corpse *and* specter

King of the Wood (Ward of the Wood; Woodward of the Wood): Merlin as, 183, 183–84n; at Nemi, 104–5, 108; in Owain story, 101–2, 109, 121, 130, 173n

Kirtlan, E. J. B., 76n

Kittredge, George Lyman, 76n, 77n

knight, as solar god, 85–86; *see also* chivalry; Round Table

Knight with the Lion, *see* Owain

Knower, *see* initiation / integration

Krishna, 113

Kshemendra: *Brikatkathāmañjari*, 217n

Kynon, 98–101, 109, 183n

L

Lady of the Fountain, in Owain story, 98, 102, 104–108, 111–113, 115, 118, 120, 122–126, 128, 147; *see also* Black Knight; Fountain of Life; life; water

Lady of the Lake (Nimue), 133–34n, 135–36, 139–41, 180

La Hire (Etienne de Vignolles), 132

lake, miraculous: Conn-eda's descent into, 29, 35–36, 43, 46, 47

Lakshmī, 250, 265, 266, 271, 272, 273, 278, 281, 282

Lamb, the, 51–52, 61; *see also* Jesus Christ

Lancelot, 122, 131–37, 143, 144, 149–81, 301n, Pl. I, II, III; as animus-archetype, 133, 159–60, 179; and chivalry, 132–33, 161, 164–77; and death, 164–79; and demonic possession, 135, 159–60, 179; and desire, 132–35, 167–81; ego of, 176–79; and fate, 136–37; Galahad as alter ego of, 180–81; guilt of, 132–35, 137, 158–61; love-spell of, 132–36, 149–81; madness of, 155–57; rebirth of, 159–61, 176–77, 180–81; redemption of Guinevere by, 170–77; and sacrifice, 176; as savior, 177; and sword-bridge, 166–67, 170–72, 301, Pl. III; and Tarot cards, 178–79; transfiguration of, 159–61, 177, 180–81; and unconscious, 159–60; *see also* cart; Guinevere; initiation/integration

Land of No Return, *see* death; initiation / integration; Mothers, the

Lao-tse, 134n

Last Judgment, 171–72

Last Supper, cup of, 151n; *see also* Holy Grail

law, Vedic, 290

legends, *see* ancient and medieval tales; epics; myth

Leodogran, King, and Arthur, 190-191

life: in Balin-Balan story, 147; as Death's bride in Gawain story, 69–73, 76–77, 268n; death implicit in, 193, 253 (Kāma), 273n; desire for, 247–48; as God's name, 77n; Guinevere as goddess of,

life (*cont.*)
165, 170, 175–80; in king and
corpse story, 222–35; in Kynon's
tale, 99–100; in Lancelot story,
136, 170–79; in myth and epic,
77–88; in Owain story, 102–8,
125–26, 128–31, 147; *see also*
fire; Fountain of Life; Lady of the
Fountain; water
life-stages, in India, 18–19; *see also*
hermit; withdrawal
Lile of Avelion, 137
lingam, Shiva as, 302
lion: Gawain and, 87; Herakles and
Nemean, 127; Lancelot and, 171–
72; Owain and, 98, 118–129; *see
also* alter ego; animal; nature
Livre d'Artus, 183–84n
Logres, realm of: Lancelot and, 158
Loomis, Roger S., 77n, 96n, 151n,
184n
Louis VII, King of France, 98n
Love, *see* desire; Kāma; Mountain
of the God of Love
love-spell, 199; of Lancelot and
Guinevere, 132–36, 149–81; of
Merlin and Niniane, 194–201; of
Paolo and Francesca, 135, 149;
of Tristan and Isolt, 134–35, 150,
196, 200; *see also* Kāma; magic
Luned (Lunete), in Owain story,
105–107, 115, 120–126
lust, *see* desire
Luther, Martin, 60–61

M

Mabinogion, see Guest, Lady Charlotte
Macleod, Fiona, *see* Sharp, William
Madden, Sir Frederic, 76n
madness: Lancelot's, 155–57;
Owain's, 115–17; Shiva's, 306,
307, 313, 316
magic: in Arthur story, 188–94; in
Arthurian romance, 133–34n; in

Balin story, 136–49; ball of Conn-
eda, 28–30, 39–41, 63; balsam of
Owain, 116–18; basket of Conn-
eda, 28; bed, 86–87, 167 (Gawain), 167 (Lancelot); belt of
Cuchullin, 79n; Dame Brisen
and, 151–54, 157; chessboard of
Conn-eda's stepmother, 27; in
Conn-eda story, 26–50, 235; girdle in Gawain story, 72–76, 79,
85; as guidance for soul, 18–19;
key of Faust, 82; in king and
corpse story, 202–35; in Kynon's
tale, 99–100; in Lancelot story,
135–37, 143, 149–80 *passim;*
Merlin and, 134n, 181–201; in
myth, 161–62; in Owain story,
100–31 *passim;* in priestly power,
61–62, 64; ring of Owain, 103; in
Romance / Myth of the Goddess,
239–316 *passim;* in Siegfried
story, 113–14; sleep of Brünnhilde, 151–52; slippers of Abu
Kasem, 9–25, 145; stone of Conn-
eda, 28; transformation of Dame
Ragnell, 94–95; *see also* demonic
possession; elixir; Fountain of
Life; love-spell
Magic Flute, The (Mozart), initiation in, 36n, 232
Magna Mater, *see* Mother Goddess
male, ideal: Balin, 148; Conn, 26,
34; Gawain, 81–88, 133; Owain,
133; Round Table, knights of,
133; *see also* archetypes *s.v.* animus
Malory: *Morte d'Arthur*, 83n, 97,
132n, 134n, 137, 149n, 150–51n,
153n, 156n, 158n, 159n, 186n,
188n, 189n, 190n, 191n
Manasa, Lake, 291, 296
Mandara, Mount, 264
Mann, Thomas, 210n
Māra: (Kāma-Māra) and Buddha,
77–78, 268n; *see also* desire;
Kāma

Marie de Champagne, 98n, 161
marriage: Arthur's, 190–92; Gawain's, to Dame Ragnell, 90–95; of Heaven and Earth, 26; Shiva's, 264–85; see also symbols s.v. perfection
Mary, Virgin, 54, 61, 68
matriarchal civilization, 82–83
Māyā, 15, 232–35, 239–40, 250, 264, 268–70, 280–81, 284–85, 293–96, 301, 303, 313; as Dawn, 255–58; as Kālī, 265–66; as Pārvatī, 294–95, 316, Pl. V; as Satī, 270, 282, 283, 291–93, 306, 313; see also Dawn; Kālī; Satī
Maynadier, G. H., 96n
McCoy, Abraham, 33n
mediation, 51–52
medicine man, Merlin as, 182
medieval tales, see ancient and medieval tales
Mediterranean religion, 128, see also animal; myth
Medusa, 20, 184
Meleagant, Prince, alter ego of Death, 173–74; Merlin as, 183; see also Bademagu, King; death
Menakā, 289, 292, 316
mendicant, see beggar ascetic
Merlin, 80–81, 134n, 181–201; in Balin story, 137, 141, 143, 144, 145, 148–49; as Bernlak de Hautdesert, 183; and Christianity, 184; and Council of Trent, 186; and fate, 137, 184–86, 188–201; and female, 194–201; and initiation / integration, 185–94; as Meleagant, 183; and prophecy, 134n, 137, 144, 185–94, 197, 199–201; and unconscious, 134n, 194–201; as Wise Old Man, 134n, 141, 144; see also Niniane; opposites, coexisting
Meru, Mount, see Axis, World
Mesopotamia, symbolism of, 129
Messiah, see Jesus Christ; savior

metamorphosis: St. John Chrysostom's 56–58, 63, 65, 116; in Golden Ass, The, 66n; Merlin's, 183–84n; Nebuchadnezzar's, 65–66n, 116; Owain's, 115–16; Dame Ragnell's, 94–95; trials as ways of, 194, 231; see also initiation / integration; rebirth; transfiguration
Middle Ages, and the animal, 128; see also animal; Celtic imagination; myth
Milky Ocean, 256, 264
miracle: St. John Chrysostom and, 54–65; hero and, 184, 185; Lancelot's cure by
miserliness, see avarice
Modred, 187
monastic life, limitations of, 64
monkey, king and, in king and corpse story, 202, 219–20; see also animal; nature
Morgan le Fay (Fata Morgana), 80–81, 134n; see also Niniane
Morris, Richard, 76n
Morte d'Arthur, see Malory
Moses, and animal worship, 127–128
Mother Goddess, 311–15; see also Diana; Ishtar; Isis; Māyā; Romance / Myth of the Goddess
Mothers, the: Balin-Balan and, 146–48; Gawain and, 81–88, 167; and mythology of Celts, 199–201; see also death; female
Mount Meru, see Axis, World
mountain, flaming, in Conn-eda story, 30, 37, 43, 46; see also fire
Mountain, World, 282
Mountain King, see Himālaya
Mountain of the God of Love, 301
Mountain of the Goddess, 301
Mozart (The Magic Flute), 36n
mysteries, see initiation / integration; Isis; Osiris

myth: adaptation to age, 81, 87, 172, 181, 307–8; animals in, 38–40, 126–29; archaic quality of, 194, 199–201 (Celtic), 284–85, 308–12 (Hindu); birth in, 113, 184–85; childhood in, 134n, 185; death and life in, 76–88, 188; of East, 171–72; ending in, 20; and individual, 310; interpretation of, 1–6, 96; as intoxicant, 309–10; moral of, 45; pagan, 62–64 (Conn-eda story); and super-human, 310; timelessness of, 188; see also animal; Celtic imagination; Christianity; creation myth; decapitation; Greek mythology; unconscious s.v. and archaic

Myth of the Goddess, see Romance / Myth of the Goddess

Myths and Symbols in Indian Art and Civilization (Zimmer), 178n, 179n

N

Nandī, Shiva's bull, 277, 285, 286, 291, 296, 305

Narcissus, 239

nature: Conn-eda and, 34–37, 39–43; forest and, 182; Greek and Hindu gods as personifications of, 284; Merlin and power of, 199–201; Owain and, 108–9, 126–31; Siegfried and, 113–14; see also animal; forest; initiation / integration; instinctual forces in man

Near East, symbolism of, 129–30

Nebuchadnezzar, 65–66n, 116

necromancy, see magic

Nemea, lion of, 127; see also flaying; Herakles; lion

Nemi, Lake, sacred grove at, 104–105, 108

Neolithic period, mother-goddess images in, 311

New Testament, 51

New Year, rebirth of, 84

Nicodemus, The Gospel of, 170–71

Nietzsche, 83, 310n

Nimue, see Lady of the Lake

Niniane: and Merlin, 80n, 134n, 194–201; see also Diana

Nirvāna, 78

Novalis, 230

O

Ocean, Cosmic, 300–301

Old Testament, 127–128, 131, 186, 258–59n

Olympus, 244

opposites, coexisting: in Conn-eda story, 33–37, 42, 44–50; in myth, 310n, 312–15 (Hindu); INSTANCES: Creation / Preservation / Destruction (Brahmā / Vishnu / Shiva), 265, 271–73, 279–85; demonic / human, 136–49 (Balin / Balan); human / instinctual (conscious / unconscious), 56–58, 63–65, 116 (St. John Chrysostom), 149–50, 159–60 (Lancelot), 65–66n, 116 (Nebuchadnezzar), 115–16, 119–22, 126 (Owain); human / superhuman, 184–85 (hero, Merlin), 233–35 (king and corpse story), 133–36, 143 (Lancelot), 102–9, 122, 126 (Owain); life / death, 77–78 (Buddha's temptation), 78–88 (Gawain), 253 (Kāma), 162–79 (Lancelot); male / female, 178–79 (Lancelot / Guinevere), 226–33 (king and corpse story); one / many, 283–84; opposition / identity, 265 (Māyā); wisdom / desire, 252–63 (Brahmā); wisdom / ignorance, 265 (Māyā)

Orient, see East

Orpheus, 79, 134n

Orphic period, see Greek mythology

Osiris, 36, 86, 232

Ovid, 161

Owain (*Le Chevalier au Lion;* The Knight with the Lion; Yvain), 98–131, 147, 169, 173*n*, 183*n;* and chivalry, 108, 110–13, 115, 119, 120–26; death in story of, 102–8, 130; and demonic possession, 129; and desire, 101, 130; ego of, 131; fear in story of, 101, 130; and female, 98, 101; guilt of, 114–15; initiation / integration of, 100–31; instinctual forces in story of, 116, 119–20, 122, 126, 128–31; intuition of, 98, 115–16, 119, 122, 126, 129–31; and life, 102–8, 125–26, 128–31, 147; lion as alter ego of, 118–20; madness of, 115–17; rebirth of, 108–9, 112–13, 119–20, 126–31; transfiguration of, 108–9, 112–15, 131; unconscious in story of, 115–16, 119–20, 122, 126, 128–31; *see also* opposites, coexisting; trials

P

Paleolithic period, mother-goddess images in, 311
Paolo, 149, Pl. I; *see also* Francesca da Rimini
Paradise, *see* Garden of Eden
parallelism of traditional stories, 1, 96
Paris, 135
Paris, Gaston, 192*n*
Parry, John Jay, 182*n*
Parsifal, 51, 130; *see also* Perceval
Pārvatī, 294–95, 306*n*, 316, Pl. V; *see also* Māyā
Paul, St. (Epistle to the Philippians) 313
Pellam (Pelles), King (Grail King): and Dolorous Stroke, 142–43, 150–51*n*, 173*n;* and Lancelot, 150–52, 156–58
Pelles, *see* Pellam, King

Pellinor, King, and Arthur, 190–91
penance, *see* repentance
Perceval, 114*n; see also* Parsifal
Percy, Bishop, 95*n*
perils, *see* trials
Perin de Mountbeliard, killed by Garlon, 141
Persephone, 165
Perseus: birth, 184; dragon-slayer, 20, 113, 119, 184; Medusa-slayer, 20, 184
personality, *see* ego
Phaeacians, island of, 81–82
Philippians, *see* Paul, St.
Phoenicians, travels to West, 129–30
Plato (*Republic*), 83*n*
Platonism, chariot symbolism in, 166*n*
Polycrates, ring of, 14
possessions, worldly: Abu Kasem's slippers, 9–25; St. John Chrysostom and, 54–55
poverty, St. John Chrysostom's, 54–55
predestination, *see* fate
priestly tradition: and Brahminism, 308–9; and Greek mythology, 307; *see also* sacerdotalism
primitive man, and the animal, 126–129; *see also* animal; myth
primum mobile, see Unmoved Mover
prophecy: in Lancelot and Galahad story, 150–53; Merlin and, 134*n*, 137, 144, 185–94, 197, 199–201; tradition of, 186
Prophets, 186; and animal worship, 127–128
psyche, *see* unconscious
psychology, attitude of toward symbols, 1–4; *see also* analytical psychology; symbols
Purānas, 240; Kālikā, 240–306, 312–16
Pyramus, 161

Q

queens, three, 81–82, 87
quest, *see* trials
Quixote, Don, *see* Don Quixote

R

Rabelais, 186*n*, 194
Rachel, 131
Radin, Paul: *The Road of Life and Death,* 43*n*
Ragnell, Dame, 90–95
Rank, Otto, 35*n*
Rati (Delight), wife of Kāma, 249–51, 254, 281; *see also* female
rebirth: Abu Kasem's, 21–25; Buddha's, 77–78; St. John Chrysostom's, 54–65; Conn-eda's, 37–38, 42–51; Galahad and, 143; Gawain's, 78–88; through initiation, 182; in king and corpse story, 216–35; Lancelot's, 159–61, 176–77, 180–81; as liberation from attachment, 17–19, 36, 78; Nebuchadnezzar's, 65–66*n;* Owain's, 108–9, 112–13, 119–20, 126–31; Shiva and, 303; of world, 177–79, 184–85; *see also* ego, abandonment of; initiation / integration; metamorphosis; redemption; transfiguration
Red Book of Hergest, 98*n*, 122, 126*n*, 183*n*
Redeemer, *see* Brünnhilde; Jesus Christ; redemption; sacrifice; savior
redemption, 239; in St. John Chrysostom story, 53, 59, 60*n*, 65; through Galahad, 143, 180; of Guinevere by Lancelot, 170–77; in king and corpse story, 215–16, 227, 230; through sacrifice, 51–52; *see also* Buddha; Jesus Christ; salvation of world; savior
reintegration, *see* integration

Renaissance, and Arthurian romance, 130, 194
renunciation, *see* ego
repentance, St. John Chrysostom's, 56–58, 61–63, 65
resignation, *see* acceptance
resurrection, *see* rebirth
Revelation, *see* Apocalypse
riddles, in king and corpse story, 204–35
ring: Lancelot's, 136; in Owain story, 103, 113, 115; Polycrates', 14; Siegfried's, 113; significance of in Gawain story, 71–72; *see also* invisibility; symbols *s.v.* ring
Rion, King, and Arthur, 190
Ripperberger Helmut, 60*n*
ritual: in Conn-eda story, 36–37, 39, 48; and Fountain of Life, 99–102, 109–10, 125; function of, 18–19; and initiation, 182; *see also* sacrifice *s.v.* Daksha's
Roger the Dane, 131
Roman Catholicism, 61–62, 64
Roman de Merlin, 86*n*, 184*n*, 186*n*, 189*n*, 190*n*, 191*n*, 196*n*, 199*n*
Roman occupation of Britain, 187
Romance / Myth of the Goddess (Māyā), from *Kālikā Purāna,* 239–316; *see also* Māyā
romances, medieval, *see* ancient and medieval tales; Arthurian romance
Rome: King Arthur and, 187; founding of, 132*n*
Round Table, 67, 71, 75–76, 79, 80, 85, 96, 98*n*, 108, 112, 115, 120, 121–22, 126, 128, 132–33, 134*n*, 138, 150, 158, 160, 163, 170; Merlin and, 182–83, 185–86, 190–94, 196, 201; mission of, 143–44, 201; *see also* evil; fate; initiation / integration; male; ideal; trials
Rūmī, *see* Jalal-ud-din Rūmī
Ryan, Granger, 60*n*

S

sacerdotalism, in Roman Catholicism, 61–62, 64; *see also* priestly tradition

sacraments, 18–19; in St. John Chrysostom story, 53–65; in Conn-eda story, 42, 48

sacrifice: Brünnhilde's, 51–52; in St. John Chrysostom story, 64; in Conn-eda story, 36, 42–51; Daksha's, 289–94, 296–99; Jesus Christ's, 51–52; in king and corpse story, 213–15, 220–23, 228–30; Lancelot and, 176; *see also* redemption; salvation of world; savior

saga, *see* epics; myth

sages, of the East, 114

Saïs, Egyptian temple of, 312

salvation of world: in Romance / Myth of the Goddess, 289–90; 292–94; Round Table's mission, 144, 201; *see also* apotheosis; initiation / integration; rebirth; redemption; sacrifice; savior

Sangreal, *see* Holy Grail

Sarah, 52

Sarastro, 197, 232

Satan, 56

Śatapatha Brāhmana, see *Brāhmanas*

Satī, and Shiva, 160, 270–79, 281–83, 285–306, 313; *see also* death; female; marriage; Māyā; suicide

Saturn (The Slow Wanderer), 300–302, 304

savior: Judaic belief in, 51–52; in king and corpse story, 229–31; Lancelot as, 170–79; *see also* Buddha; Jesus Christ; redemption; sacrifice; Vishnu

Sāvitrī, 265, 271, 272, 273, 275, 281

Scathach, realm of, 40n

Schiller, 308

Scottish invasion of Britain, 187; *see also* Britain

seat perilous, of Round Table, 191

Self, realization of: in king and corpse story, 233–35; Shiva and, 303–4; *see also* apotheosis; initiation / integration; rebirth; transfiguration

sensuality, *see* desire; Kāma; love-spell

serpent: in Conn-eda story, 29, 36, 42, 43, 46; in Garden of Eden, 258n; Herakles and, 127; in Owain story, 101, 118, 119, 129; Shiva and, 277, 288, 305; *see also* animal; dragon; Hydra; myth

Sharp, William (Fiona Macleod), 130

shield: as symbol of ego, 146; in Balin story, 146–48; *see also* symbols

Shiva, 233–34, 239–40, 243, 244, 245, 246, 248–49, 250, 251, 265; as ascetic, 215–16, 243, 246, 249, 254, 271, 272–73, 290–91, 302, 303, 313; as bisexual symbol, 178–79; dancing, 178–179, 307, frontispiece; and desire, 253–56, 263, 266–306, 313, 315–16; as lingam, 302; *see also* Hermaphrodite, Cosmic / Dancing; madness; marriage; rebirth; Satī

Siegfried, 113–114, 119

sin, *see* evil; guilt

Siprā lake, 306n, 315–16

Sisyphus, 223

Sivadāsa, 217n

sleep, enchanted, *see* Brünnhilde

Slow Wanderer, The, *see* Saturn

snake, *see* dragon; Hydra; serpent

soma, 309–10

Somadeva: *Kathāsaritsāgara,* 217n

Sommer, H. O., 184n, 186n, 189n, 190n, 191n, 196n, 199n

Sophocles, 308

sorcery, *see* magic

specters, *see* ghosts
Spring, in Romance / Myth of the Goddess, 254–55, 268, 273, 287, 299
stepmother, Conn-eda's wicked, 27–28, 32–35, 48
stone, Conn-eda's magic, 28
Stonehenge, 134*n*
Strindberg, August, 24*n*
suicide, Satī's, 292, 294–96; *see also* ego *s.v.* suicide
sun-god, *see* Hinduism; knight; symbols *s.v.* chariot
superhuman, myth and, 310; *see also* apotheosis; transfiguration
supernatural, *see* magic
Swedenborg, Emanuel, 24*n*
sword, as symbol of ego and power, 136, 146; Arthur's three swords, 188–90; of Balin and Lancelot, 136–49; in king and corpse story, 203–10, 216, 233, 235; Shiva's, 234; Siegfried's 113–14; *see also* Excalibur; symbols
sword-bridge, Lancelot and, 166–67, 170–72, 301, Pl. III
symbols: in Arthurian romance, 194–201; in Conn-eda story, 26–51; in Eastern culture, 129–30; in Hindu myth, 285; interpretation of, 1–6, 80*n*, 96–98, 161–62; in Lancelot story, 177–81; persistence of, 81; of unconscious, 80*n;* INSTANCES: Abu Kasem's slippers (attachment), 14–25, 145, 221; Brünnhilde (humanity), 51; chariot, 166*n;* corpse, in king and corpse story (forgotten part of self), 222–35; gifts (essential in seemingly valueless), 218–20, 224–25, 233, 235; marriage of Arthur (attainment of perfection), 192; Owain's new name (rebirth), 126; ring (personality), 71–72; son (higher transformation of personality), 180;

specter, in king and corpse story (inner guide), 226–35; *see also* animal; cart; centaur; Fountain of Life; Lady of the Fountain; Mesopotamia; ring; shield; sword; trials; water
Synge, John Millington, 130
Syria, symbolism of, 129

T

talisman, *see* magic
Tamino, 232
Tammuz / Adonis, 177*n*
Tao: in Conn and Eda, 26; in Conn-eda, 34–35, 42
Taraka, 283
Tarot cards, 177–79, Pl. IV; *Tarot de Marseilles,* 177; *see also* death; "Fool, The"; "Hanged One, The" (*Le Pendu*); Hermaphrodite, Cosmic / Dancing
Teh, in Conn and Eda, 26; in Conn-eda, 34–35
temptation, *see* trials
Tempter, *see* Satan
Tennyson, Alfred, 159*n*
Theseus, 79, 194
Thisbe, 161
Thompson, Henry Yates: *Illustrations from One Hundred Manuscripts,* ix, Pl. I, II, III
Thor, 190
thread, Brahminic, 277
Tibet, Buddhist art of, 76; Buddhist priests in, 185
titans, warring against Hindu gods, 271–72, 282–83; *see also* giants; Golden Garment
totem animal: and forest, 182; Owain's, 119–20
tragedy, *see* Greek tragedy
transcendence, *see* initiation / integration; opposites, coexisting; transfiguration

transfiguration, 48, 51, 226; Conn-eda's, 44–45; Gawain's, 87–88; Guinevere's, 159–61; of hero, 184–85, 188; in king and corpse story, 216–17, 221–35; Lancelot's, 159–61, 177, 180–181; Owain's, 108–9, 112–15, 131; Siegfried's, 113–14; and Siprā lake, 316; *see also* apotheosis; initiation / integration; metamorphosis; rebirth

transformation, *see* apotheosis; metamorphosis; rebirth; transfiguration

Transposed Heads, The (Mann), 210n

tree: of everlasting life, 46, 258n; in king and corpse story, 204–10, 222–30; of knowledge of good and evil, 258n

trials, symbols of process of initiation / integration, 193–94; Abu Kasem's, 9–25; Arthur's, 187–94; Balin's, 136–49; Buddha's, 77, 79, 268n; St. John Chrysostom's, 54–65; Conn-eda's, 35, 38–45; Gawain's, 68–95, 96n, 163–67, 173–74, 268n; Hindu gods', 252–306; king's, in king and corpse story, 202–35; Lancelot's, 132–37, 149–81; Merlin and, 182–201; Owain's, 98–131; Round Table's, 191–94; Siegfried's, 113–14; *see also* sword-bridge; water-bridge

tribal religion, 51–52; *see also* Jehovah; Wotan

Trinity, Hindu, *see* opposites, coexisting *s.v.* Creation / Preservation / Destruction

Trinity, Holy: mystical union with, 178

Tristan, 119, 130, 134–35, 141, 150, 196; *see also* demonic possession; desire; fate; guilt; Isolt; love-spell

Troy, 132

truth, Brahmā's essence, 252, 260; *see also* Brahmā

Twice-born, the, *see* rebirth

Twilight of the Gods (Wagner), 113–114

U

Ulrich, Jacob, 192n

Ulysses, 81, 190, 194, 200

unconscious, 2–6, 96–98, 128–29, 193; in Abu Kasem story, 14–25; and archaic, 310–11; Balin and, 144–49; in Conn-eda story, 38–51; Gawain and, 144; in king and corpse story, 224–35; in Lancelot and Guinevere story, 159–60; Merlin and, 134n, 194–201; in Owain story, 115–16, 119–20, 122, 126, 128–31; symbols of, 80n; *see also* initiation / integration; instinctual forces in man; intuition

Universal Goddess, *see* Mother Goddess

universality: of Holy Ghost, 51–52; of Mahāyāna Buddhism, 52

Unmoved Mover, 40; Mother Goddess as, 311–12

Upanishads, 5, 83n; *Katha*, 172n, 270n

Uther Pendragon, King, 186–88, 190

V

Vaitarani, 301

Valley of No Return, *see* death; initiation / integration; Mothers, the

Vedas, 240, 246, 268n, 277, 290; *Rig*, 257n

Vijayā, 291–93, 296–97, 305

Vikings, Arthur and, 187

Vikramāditya (The Sun of Valor), 217n

Virabhadra, 297–98

Virana, 270

Vīranī, 270

Virgil, 222
Virgin, *see* Mary
virgin birth: of Indra, 184; of Merlin, 184; as mythological motif, 184
Vishnu, 126–27, 239–40, 243, 244, 245, 249, 250, 251, 254, 255–56, 264–68, 271, 273, 278–85, 290, 298–99, 301–2, 306, 312, 316; Incarnation as Boar, 306n
Voragine, Jacobus de, *see* Jacobus de Voragine
Vortigern, King, 185, 187
Vritra, 268n
Vyāsa, 4

W

Wagner, Richard, 51–52, 130, 199–200
Wales, Merlin and, 186–87
Ward of the Wood, *see* King of the Wood
War God, son of Shiva and Satī, 283
water: as infrahuman power in Conn-eda story, 29, 35–36, 43, 46, 47; as symbol of life, 129; *see also* Fountain of Life; Lady of the Fountain; lake, miraculous; life; symbols
water-bridge, Gawain and, 166–67, 173–74
Webster, K. G. T., 76n
well, *see* Fountain of Life; water
Weston, Jessie L., 76n, 81n, 96n, 133n

Whiting, Bartlett J., 96n
Wise Old Man, as archetypal teacher: Conn-eda and, 39; Merlin as, 134n, 141, 144; *see also* archetypes; Merlin
witches, in Conn-eda story, 27; *see also* demon; magic
withdrawal, 18, 198–201; *see also* hermit; life-stages
Wolfram von Eschenbach, 81n, 97
woman, *see* archetypes; female; Mothers, the
Woodward of the Wood, *see* King of the Wood
World Axis, Mountain, *see under respective nouns*
World Mother, *see* Mother Goddess
Wotan, 51, 113–14, 260
Wu Wei, 41n

Y

Yang, 35
Yeats, William Butler, 33n, 130
Yin, 35
yoga: Brahmā's, 261n, 262–63; and Māyā, 256; Shiva's, 253–54, 272–73, 295
Yvain, *see* Owain

Z

Zeus, 113, 184, 190, 260
Zimmer, Heinrich: *Myths and Symbols in Indian Art and Civilization*, 178n, 179n

Index by Arnold Canell

MYTHOS: The Princeton/Bollingen Series in World Mythology

J. J. Bachofen / MYTH, RELIGION, AND MOTHER RIGHT

George Boas, trans. / THE HIEROGLYPHICS OF HORAPOLLO

Anthony Bonner, ed. / DOCTOR ILLUMINATUS: A RAMON LLULL READER

Jan Bremmer / THE EARLY GREEK CONCEPT OF THE SOUL

Martin Buber / THE LEGEND OF THE BAAL-SHEM

Kenelm Burridge / MAMBU: A MELANESIAN MILLENNIUM

Joseph Campbell / THE HERO WITH A THOUSAND FACES

Henry Corbin / AVICENNA AND THE VISIONARY RECITAL

F. M. Cornford / FROM RELIGION TO PHILOSOPHY

Marcel Detienne / THE GARDENS OF ADONIS: SPICES IN GREEK MYTHOLOGY

Mircea Eliade / IMAGES AND SYMBOLS

Mircea Eliade / THE MYTH OF THE ETERNAL RETURN

Mircea Eliade / SHAMANISM: ARCHAIC TECHNIQUES OF ECSTASY

Mircea Eliade / YOGA: IMMORTALITY AND FREEDOM

Garth Fowden / THE EGYPTIAN HERMES

Erwin R. Goodenough (Jacob Neusner, ed.) / JEWISH SYMBOLS IN THE GRECO-ROMAN PERIOD

W.K.C. Guthrie / ORPHEUS AND GREEK RELIGION

Jane Ellen Harrison / PROLEGOMENA TO THE STUDY OF GREEK RELIGION

Joseph Henderson & Maud Oakes / THE WISDOM OF THE SERPENT

Erik Iversen / THE MYTH OF EGYPT AND ITS HIEROGLYPHS IN EUROPEAN TRADITION

Jolande Jacobi, ed. / PARACELSUS: SELECTED WRITINGS

C. G. Jung & Carl Kerényi / ESSAYS ON A SCIENCE OF MYTHOLOGY

Carl Kerényi / DIONYSOS: ARCHETYPAL IMAGE OF INDESTRUCTIBLE LIFE

Carl Kerényi / ELEUSIS: ARCHETYPAL IMAGE OF MOTHER AND DAUGHTER

Stella Kramrisch / THE PRESENCE OF ŚIVA

Jon D. Levenson / CREATION AND THE PERSISTENCE OF EVIL: THE JEWISH DRAMA OF DIVINE OMNIPOTENCE

Roger S. Loomis / THE GRAIL: FROM CELTIC MYTH TO CHRISTIAN SYMBOL

Bronislaw Malinowski (Ivan Strenski, ed.) / MALINOWSKI AND THE WORK OF MYTH

Louis Massignon (Herbert Mason, ed.) / HALLAJ: MYSTIC AND MARTYR

Erich Neumann / AMOR AND PSYCHE

Erich Neumann / THE GREAT MOTHER

Erich Neumann / THE ORIGINS AND HISTORY OF CONSCIOUSNESS

Maud Oakes with Joseph Campbell / WHERE THE TWO CAME TO THEIR FATHER

Dora & Erwin Panofsky / PANDORA'S BOX

Paul Radin / THE ROAD OF LIFE AND DEATH

Otto Rank, Lord Raglan, Alan Dundes / IN QUEST OF THE HERO

Gladys Reichard / NAVAHO RELIGION

Géza Róheim (Alan Dundes, ed.) / FIRE IN THE DRAGON

Robert A. Segal, ed. / THE GNOSTIC JUNG

Jean Seznec / THE SURVIVAL OF THE PAGAN GODS: THE MYTHOLOGICAL TRADITION AND ITS PLACE IN RENAISSANCE HUMANISM AND ART

Miranda Shaw / PASSIONATE ENLIGHTENMENT: WOMEN IN TANTRIC BUDDHISM

Philip E. Slater / THE GLORY OF HERA

Daisetz T. Suzuki / ZEN AND JAPANESE CULTURE

Jean-Pierre Vernant (Froma I. Zeitlin, ed.) / MORTALS AND IMMORTALS

Jessie L. Weston / FROM RITUAL TO ROMANCE

Hellmut Wilhelm and Richard Wilhelm / UNDERSTANDING THE *I CHING*: THE WILHELM LECTURES ON THE BOOK OF CHANGES

Heinrich Zimmer (Joseph Campbell, ed.)/ THE KING AND THE CORPSE: TALES OF THE SOUL'S CONQUEST OF EVIL

Heinrich Zimmer (Joseph Campbell, ed.) / MYTHS AND SYMBOLS IN INDIAN ART AND CIVILIZATION